Philippines Via Old Pics (PVOP) - 7

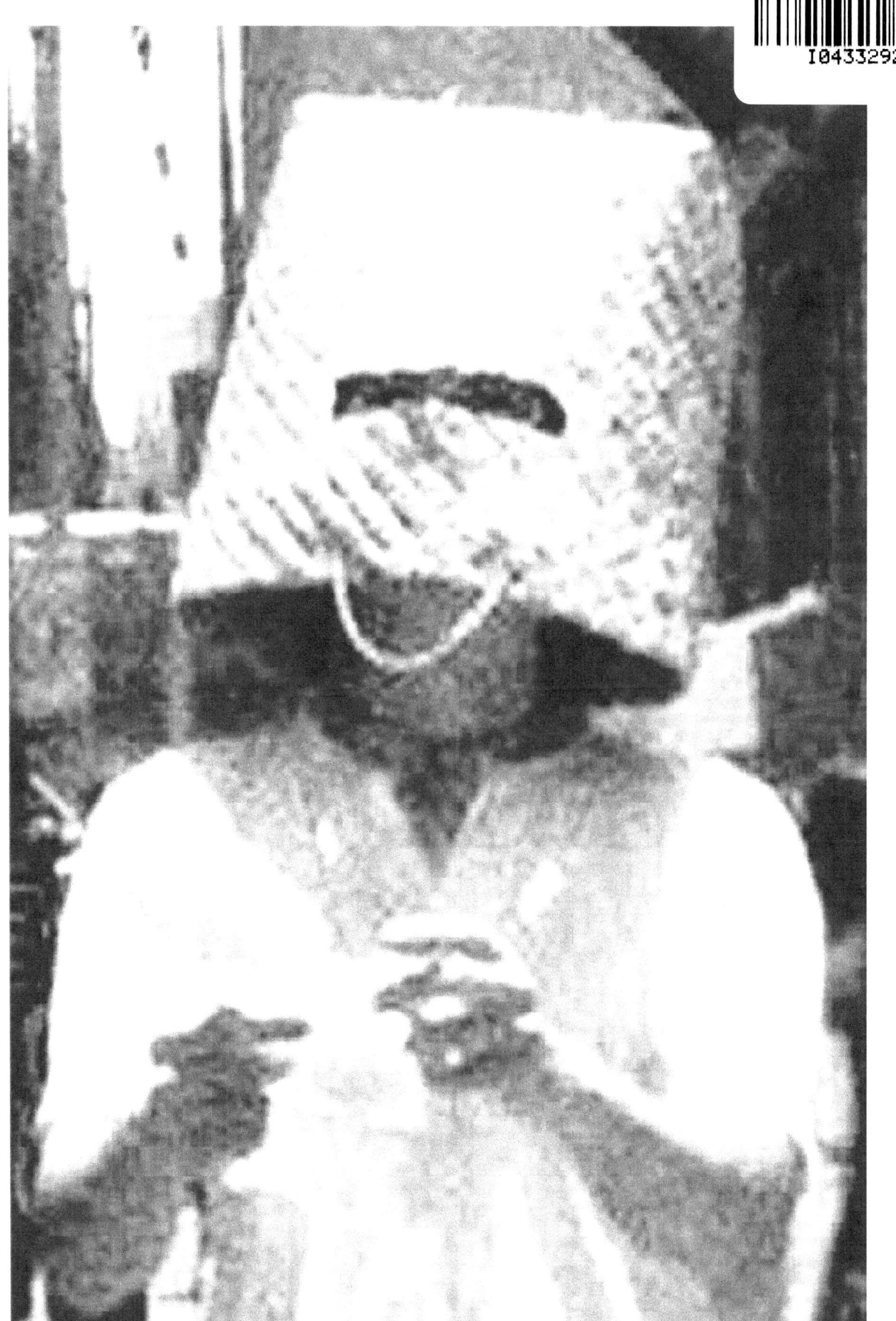

A Collaborator, willing or not, during World War II Occupation of the Philippines. His face is covered to help Japanese identify fellow Filipinos.

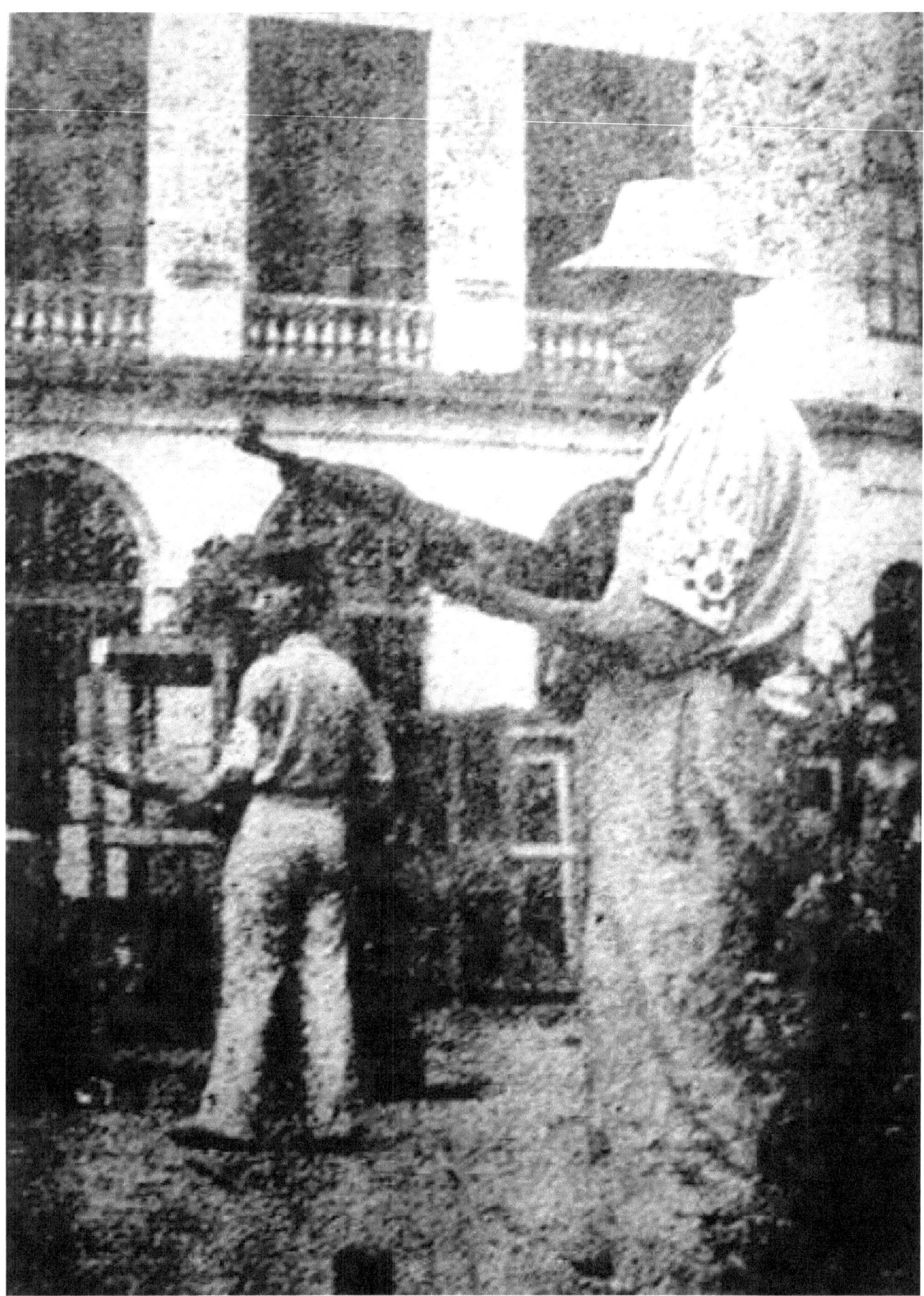
Real open Filipino Collaborators helping the Japanese in WWII

Philippines Via Old Pics (PVOP) - 7

WELCOME! Thank you for viewing these heritage or nostalgic pictures of individuals, places and events in the history of our beloved country, The Philippines. They say, a picture is worth a thousand words. More info about the person/event can easily be searched in the internet. These old pictures are available in prints, galleries, museums, magazines, and other forms of media. We record them as archives in this format for posterity.

This book can be displayed as coffee table book for family and guests. Each picture can be cut and framed, by buying extra copies. This book is suitable for libraries and schools in Philippines and USA. It is ideal reference material for study of history and celebrities. It is suitable as gift for any occasion. It's a collector's item. Heirs of those shown in pictures may want to own this book for their own families. Pictures are arranged in no particular order. Browse at random.

Most pictures are courtesy of Philippines My Philippines facebook website, but some were derived from various sources, like Museums, Wikipedia and historical websites.

Self-Publisher - Tatay Jobo Elizes
Printed, Sept., 2017 in the United States of America under ISBN codes below.
ISBN-13: 978 - 1975898281   +   ISBN-10: 1975898281
Book List - Buy online as paperback or kindle - Contact: job_elizes@yahoo.com
Websites: http://tinyurl.com/mj76ccq + www.jobelizes6.wix.com/mysite

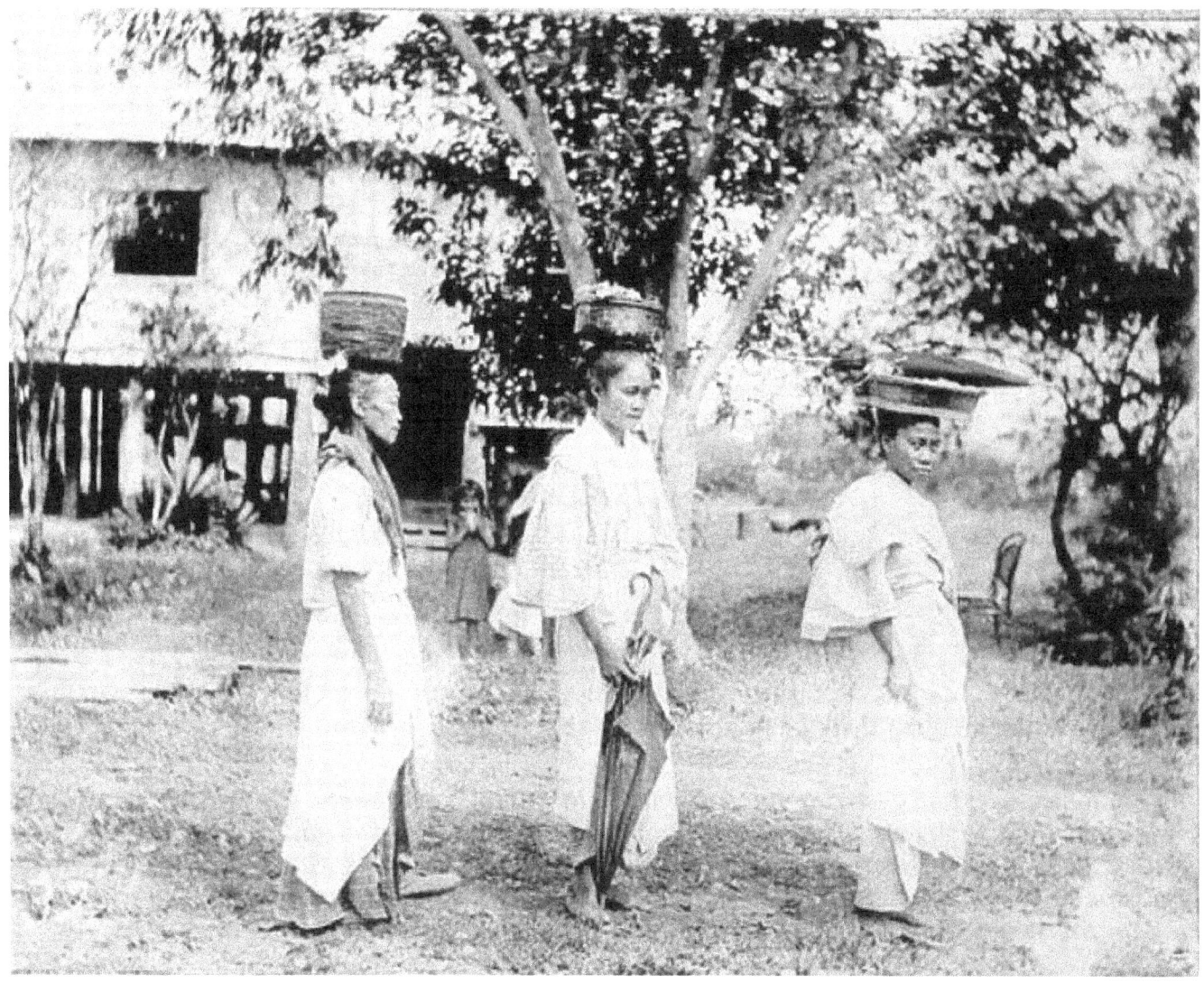

Typical Filipina Women Going to the Market, Early 1900s

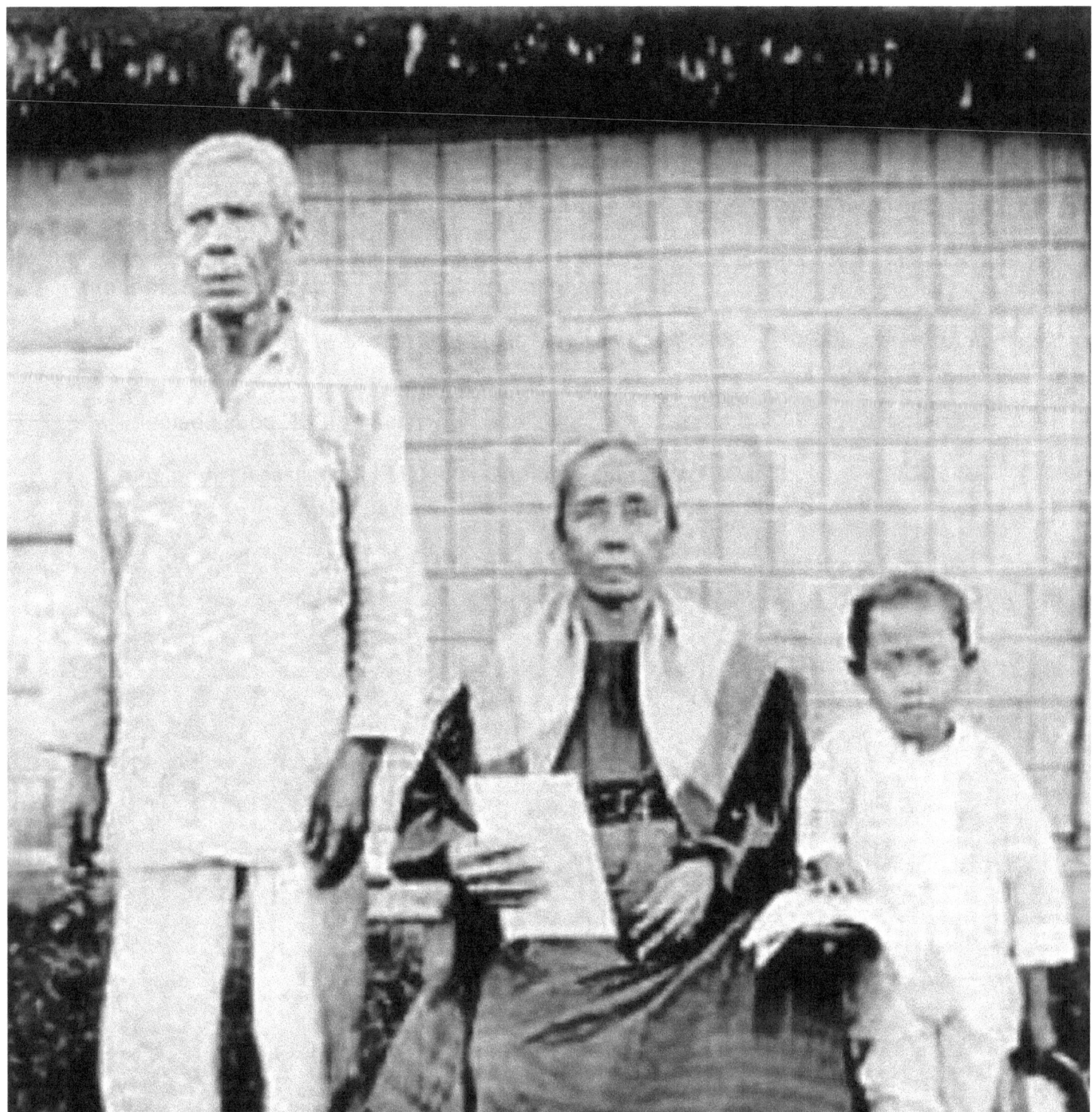

Typical Filipino grandparents and grandson in their normal attire, early 1900s

This book can be displayed as coffee table book for family and guests. Each picture can be cut and framed, by buying extra copies. This book is suitable for libraries and schools in Philippines and USA. It is ideal reference material for study of history and celebrities. It is suitable as gift for any occasion. It's a collector's item. Heirs of those shown in pictures may want to own this book for their own families. Pictures are arranged in no particular order. Browse at random.

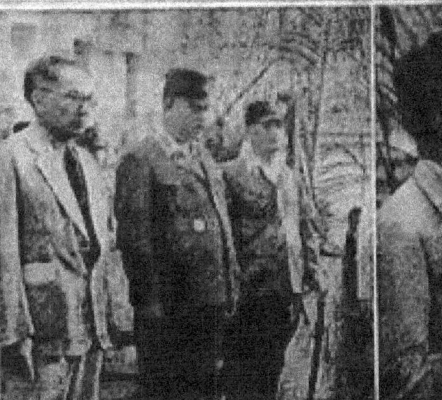

News about Filipino collaboration in WWII

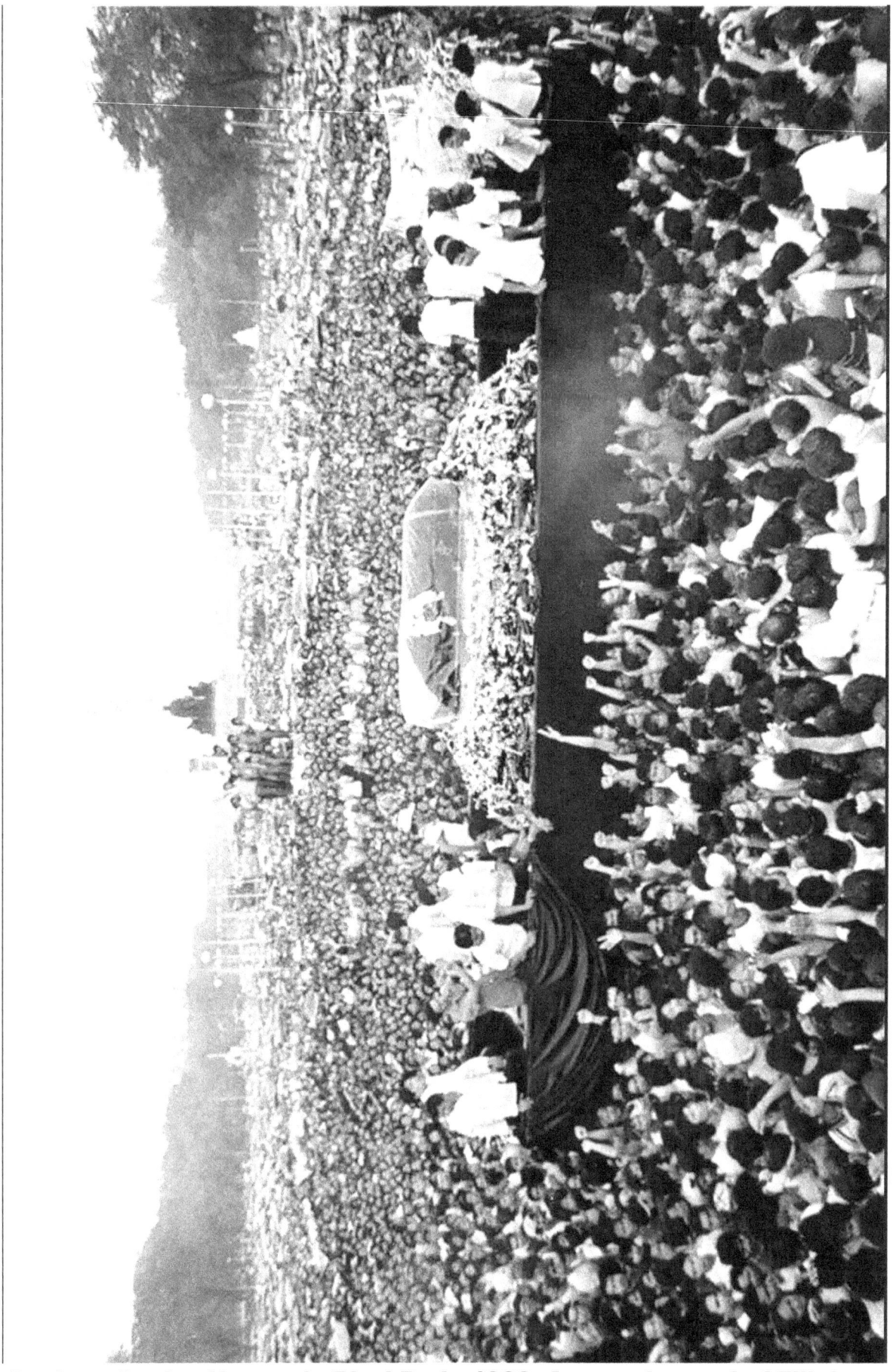

Benigno Aquino Hearse in Rizal Park, 1983. A record crowd of Filipinos

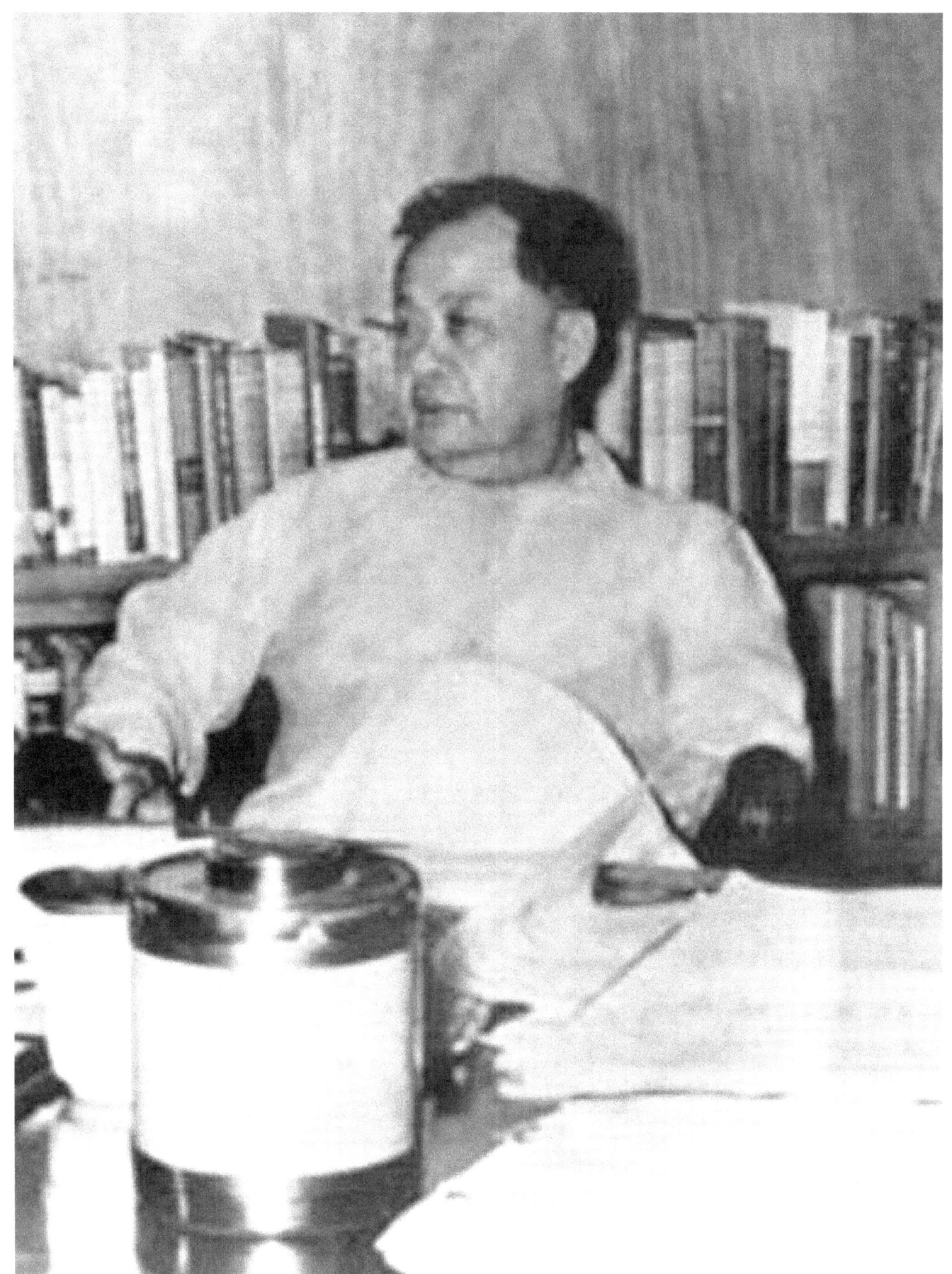

Claro M. Recto, Prominent Filipino Leader, Senator, Patriot & Nationalist

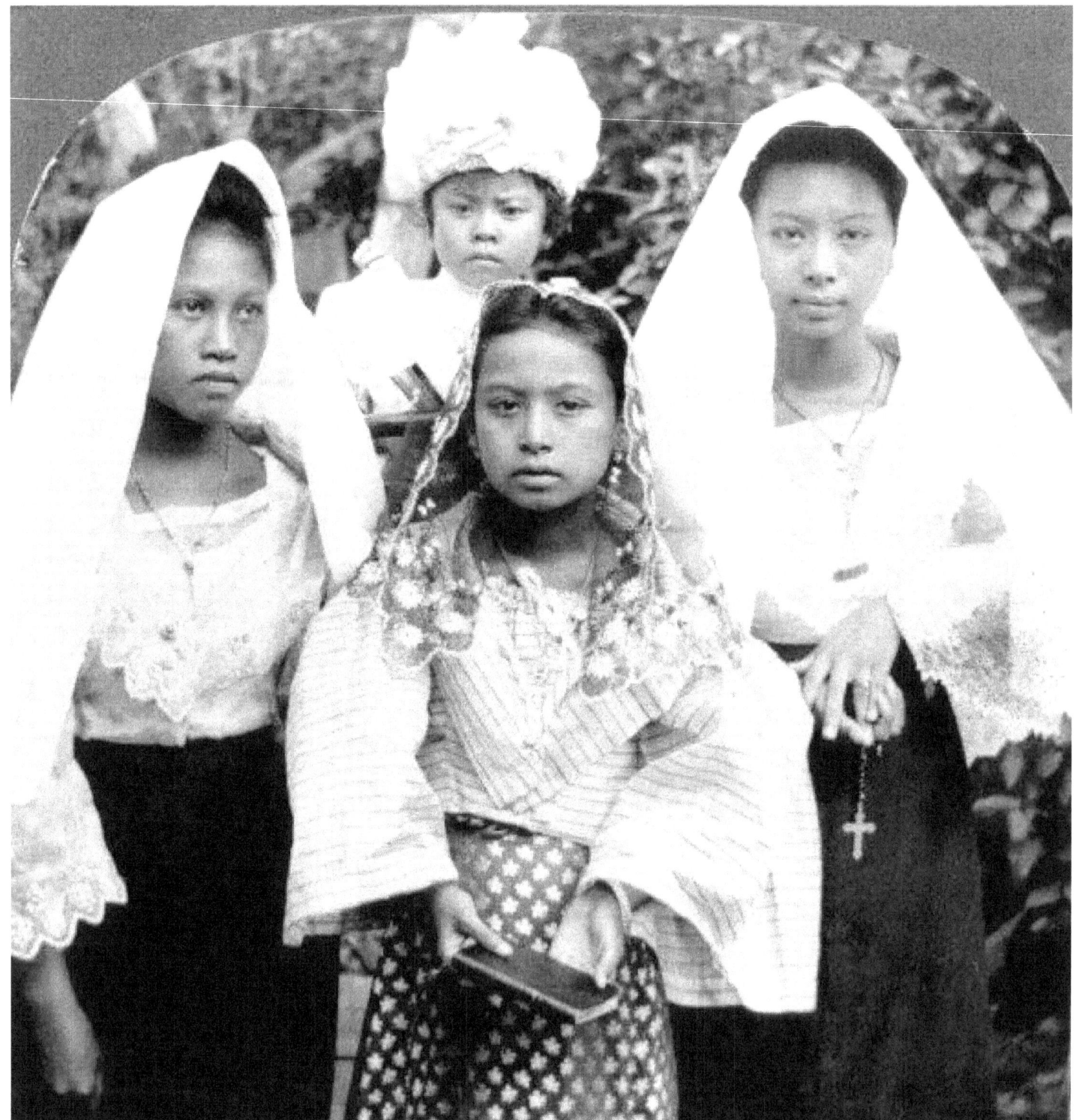

Typical Catholic Faithful Filpina Women, early 1900s. Note elitist fashion.

This book can be displayed as coffee table book for family and guests. Each picture can be cut and framed, by buying extra copies. This book is suitable for libraries and schools in Philippines and USA. It is ideal reference material for study of history and celebrities. It is suitable as gift for any occasion. It's a collector's item. Heirs of those shown in pictures may want to own this book for their own families. Pictures are arranged in no particular order. Browse at random.

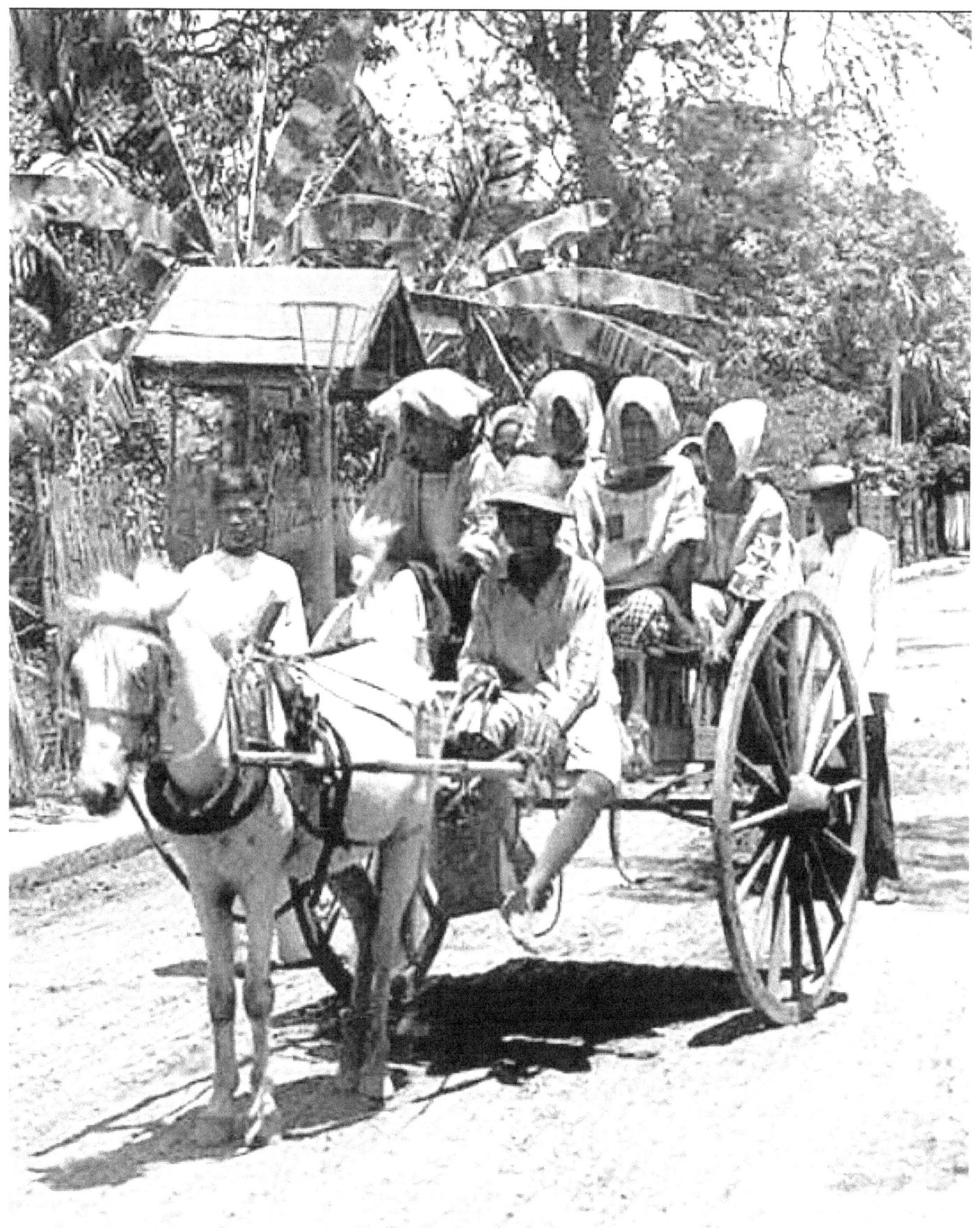

Typical Horse-drawn cart as mode of transport, early 1900s

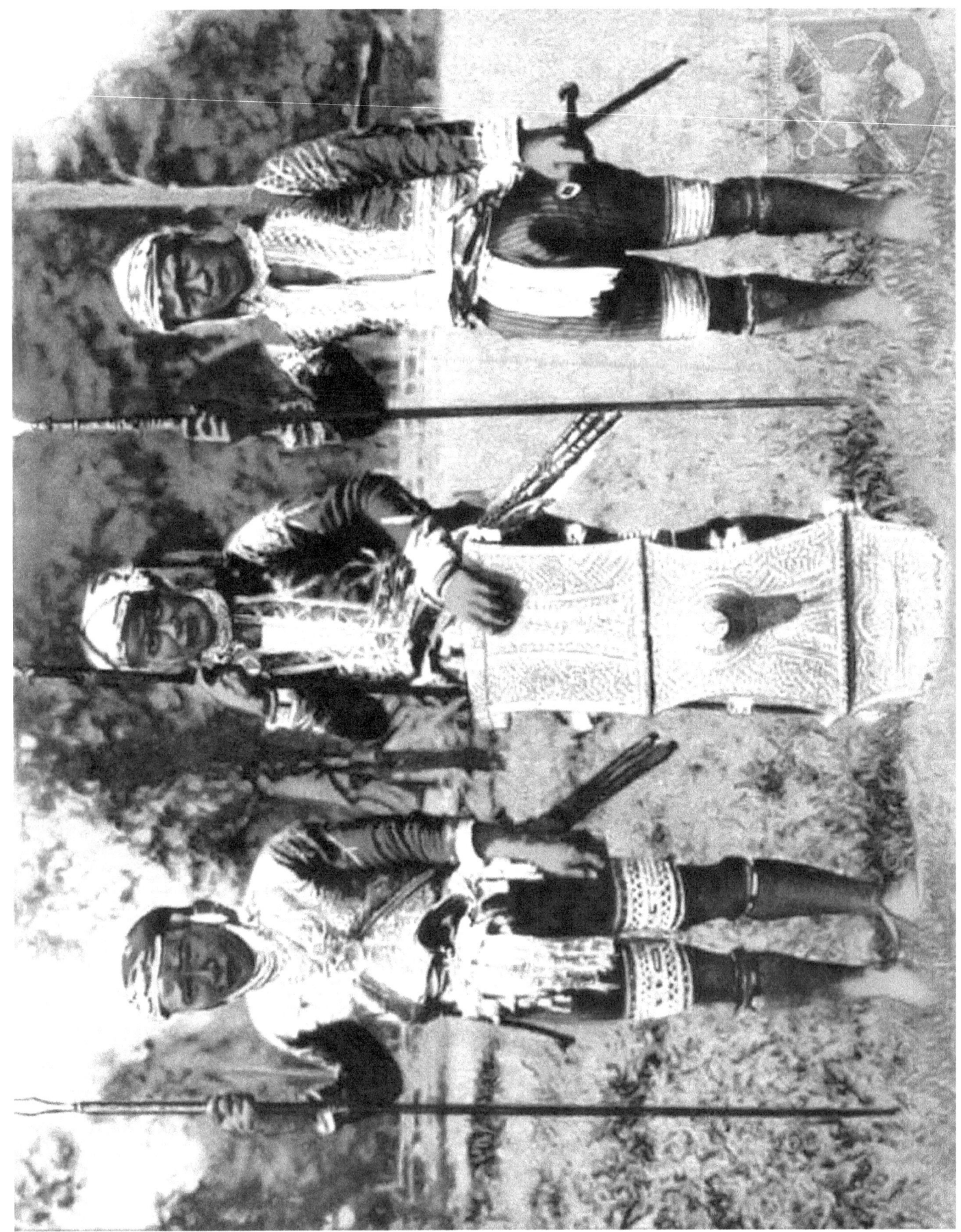

Typical Leaders & Attire in Mindanao Moro Tribes of Philippines, many years

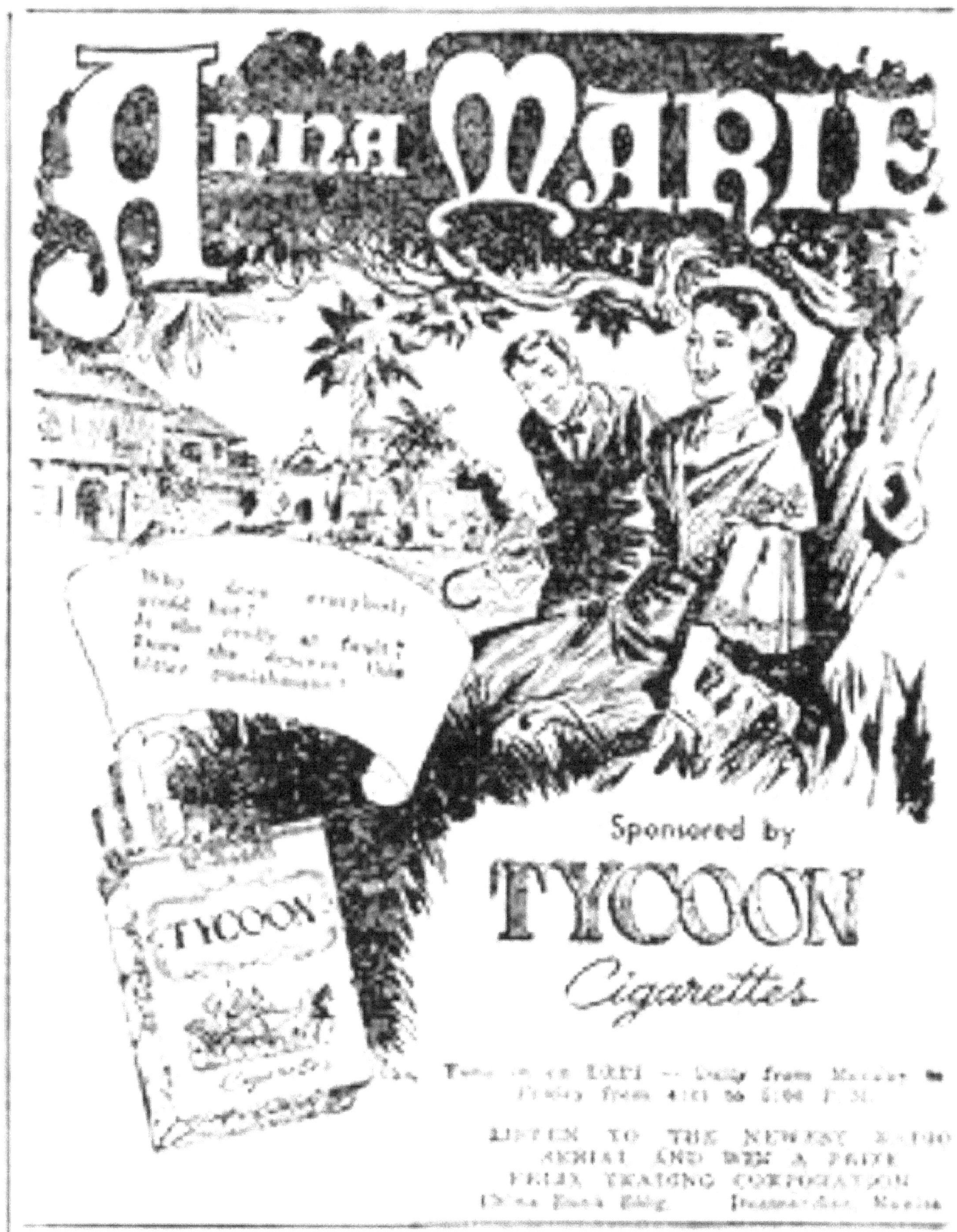

Typical Philippine Ad, maybe 1940s-1950s

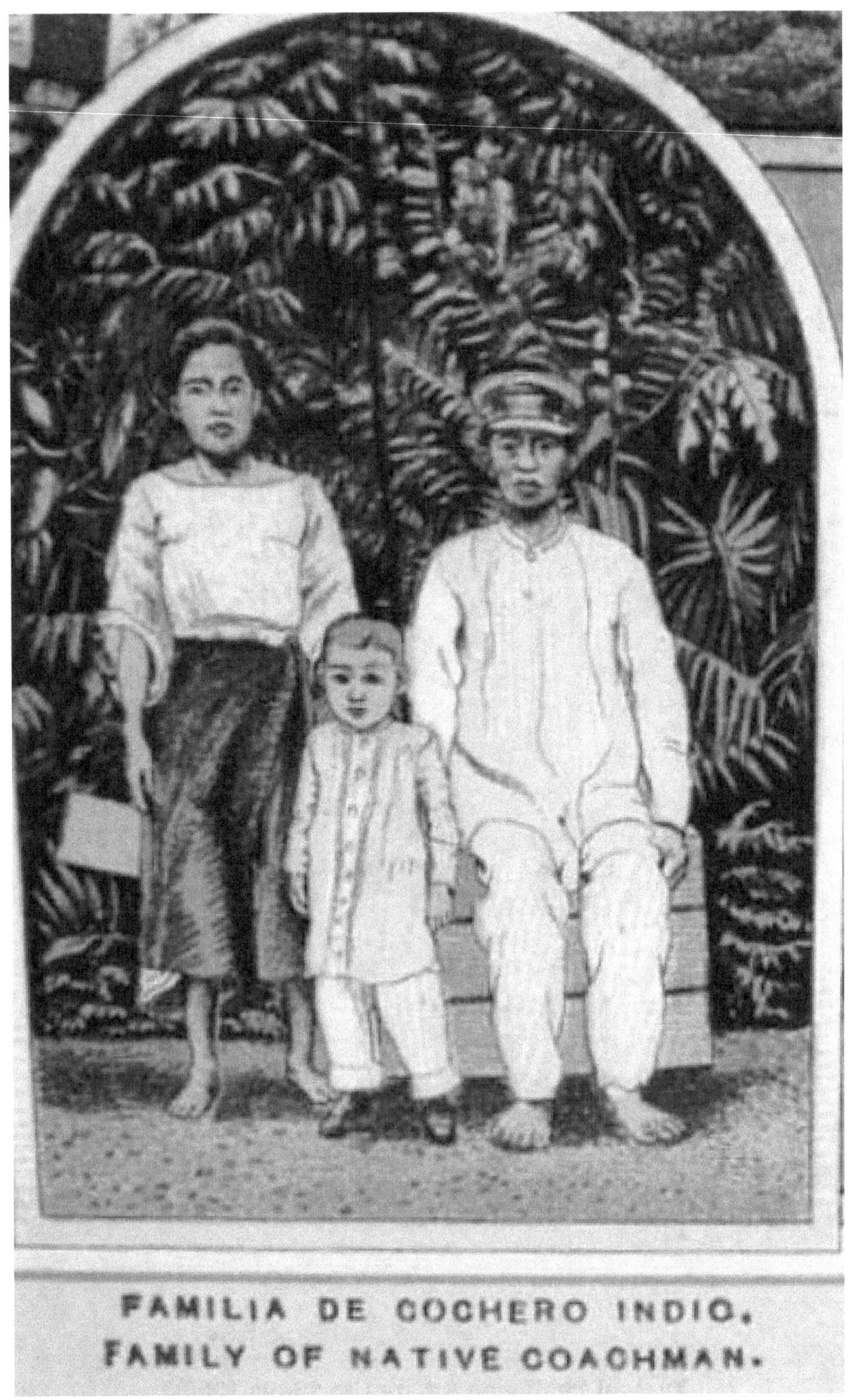

FAMILIA DE COCHERO INDIO,
FAMILY OF NATIVE COACHMAN.

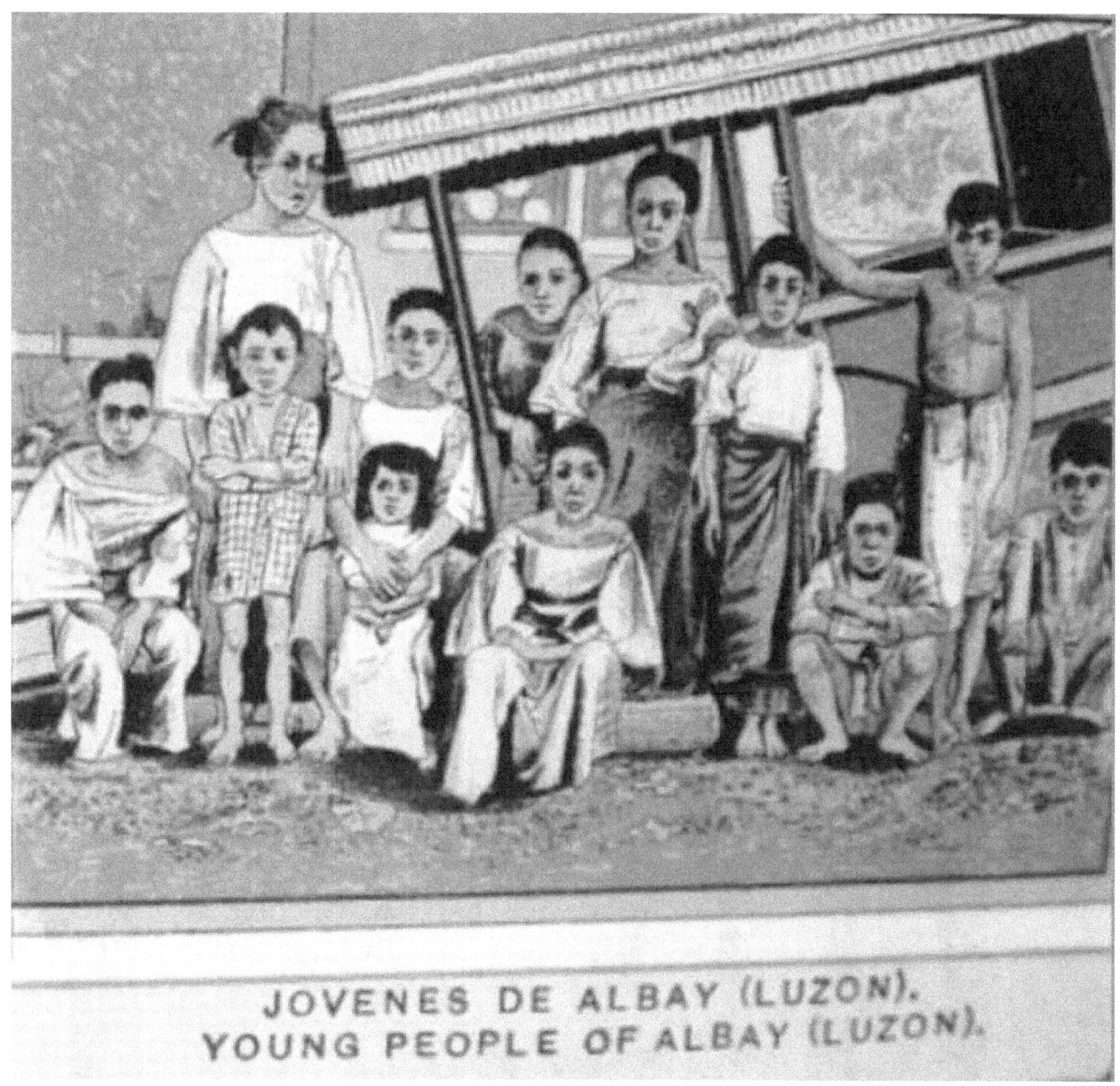

A drawing

This book can be displayed as coffee table book for family and guests. Each picture can be cut and framed, by buying extra copies. This book is suitable for libraries and schools in Philippines and USA. It is ideal reference material for study of history and celebrities. It is suitable as gift for any occasion. It's a collector's item. Heirs of those shown in pictures may want to own this book for their own families. Pictures are arranged in no particular order. Browse at random.

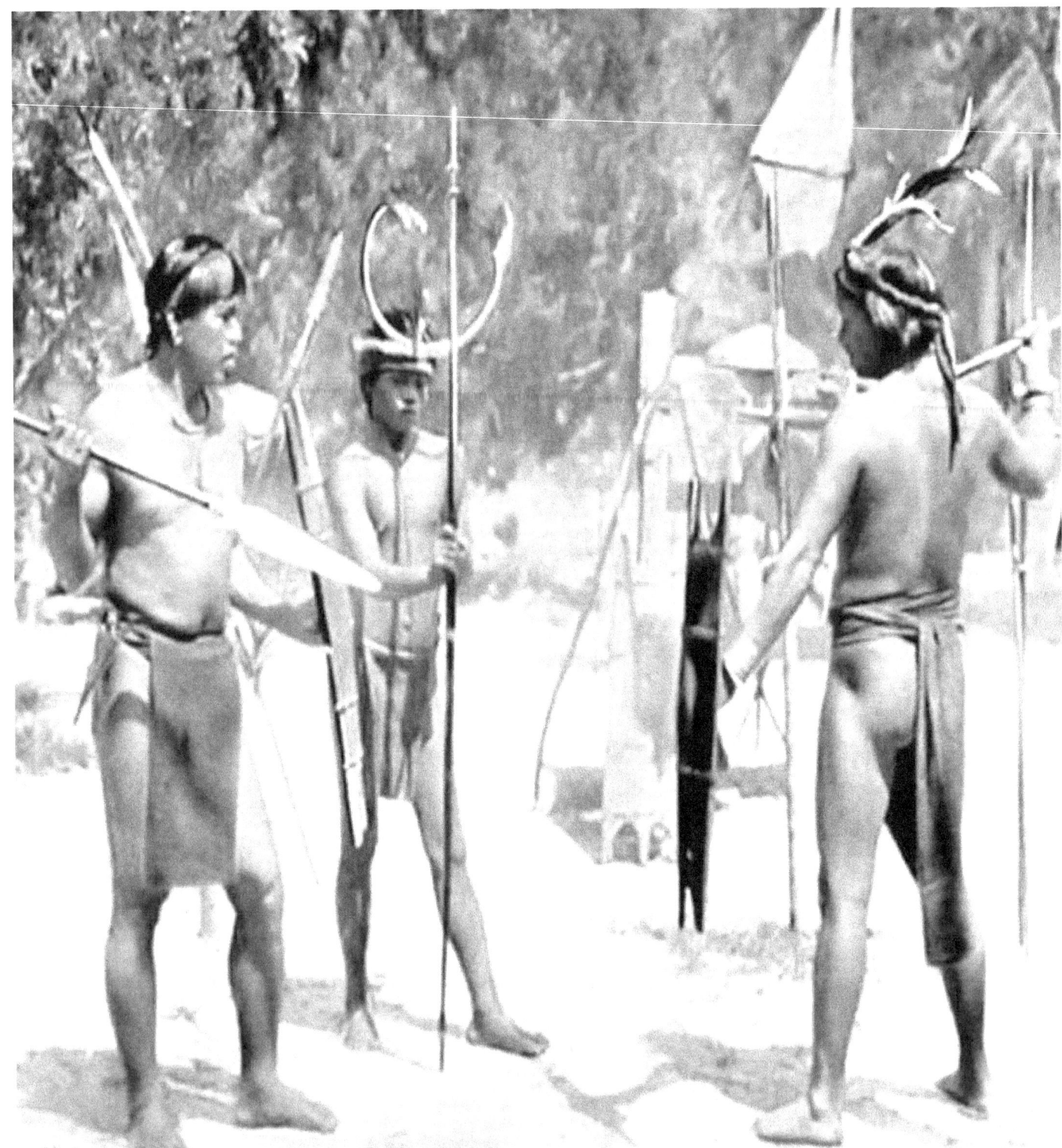

Typical Igorot warriors from Mountain Provinces, Phl for many centruies

This book can be displayed as coffee table book for family and guests. Each picture can be cut and framed, by buying extra copies. This book is suitable for libraries and schools in Philippines and USA. It is ideal reference material for study of history and celebrities. It is suitable as gift for any occasion. It's a collector's item. Heirs of those shown in pictures may want to own this book for their own families. Pictures are arranged in no particular order. Browse at random.

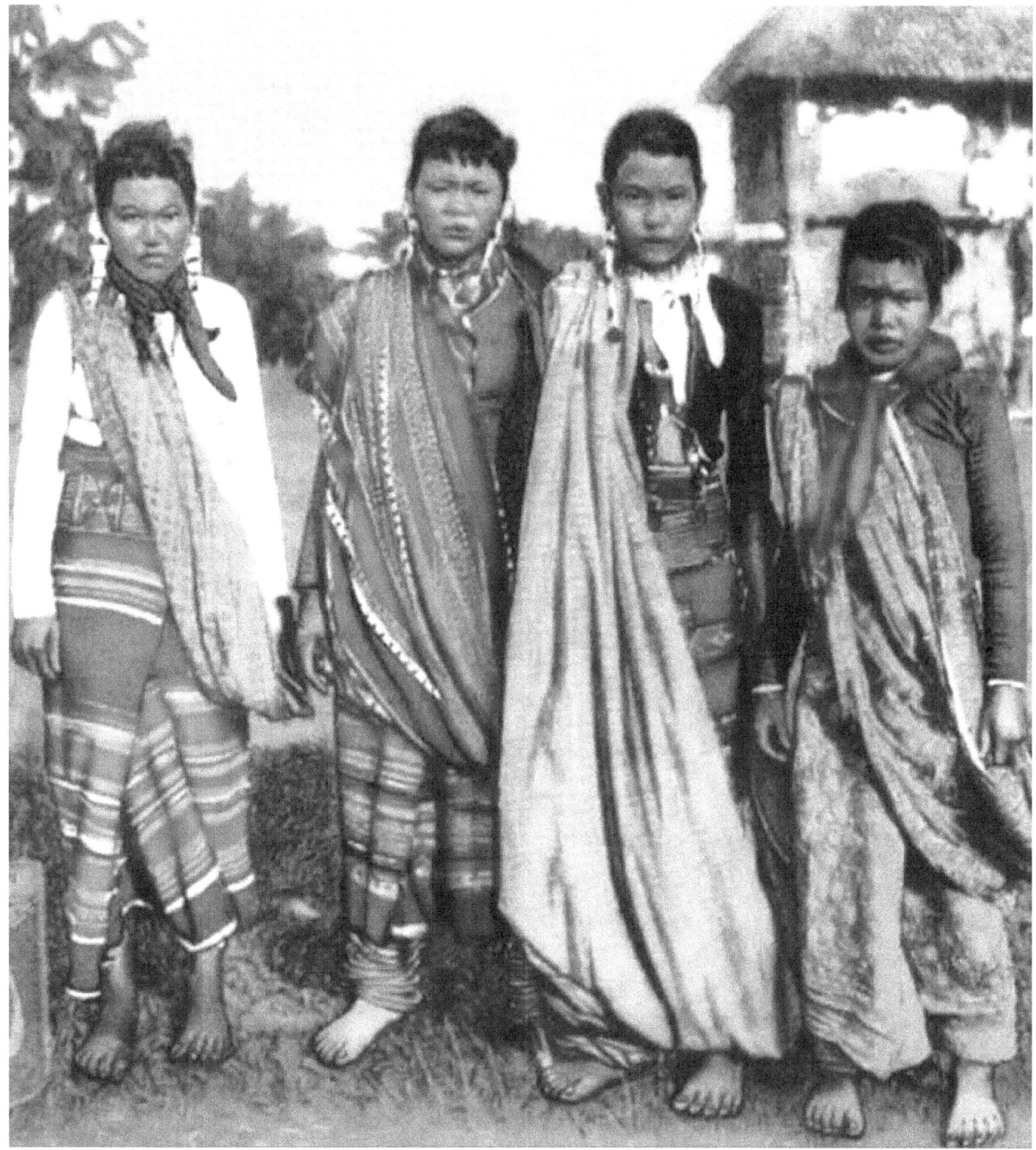

Moroland Ladies Attire ins Mindanao, Phl. For many centuries

This book can be displayed as coffee table book for family and guests. Each picture can be cut and framed, by buying extra copies. This book is suitable for libraries and schools in Philippines and USA. It is ideal reference material for study of history and celebrities. It is suitable as gift for any occasion. It's a collector's item. Heirs of those shown in pictures may want to own this book for their own families. Pictures are arranged in no particular order. Browse at random.

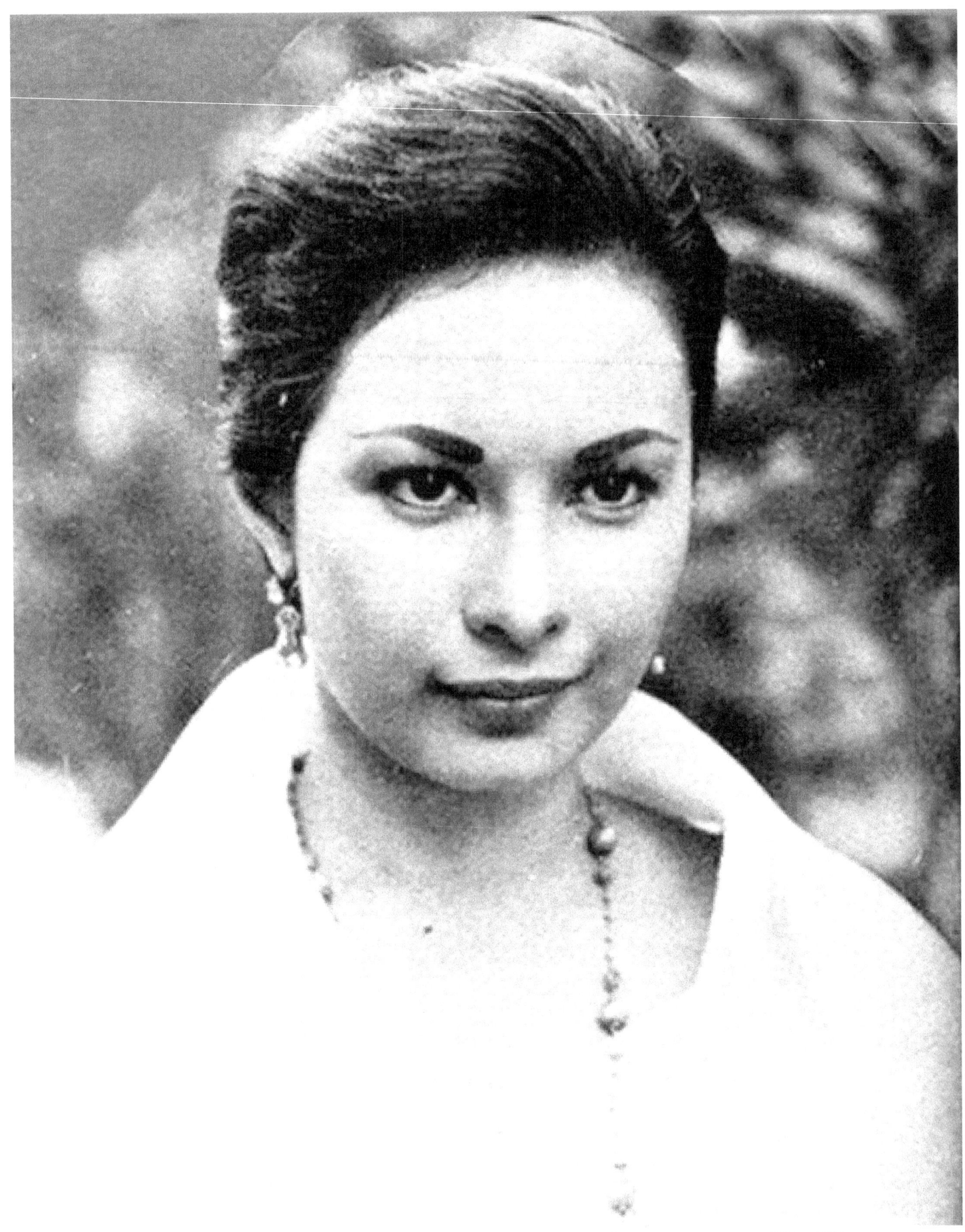

Charito Solis - Beauteous & talented Actress of yesteryears, 50s-70s

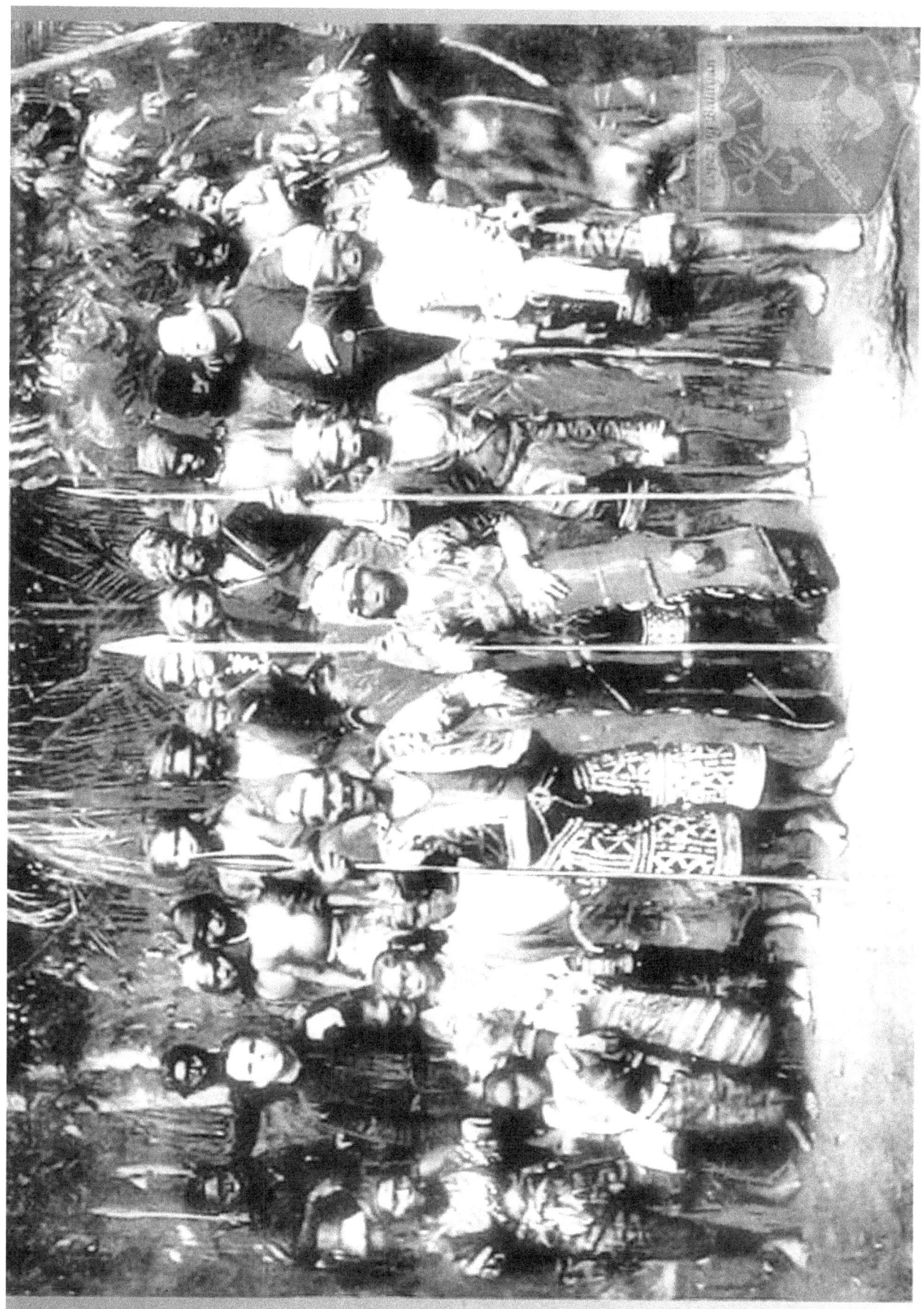

Moroland Tribal Clan with 2 Catholic Priests, early 1900s

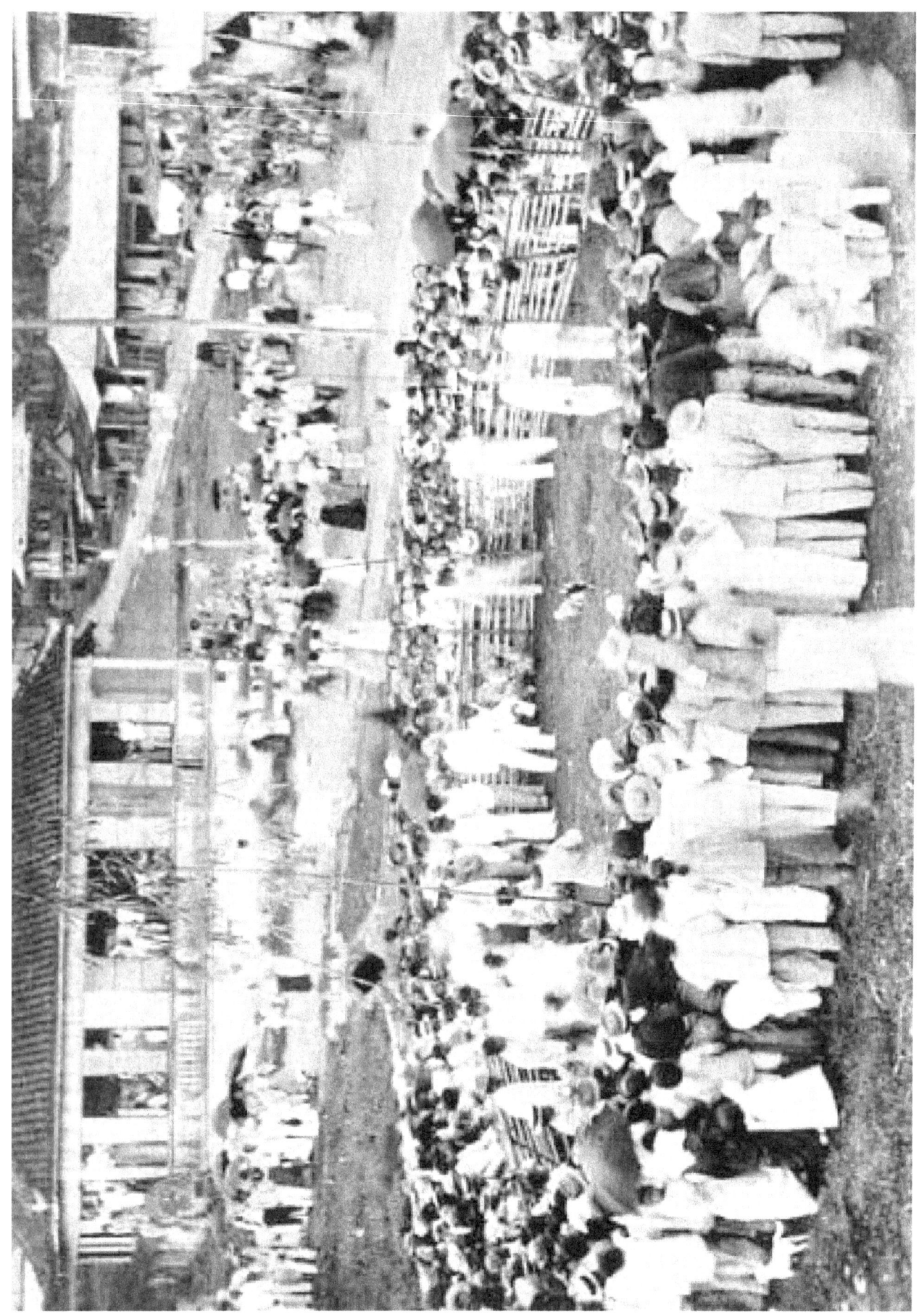
Typical Cock-Fight Gathering of Filipinos, early 1900s pic

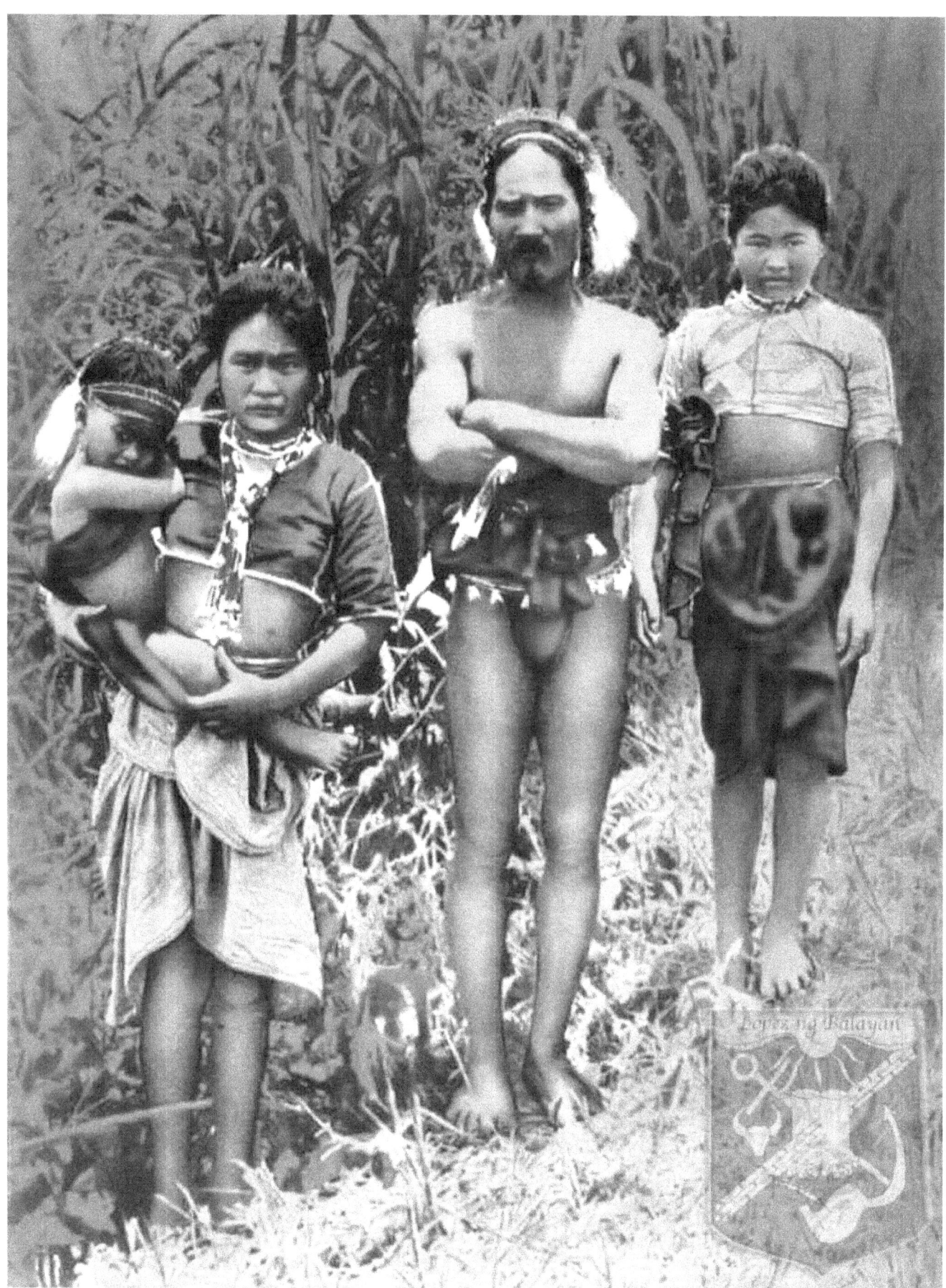
Typical Igorot Family and Attire for many years, 1900s pic

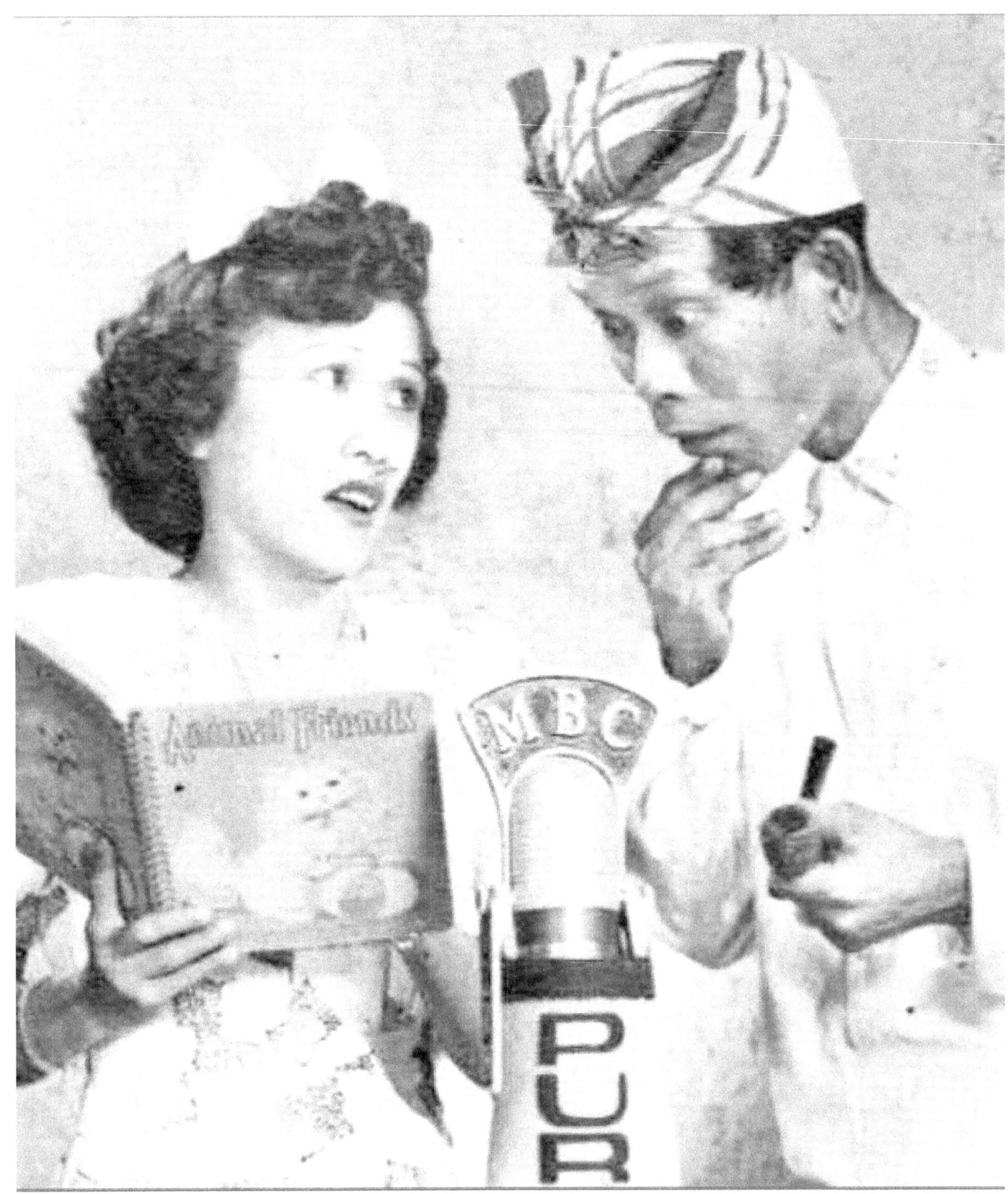

Chichay & Tolindoy, famous comedy team, 1050s-60s

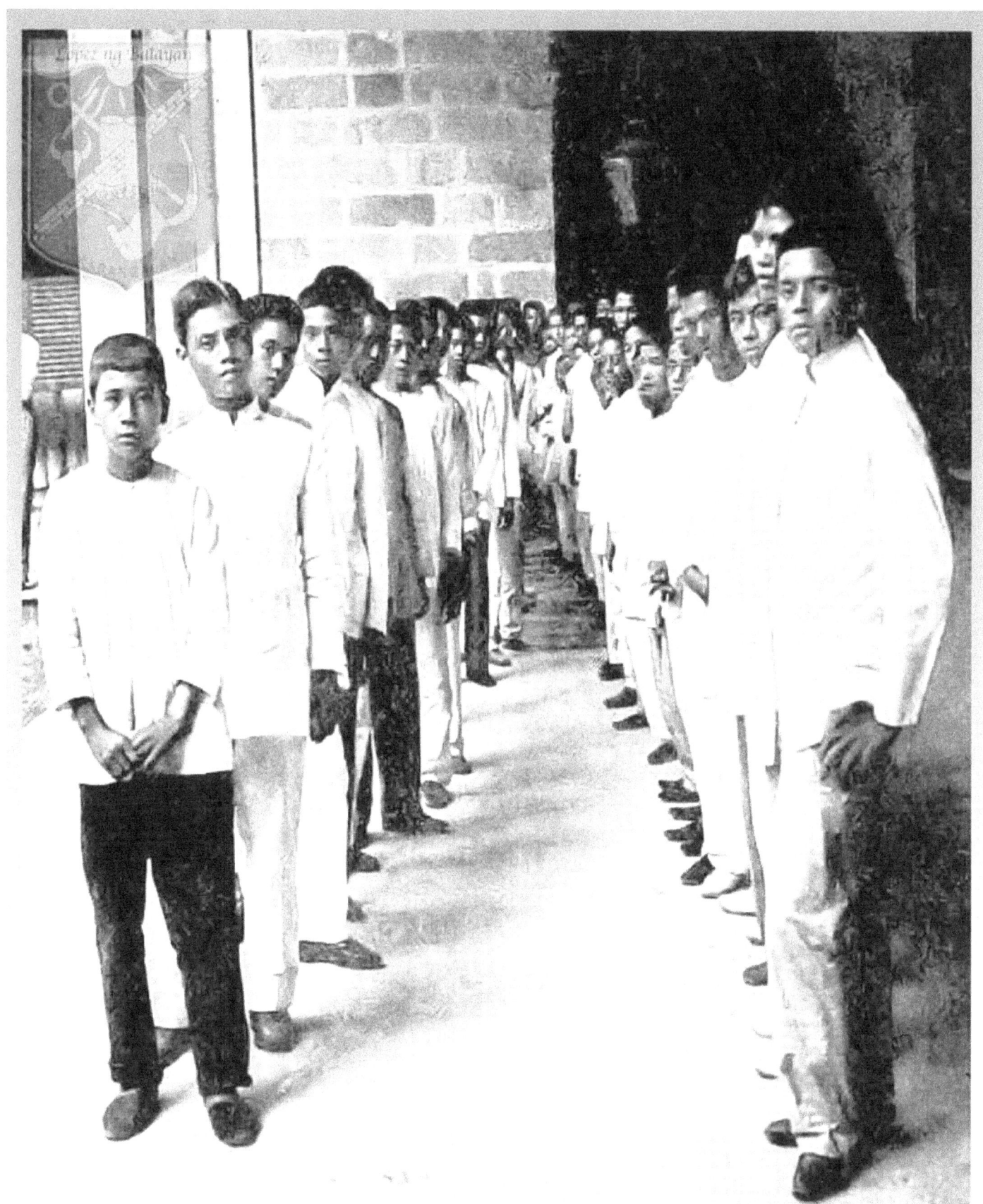

Typical Filipino Students of an Elite School, early 1900s

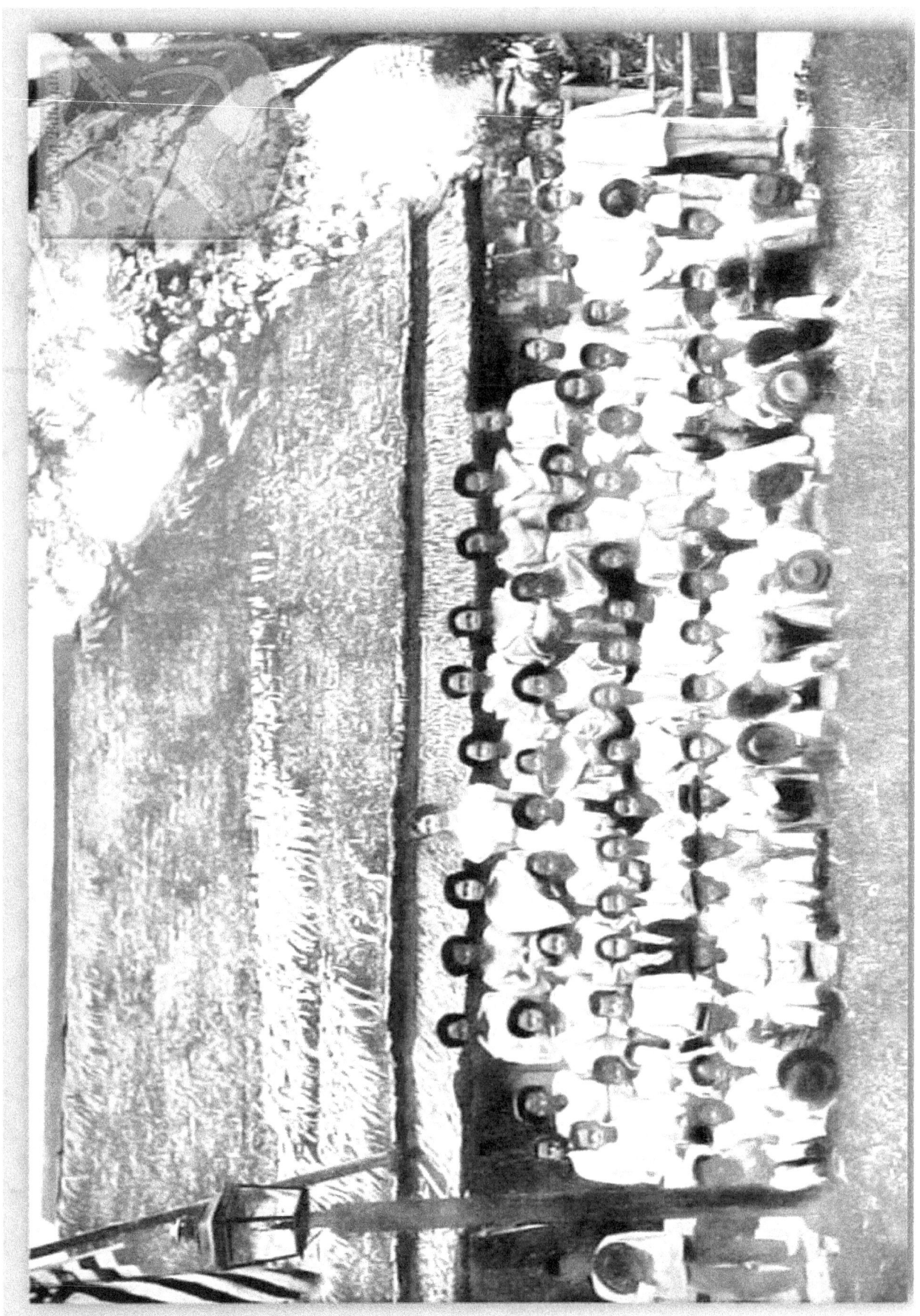

American Thomasite Teacher with her school children, early 1900s

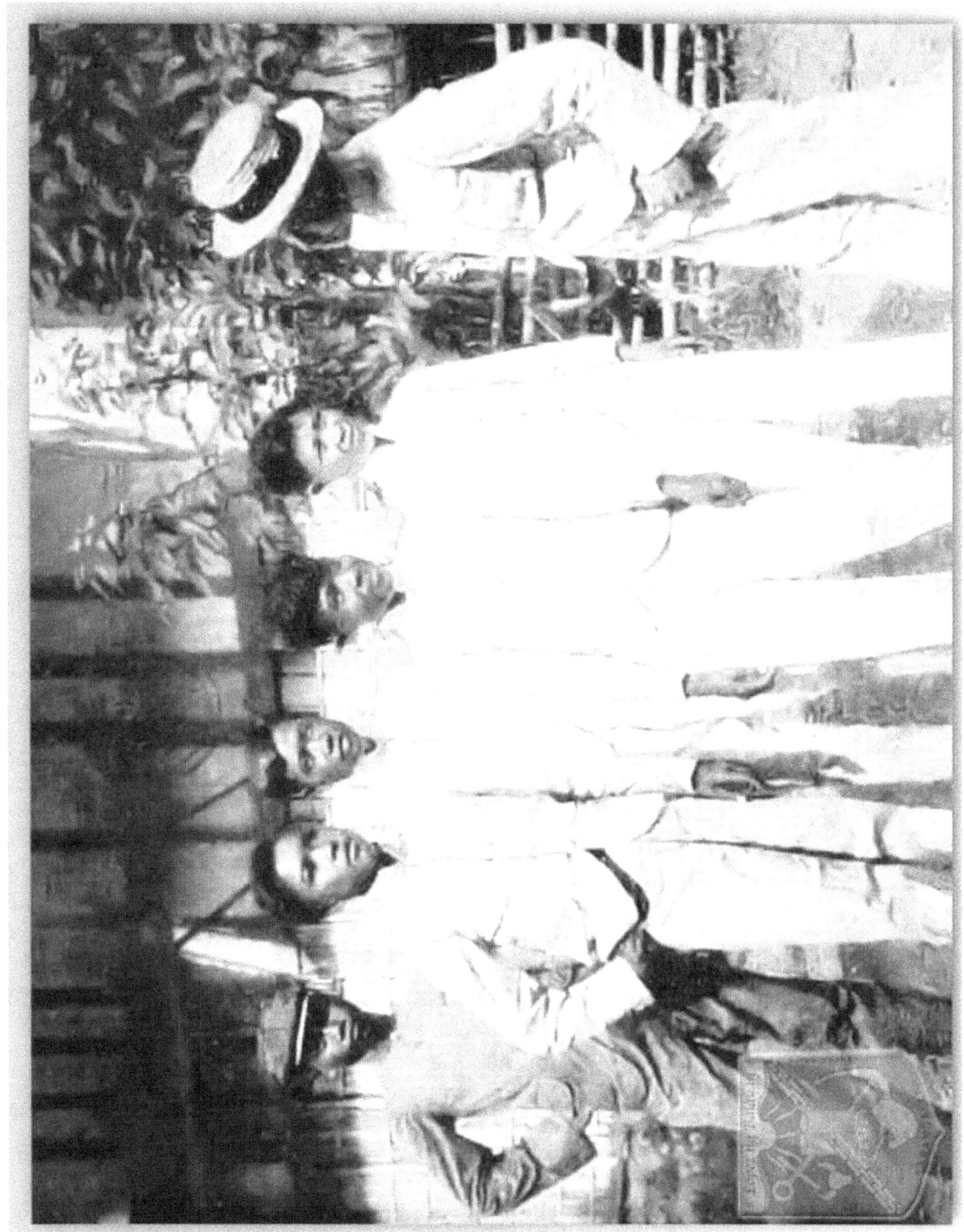

Young Filipino gentlemen from a prestigious school, early 1900s

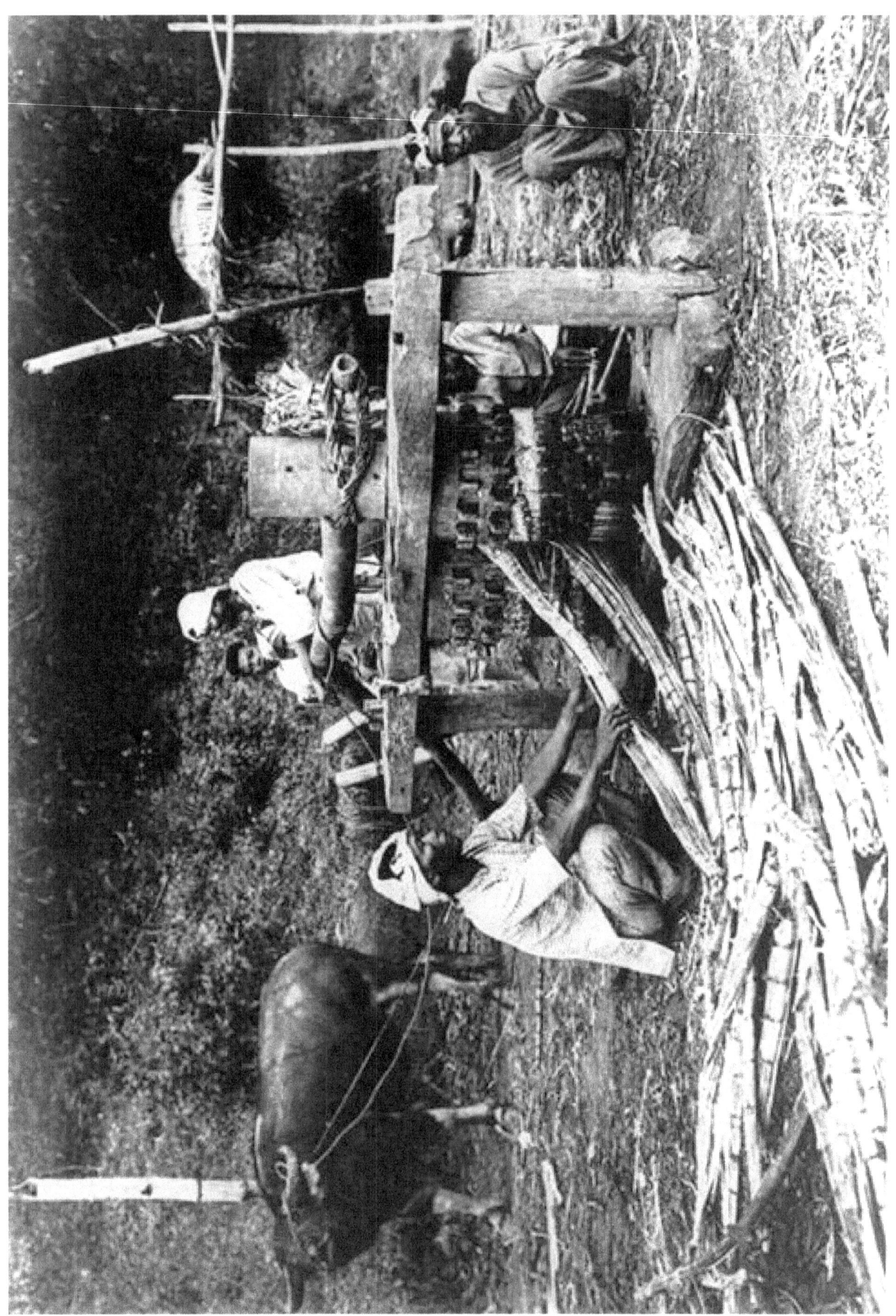

Sugarcane Juicer by carabao-driven crude rotary system, early 1900s

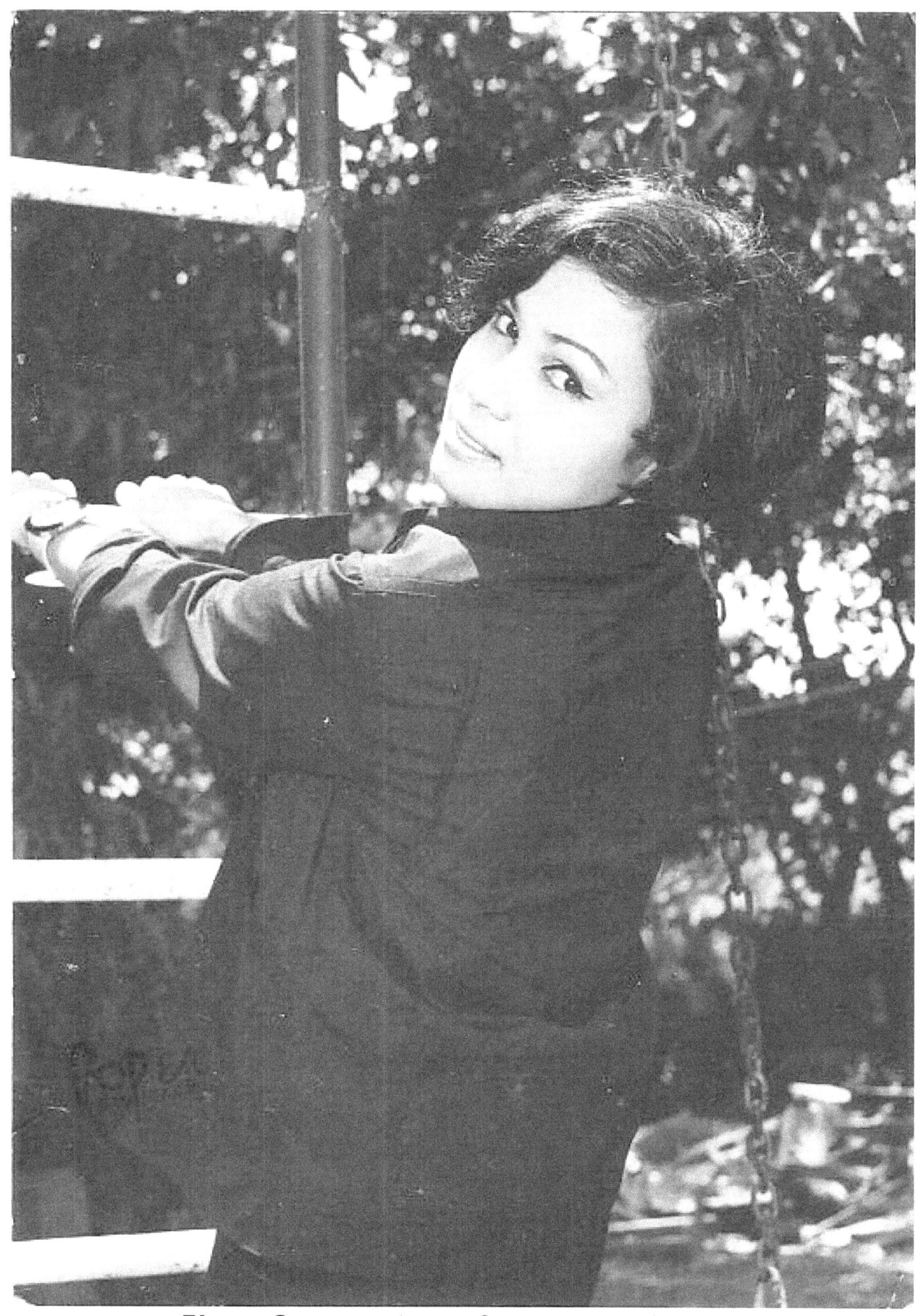

Blanca Gomez, actress of yesteryears, 60s-70s

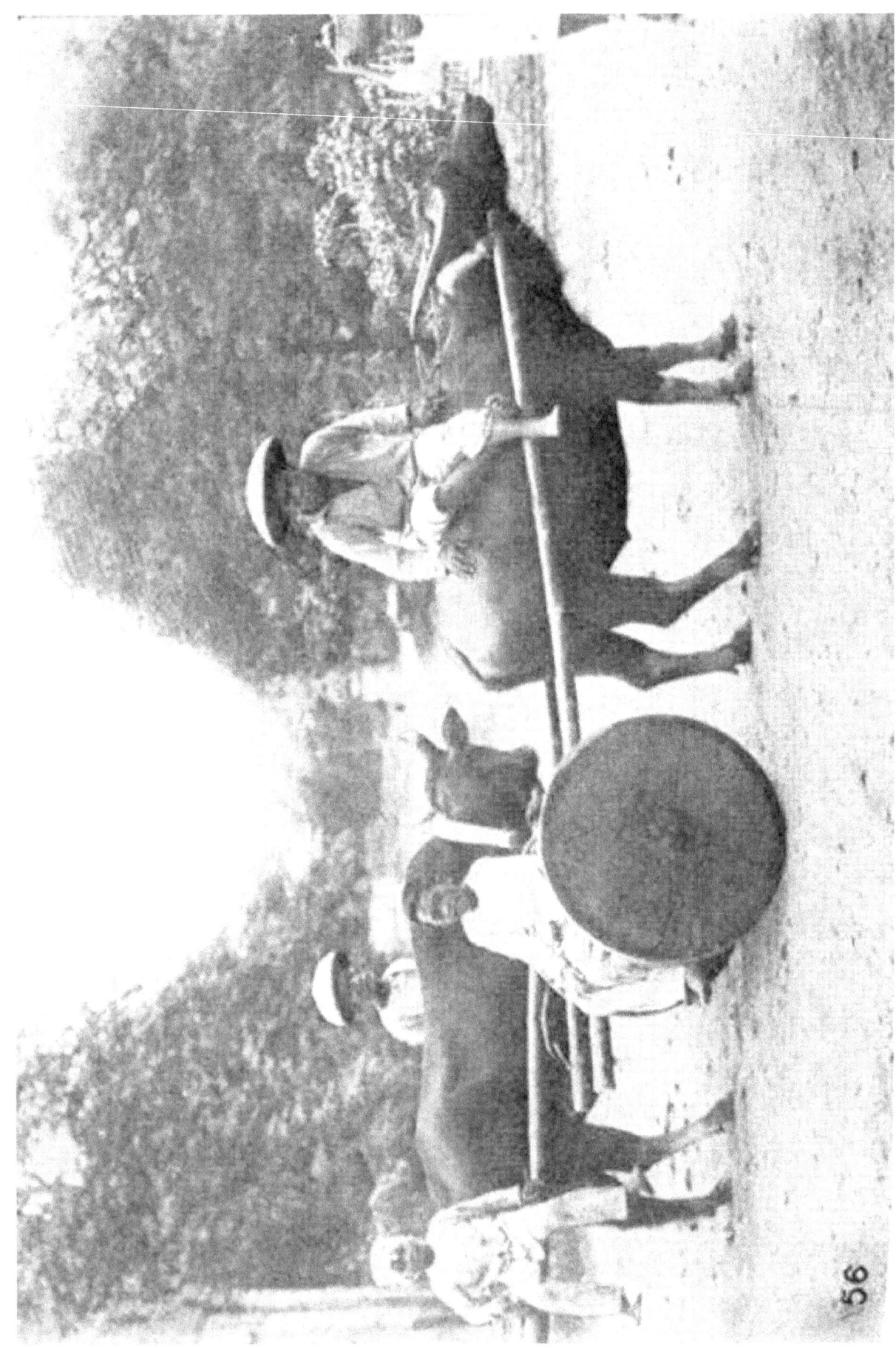
Mode or rural transport, carabao cart, many centuries

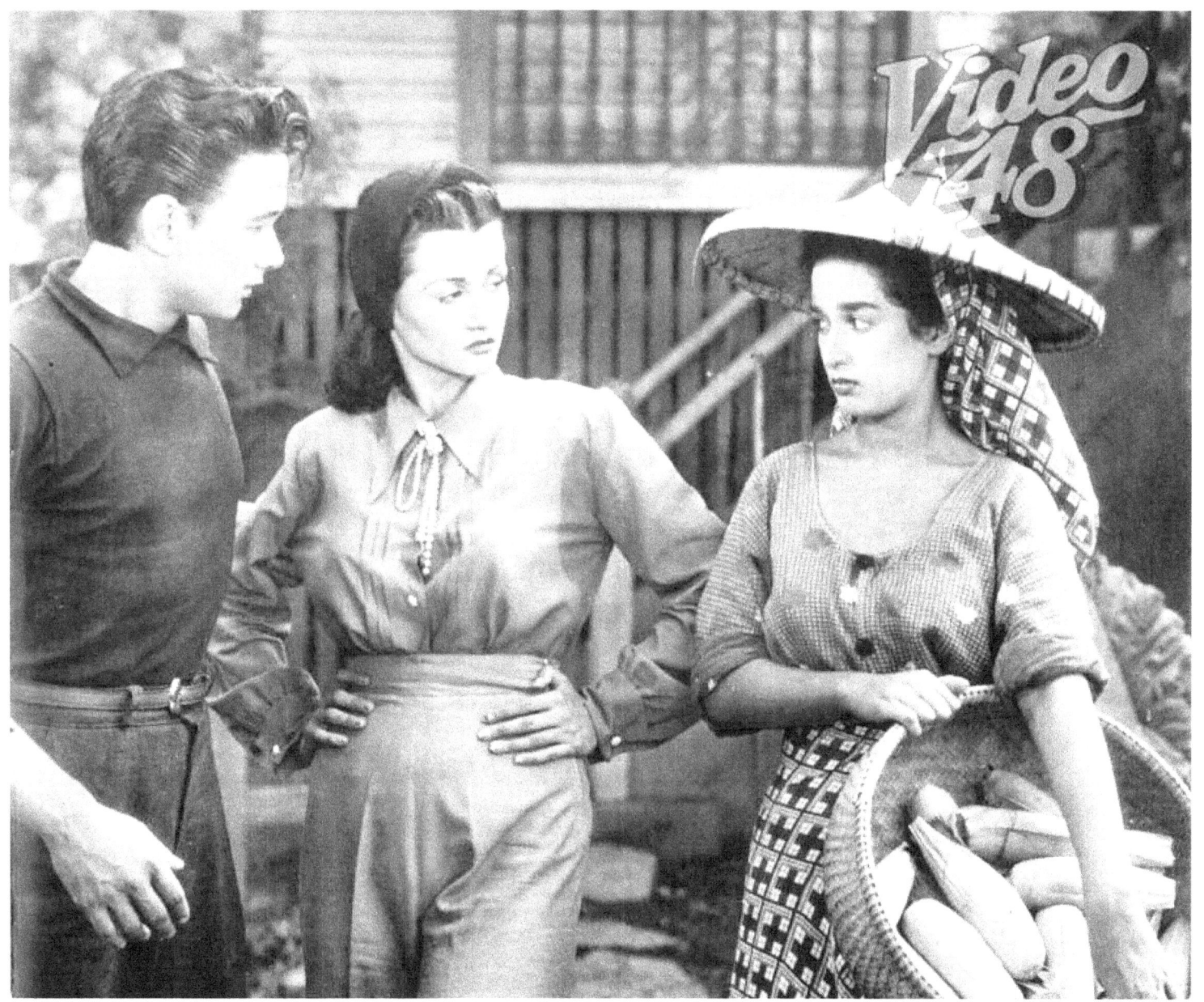

Armando Goyena+ Rosal Rosal+ Tessie Quintana
Famous Filipino Movie Stars of yesteryears, 50s to 70s

WELCOME! Thank you for viewing these heritage or nostalgic pictures of individuals, places and events in the history of our beloved country, The Philippines. They say, a picture is worth a thousand words. More info about the person/event can easily be searched in the internet. These old pictures are available in prints, galleries, museums, magazines, and other forms of media. We record them as archives in this format for posterity.

This book can be displayed as coffee table book for family and guests. Each picture can be cut and framed, by buying extra copies. This book is suitable for libraries and schools in Philippines and USA. It is ideal reference material for study of history and celebrities. It is suitable as gift for any occasion. It's a collector's item. Heirs of those shown in pictures may want to own this book for their own families. Pictures are arranged in no particular order. Browse at random.

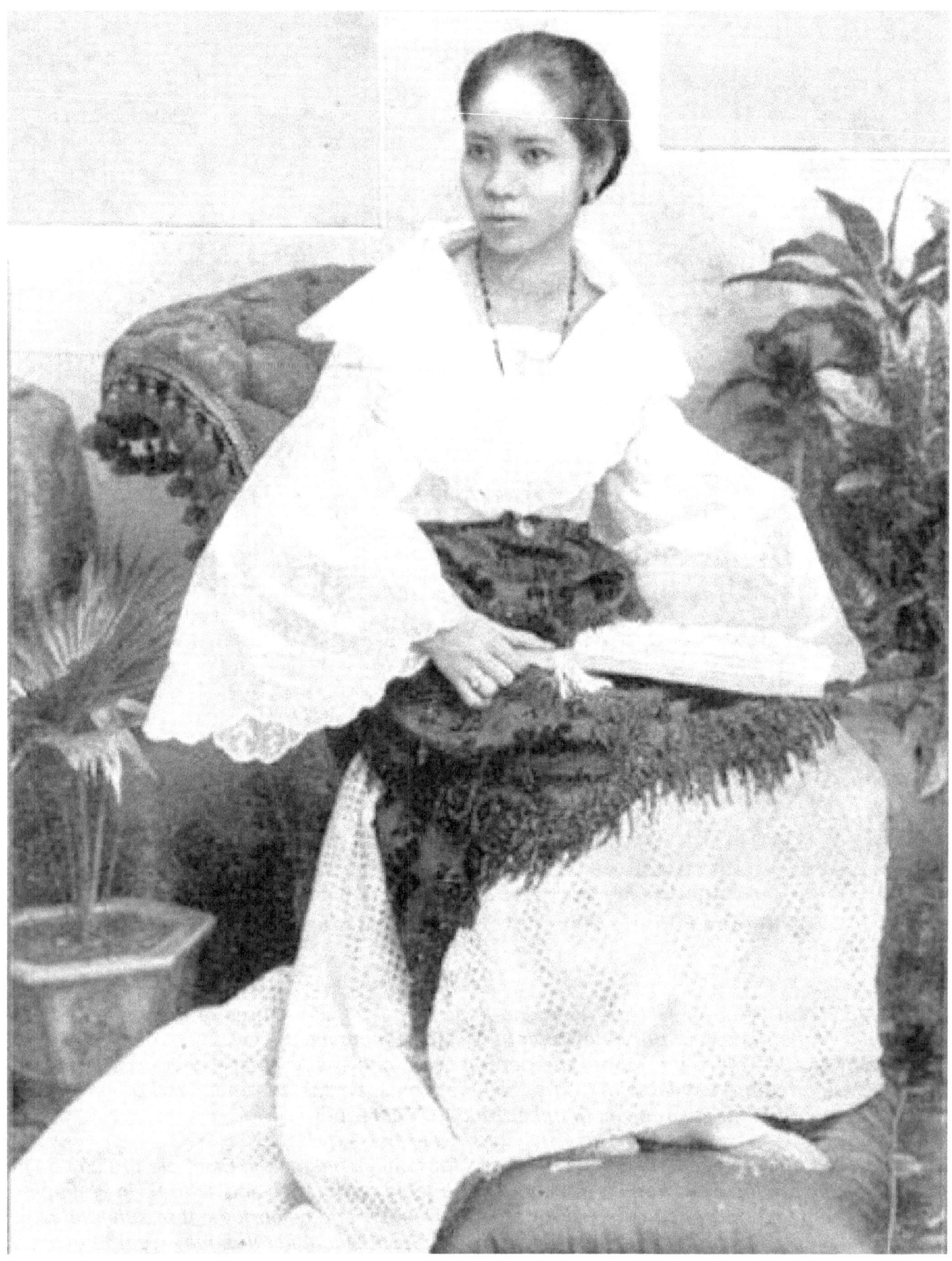

A Spanish Mestiza, with Spanish father and native Filipina mother, revered because of their western features. Early 1900s pic.

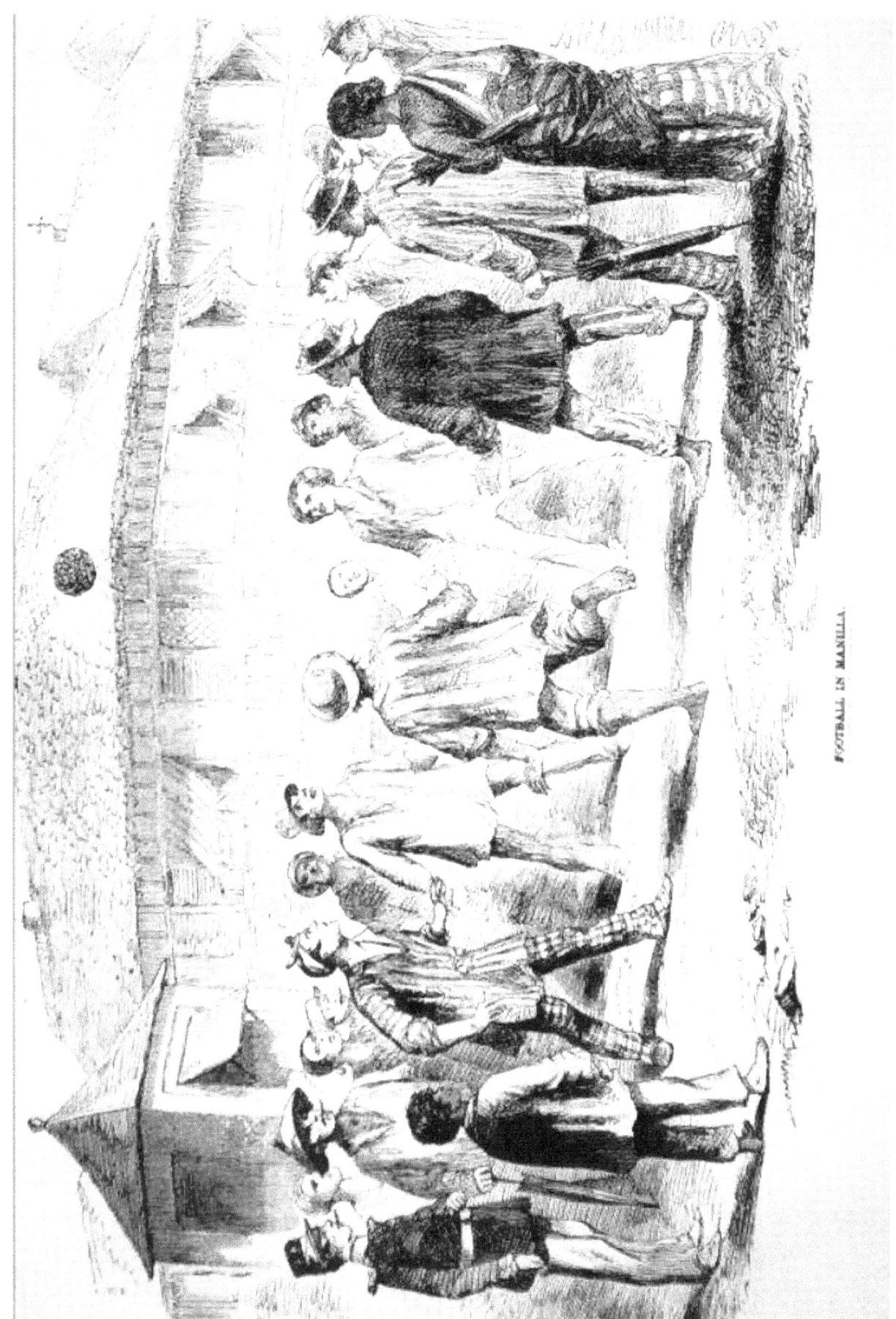

Illustration, football in Manila, 19th – 20th century

Philippines Via Old Pics (PVOP) - 7

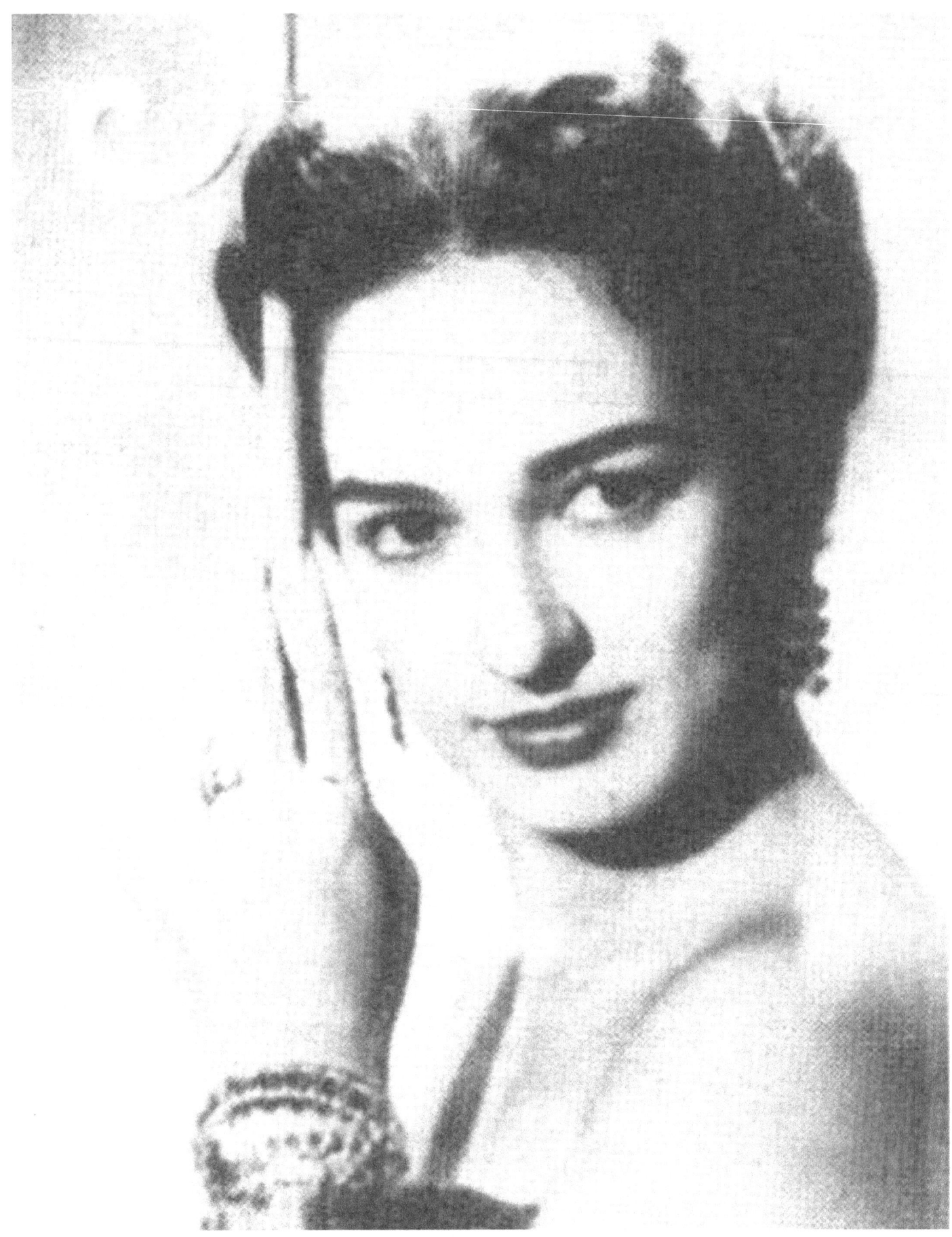

Tessie Quintana, famous movie star, 50s-70s

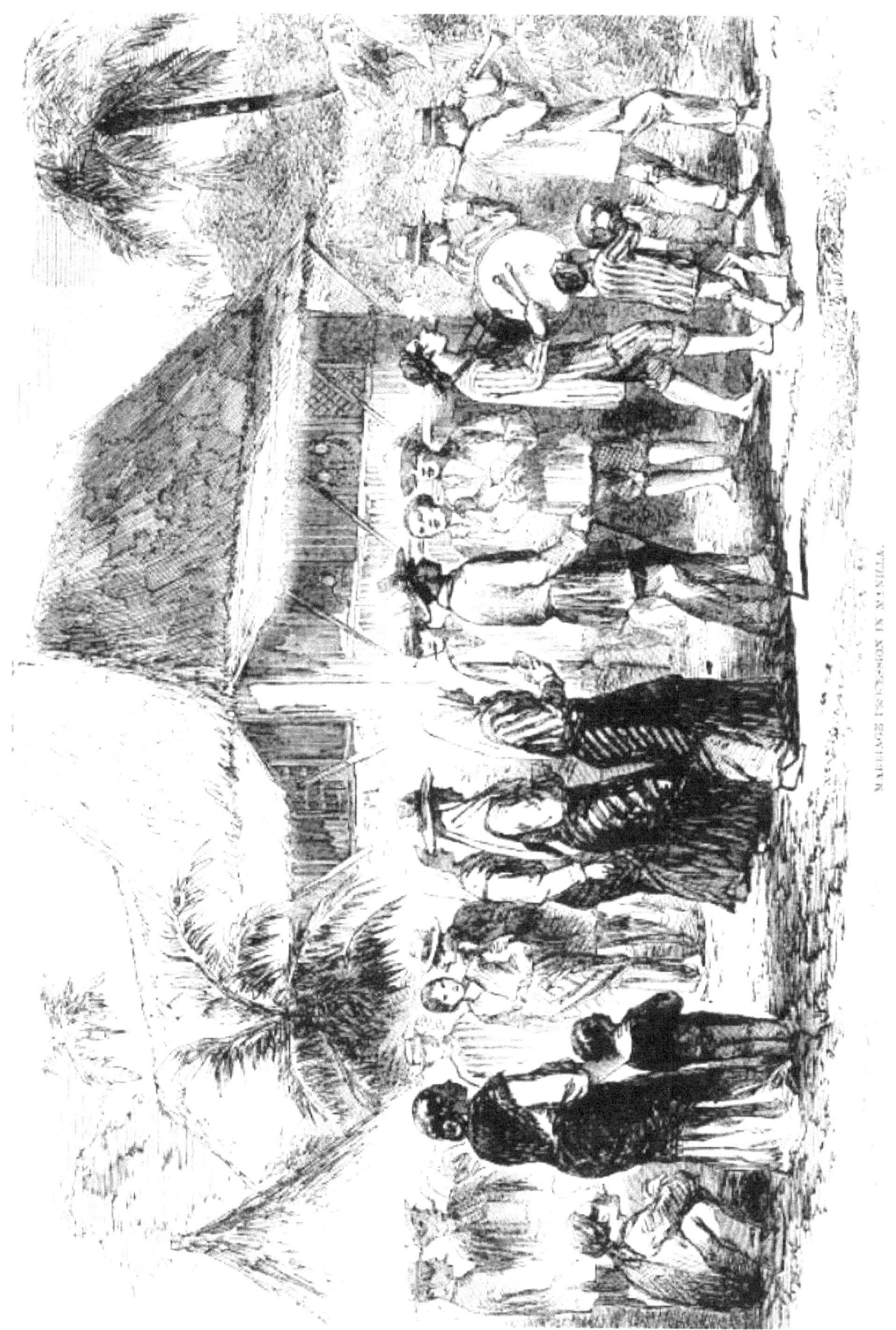

Illustration – Marriage Custom via procession in Manila, 19th-20th century

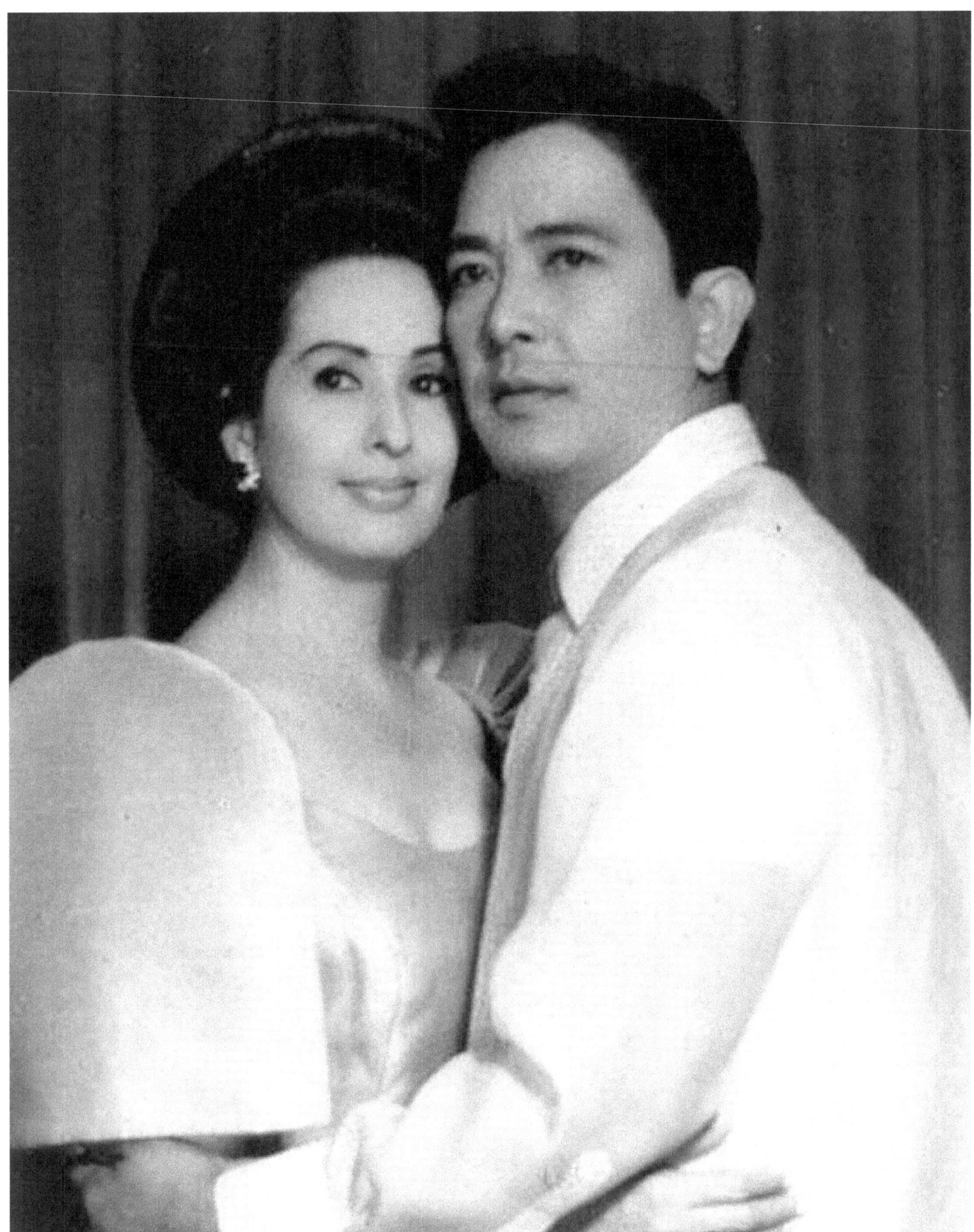

Gloria Romero and Luis Gonzales, Famous movie team, 50s-70s

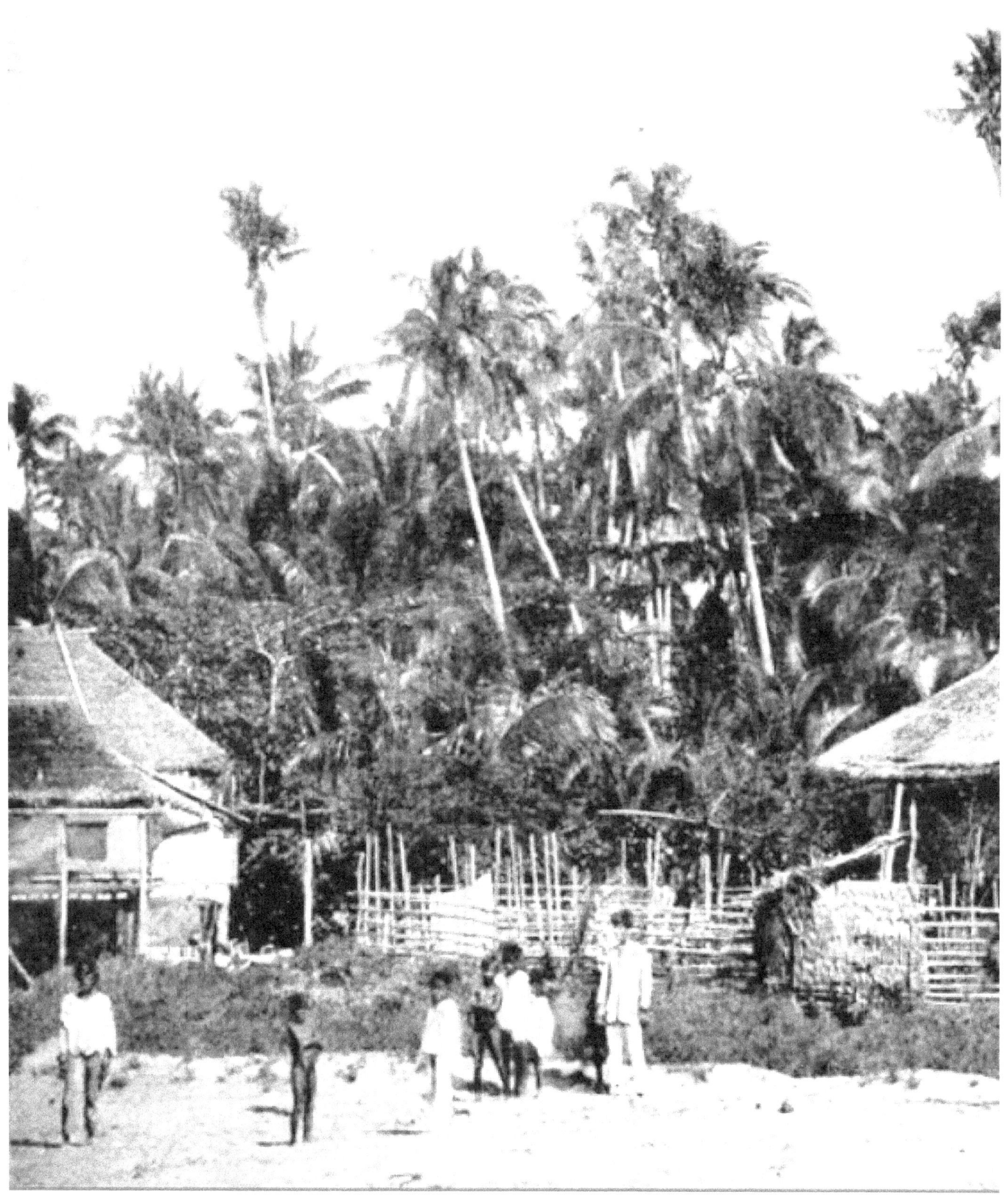
Rural Scene along seacoast, early 1900s pic

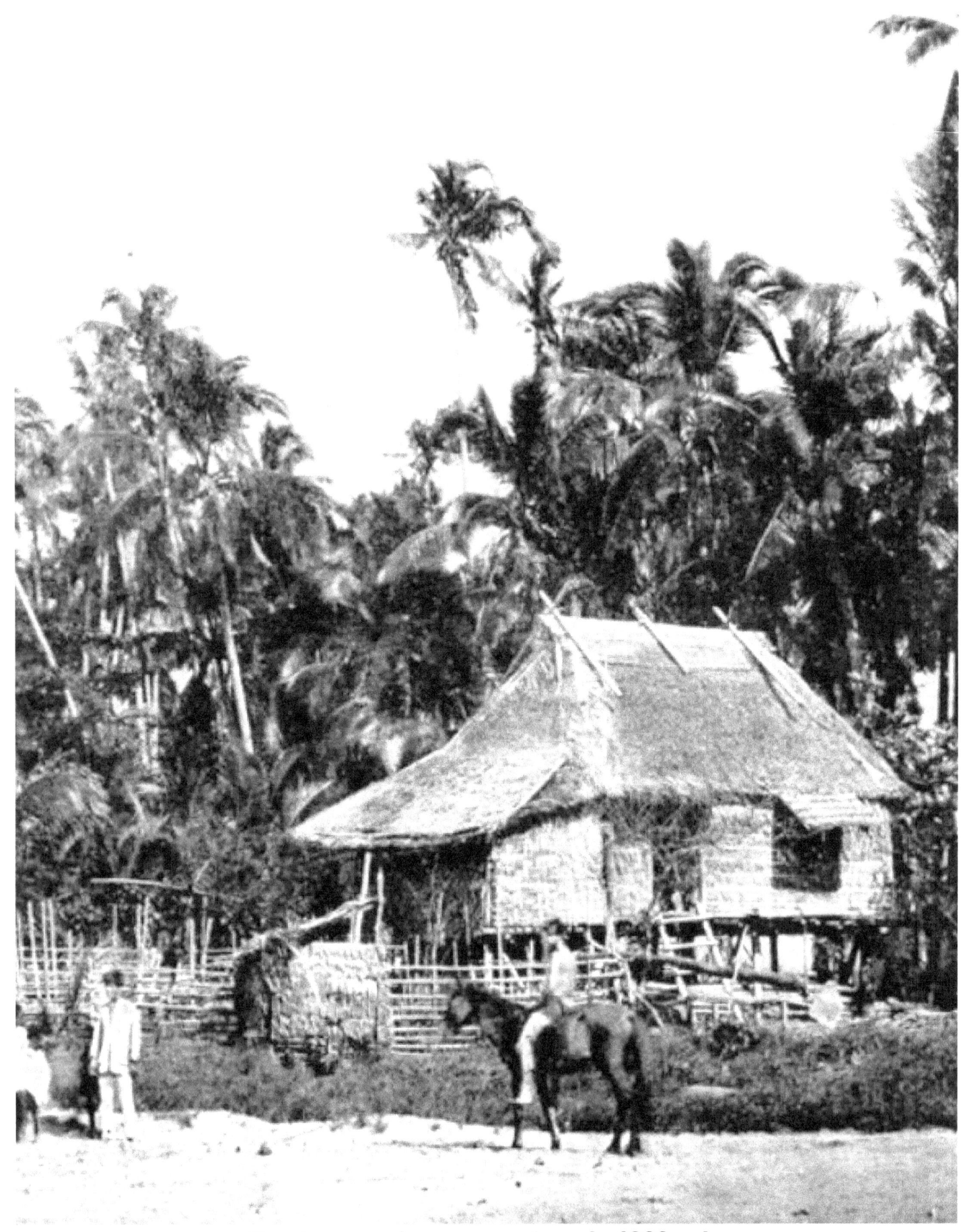
Rural scene along seacost, early 1900s pic

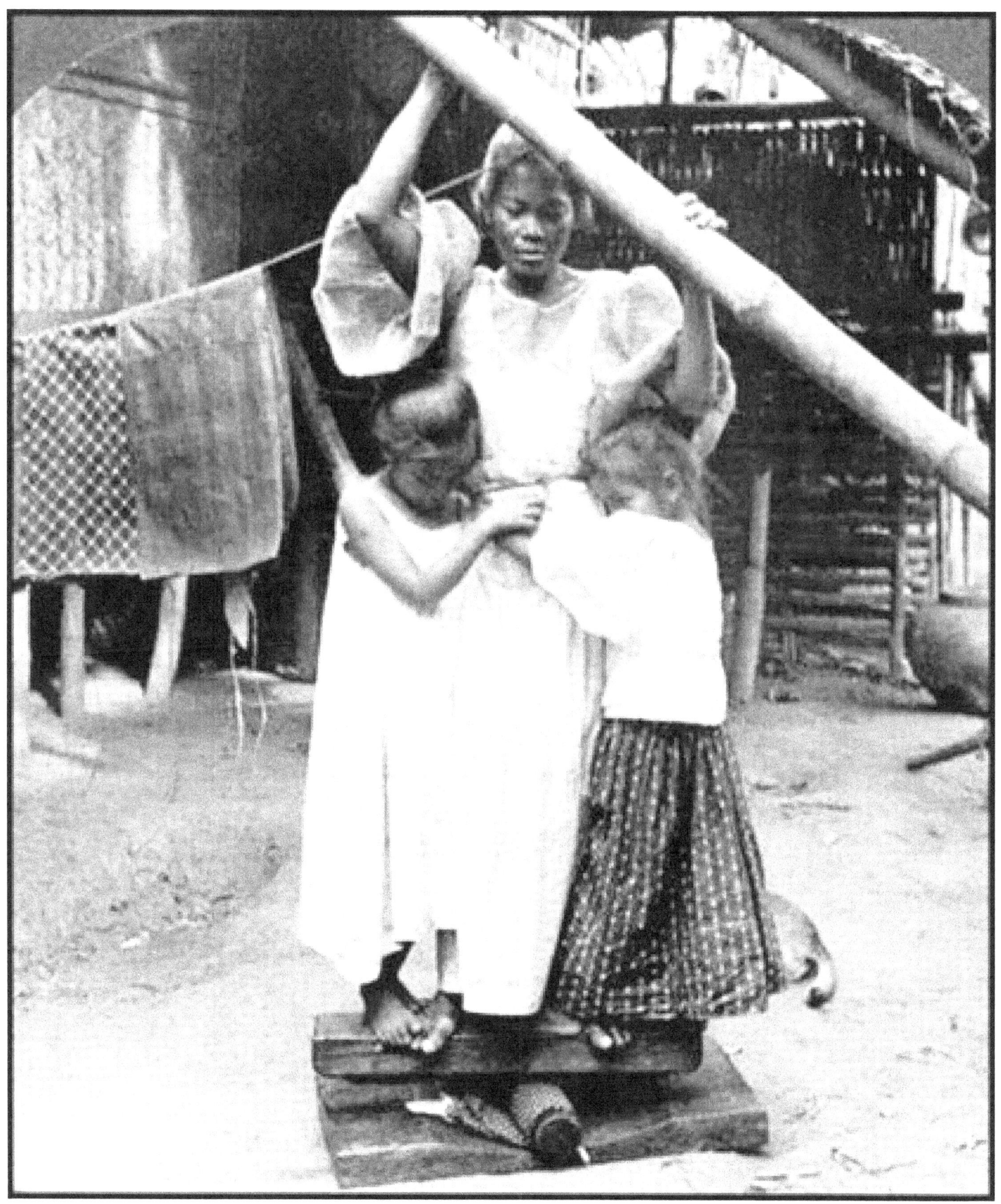
Crude method of ironing clothes, using foot roller, early 1900s pic

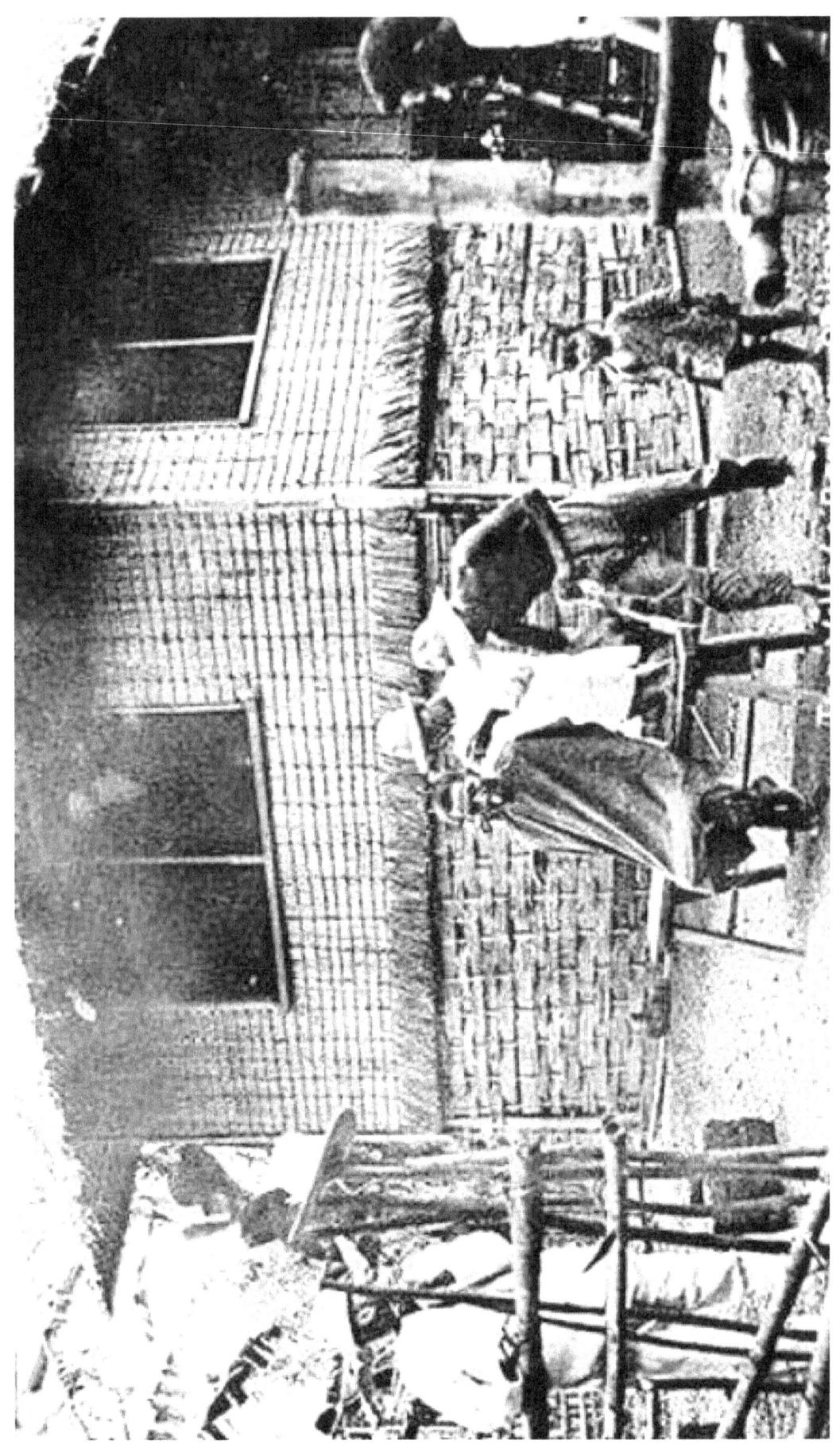

The Village Barber, early 1900s pic

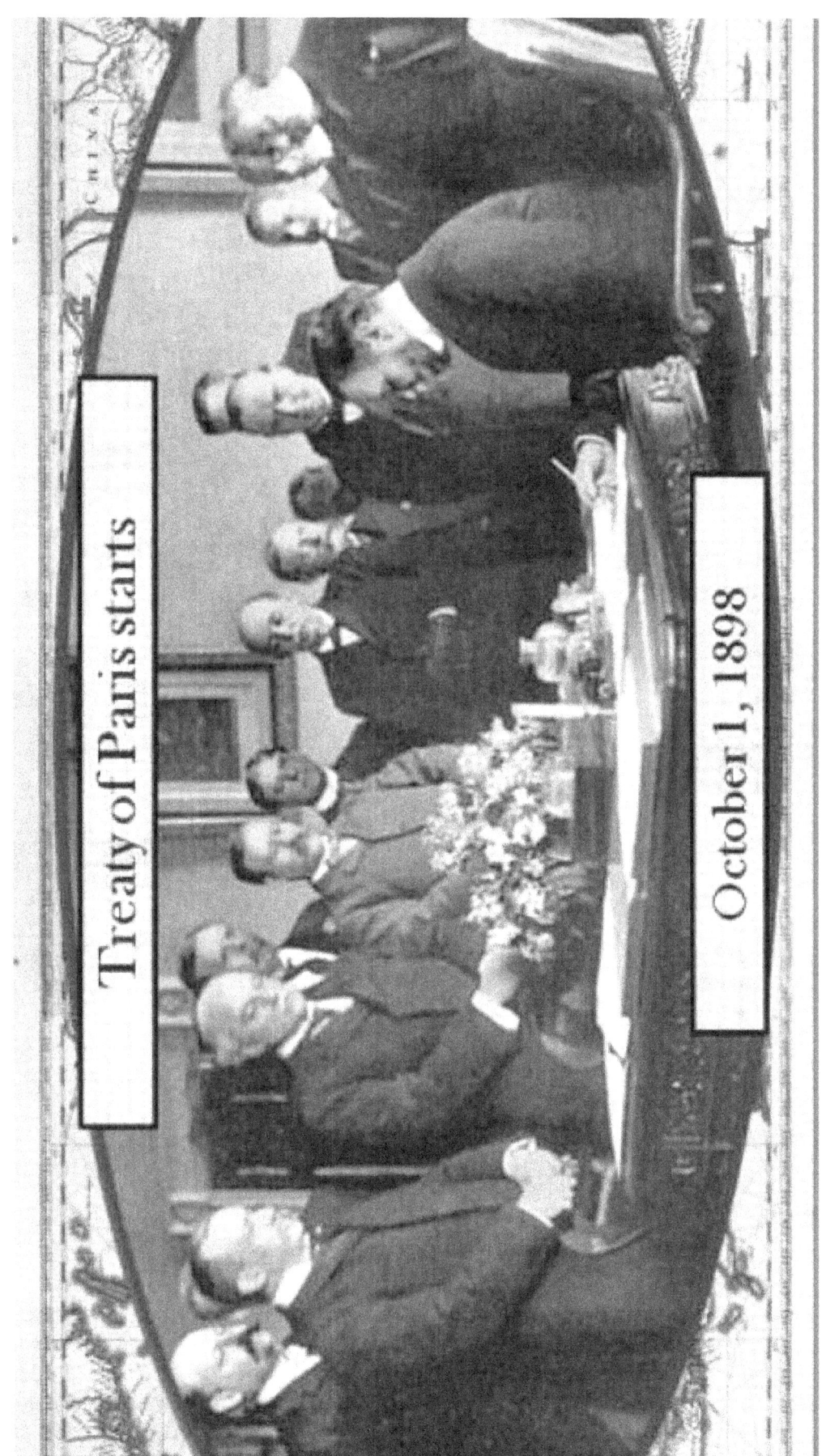

Treaty of Paris, USA-Spain, $20 Million Sale (Unpopular), 1898

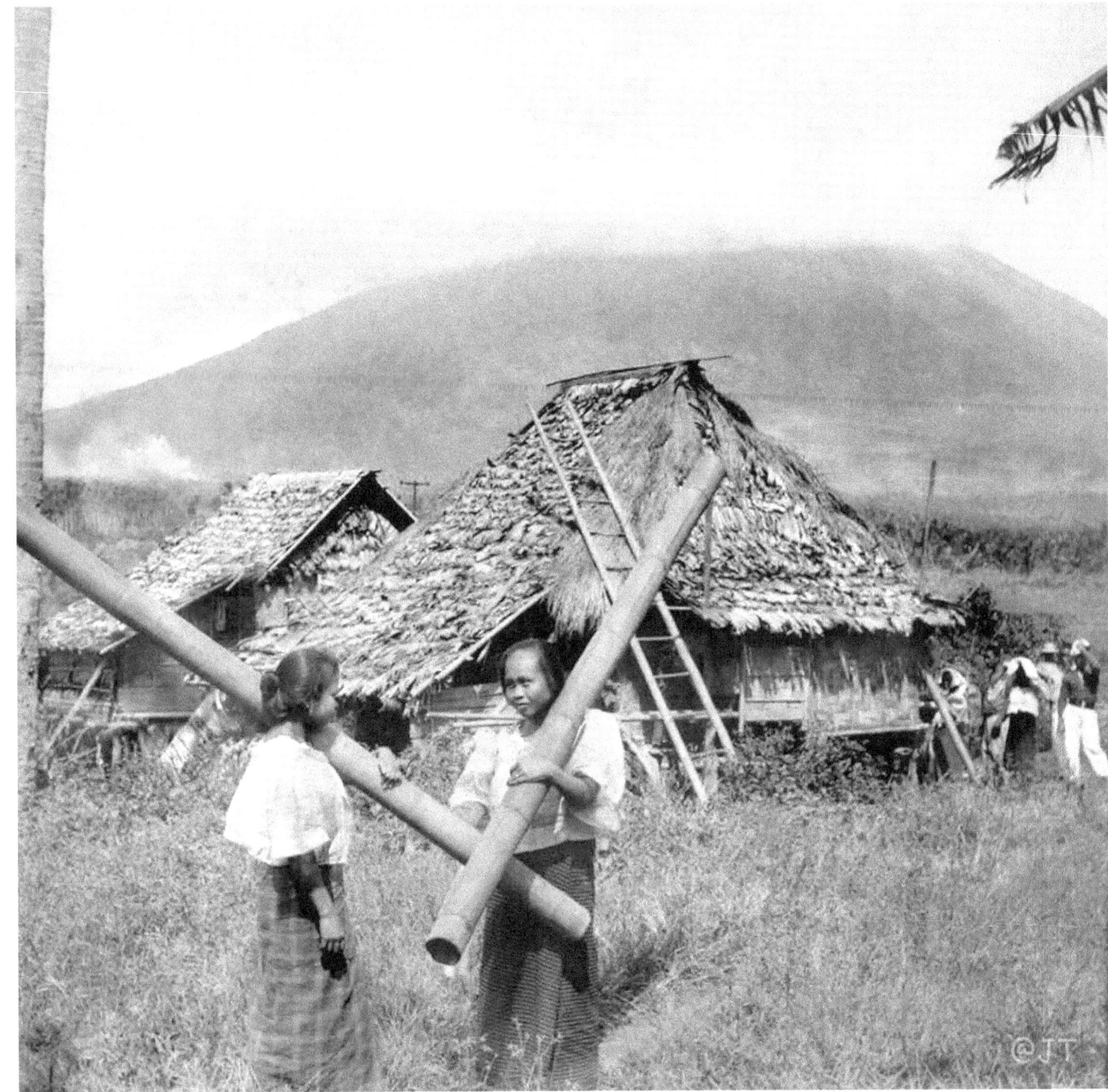

Rural Scene at foot of Mayon Volcano, early 1900s pic. Note long bamboo water containers carried by 2 women.

This book can be displayed as coffee table book for family and guests. Each picture can be cut and framed, by buying extra copies. This book is suitable for libraries and schools in Philippines and USA. It is ideal reference material for study of history and celebrities. It is suitable as gift for any occasion. It's a collector's item. Heirs of those shown in pictures may want to own this book for their own families. Pictures are arranged in no particular order. Browse at random.

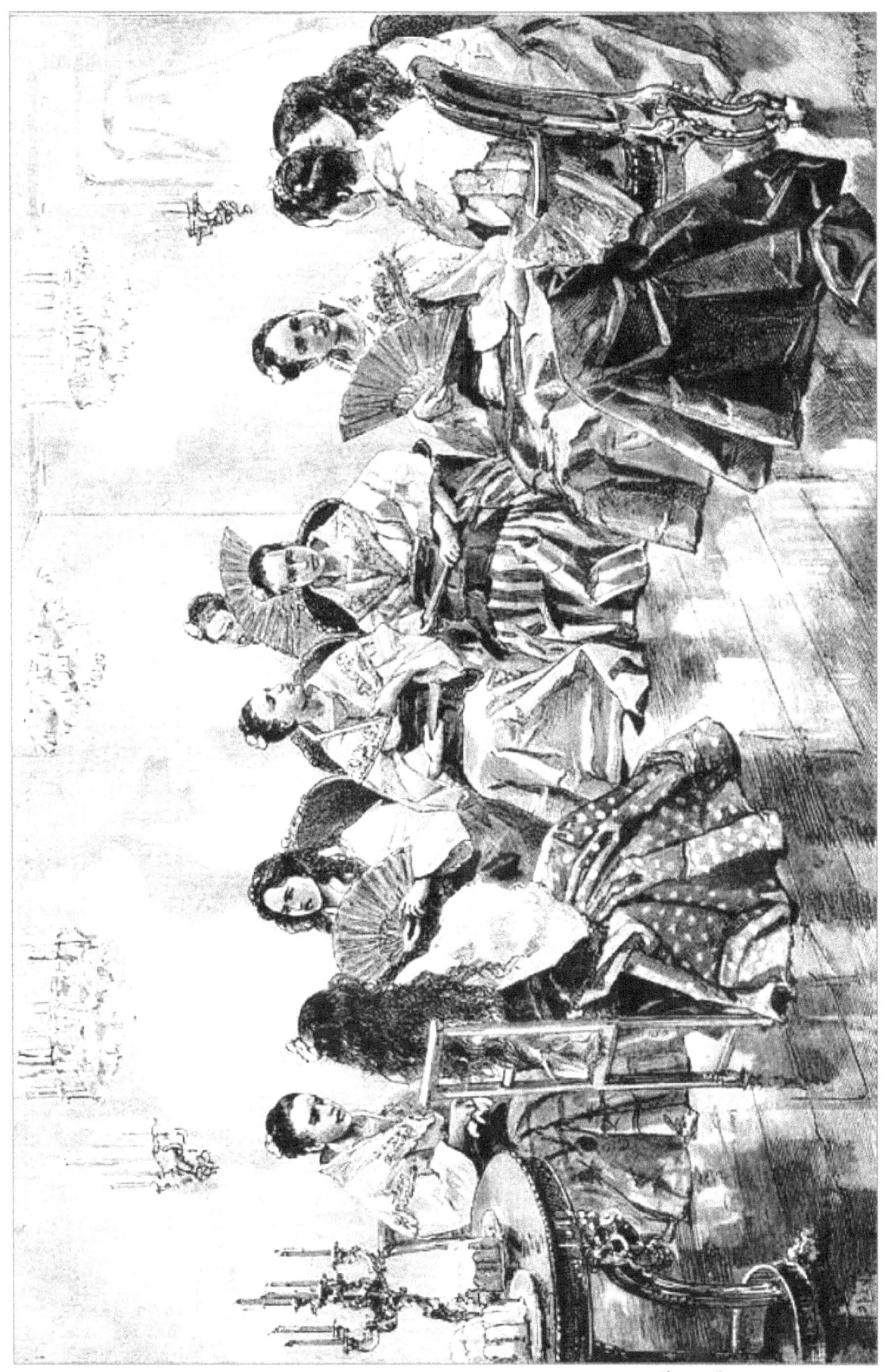

Sketch - Ladies Social Circle of the Elite class, 19th-20th centuries

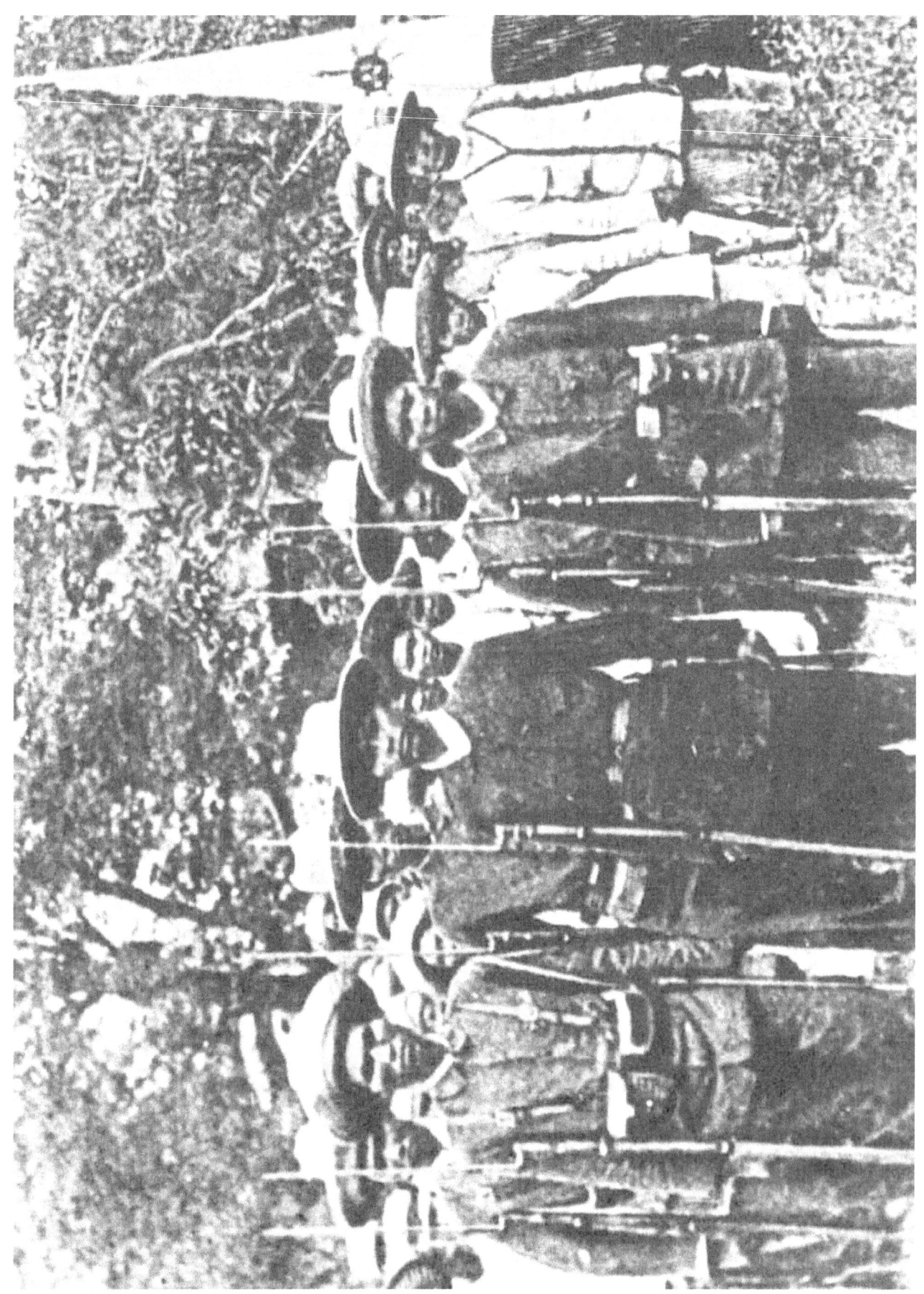

Philippine Revolionary Army, 1898-1901

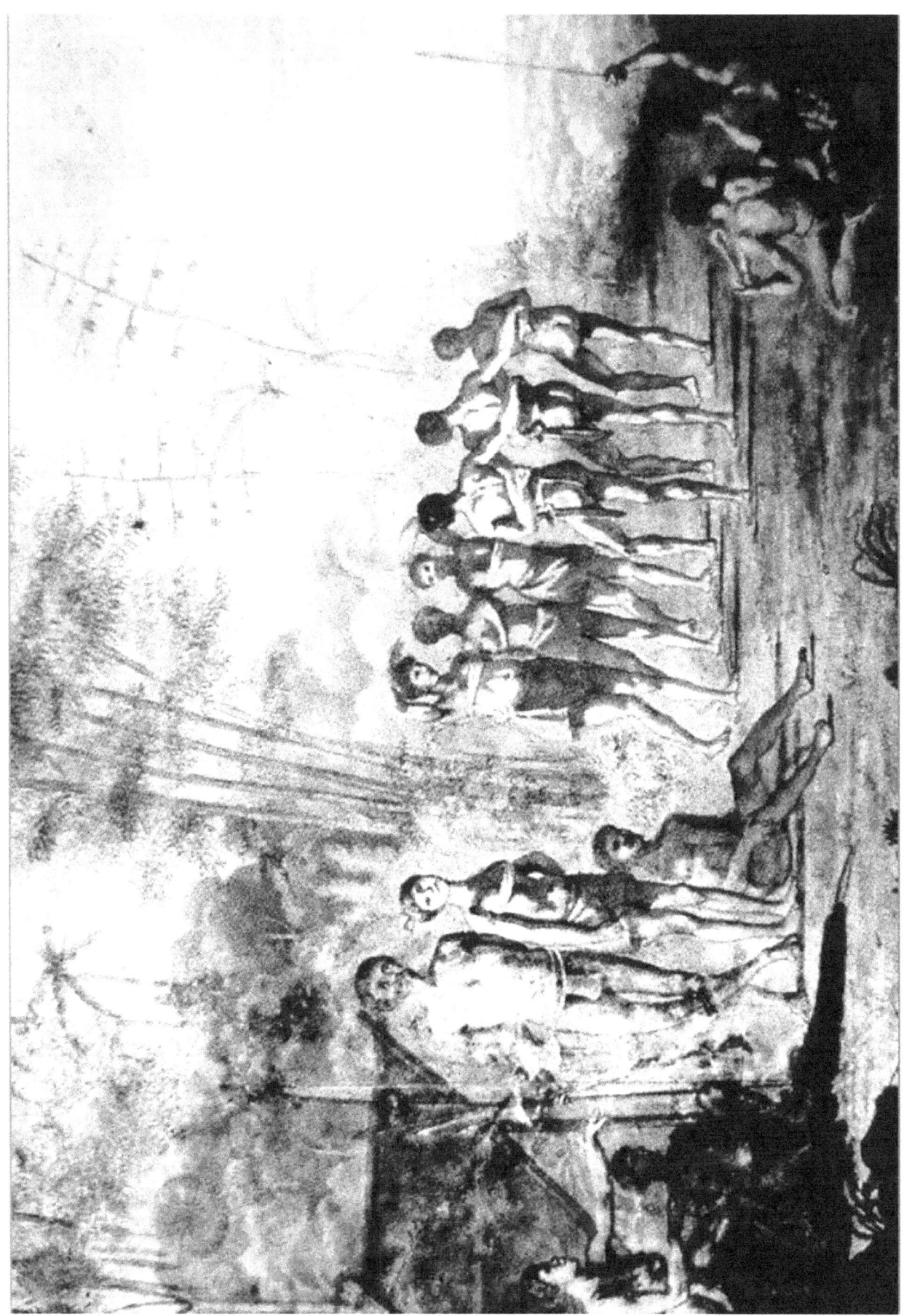

Sketch – Custom ritual dancing (maybe wedding), 19th-20th centuries

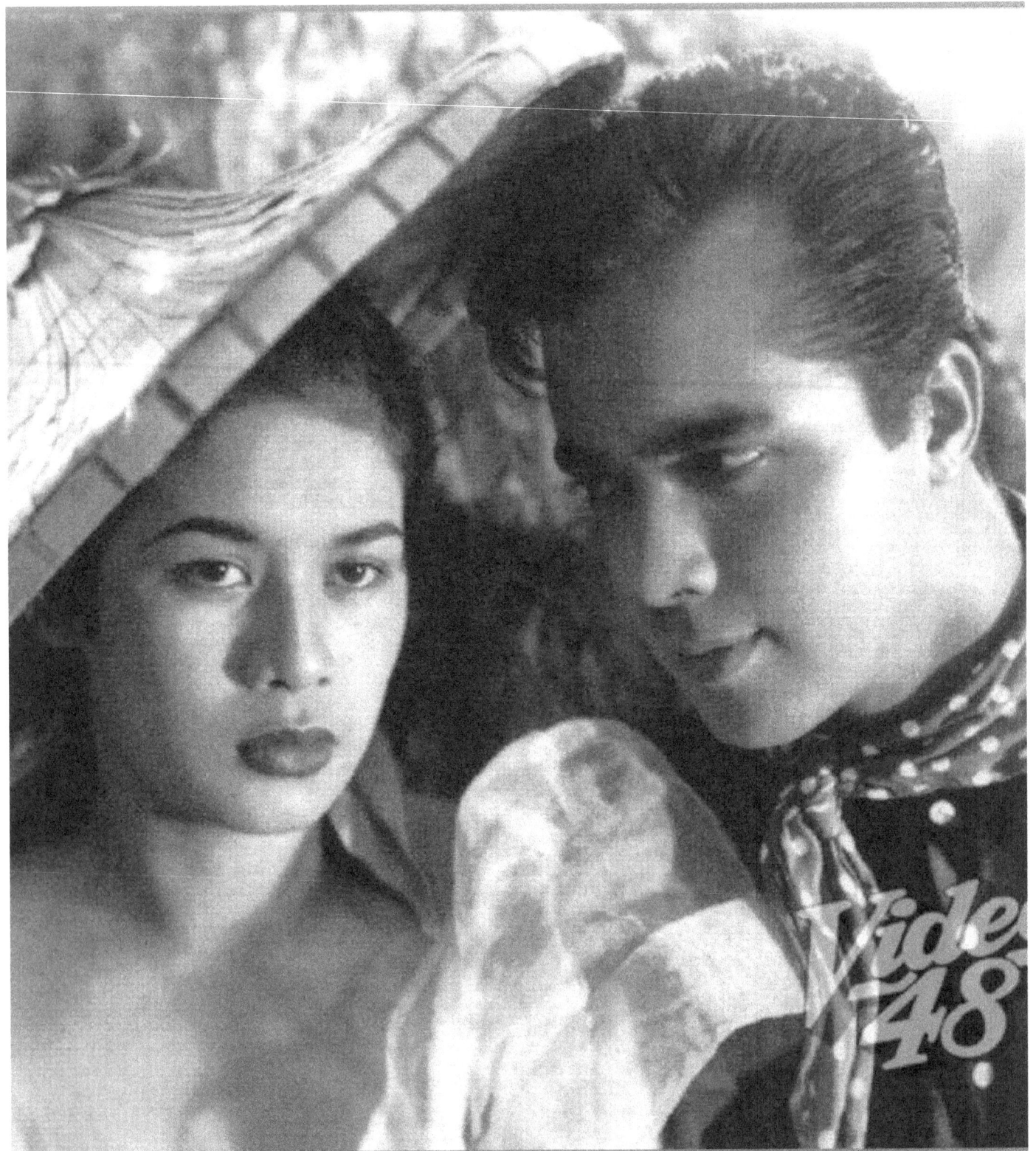

Emma Alegre & Mario Montenegro, famous love team movie stars, 50s-70s

This book can be displayed as coffee table book for family and guests. Each picture can be cut and framed, by buying extra copies. This book is suitable for libraries and schools in Philippines and USA. It is ideal reference material for study of history and celebrities. It is suitable as gift for any occasion. It's a collector's item. Heirs of those shown in pictures may want to own this book for their own families. Pictures are arranged in no particular order. Browse at random.

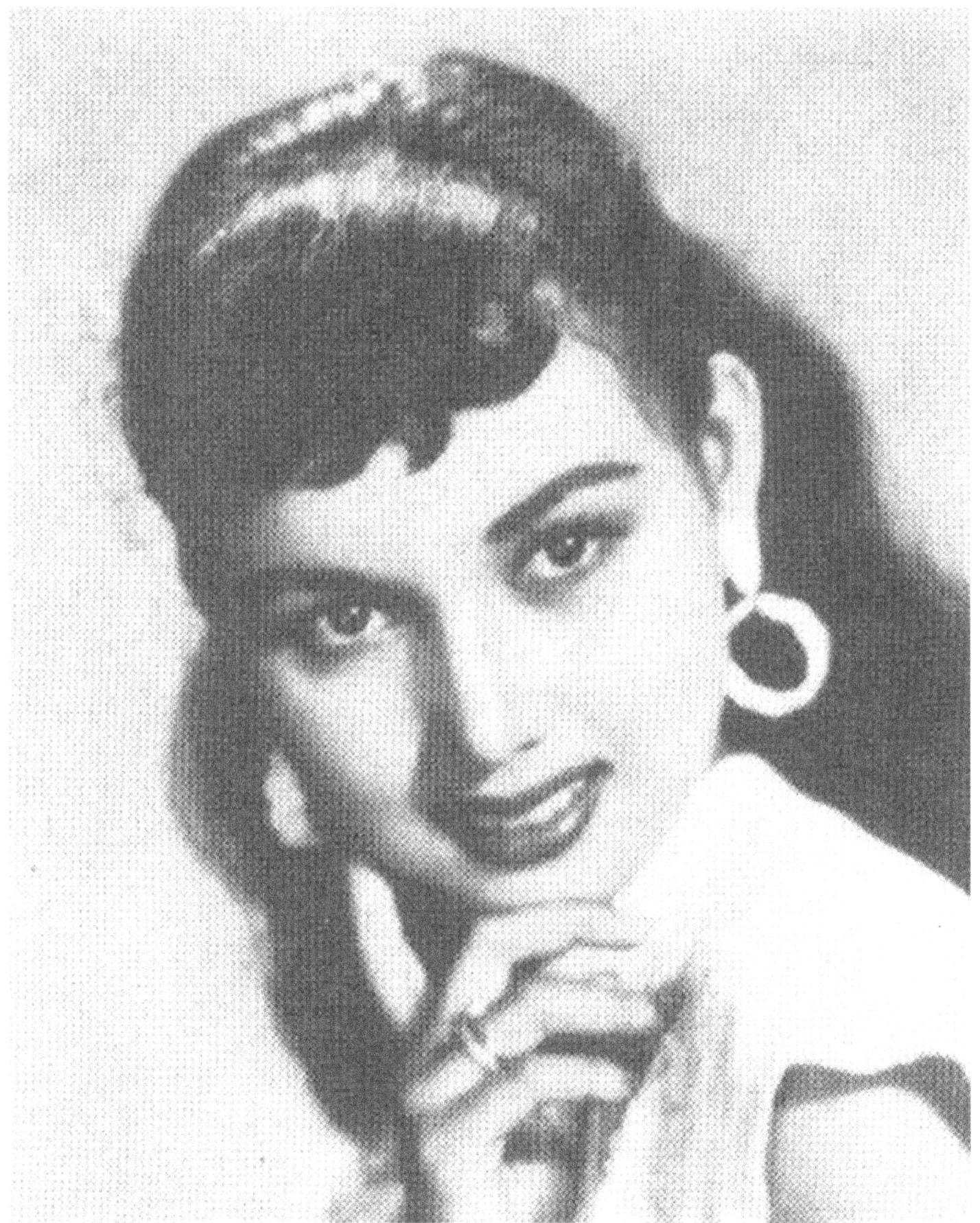

Edna Luna, famous movie star, 50s-70s

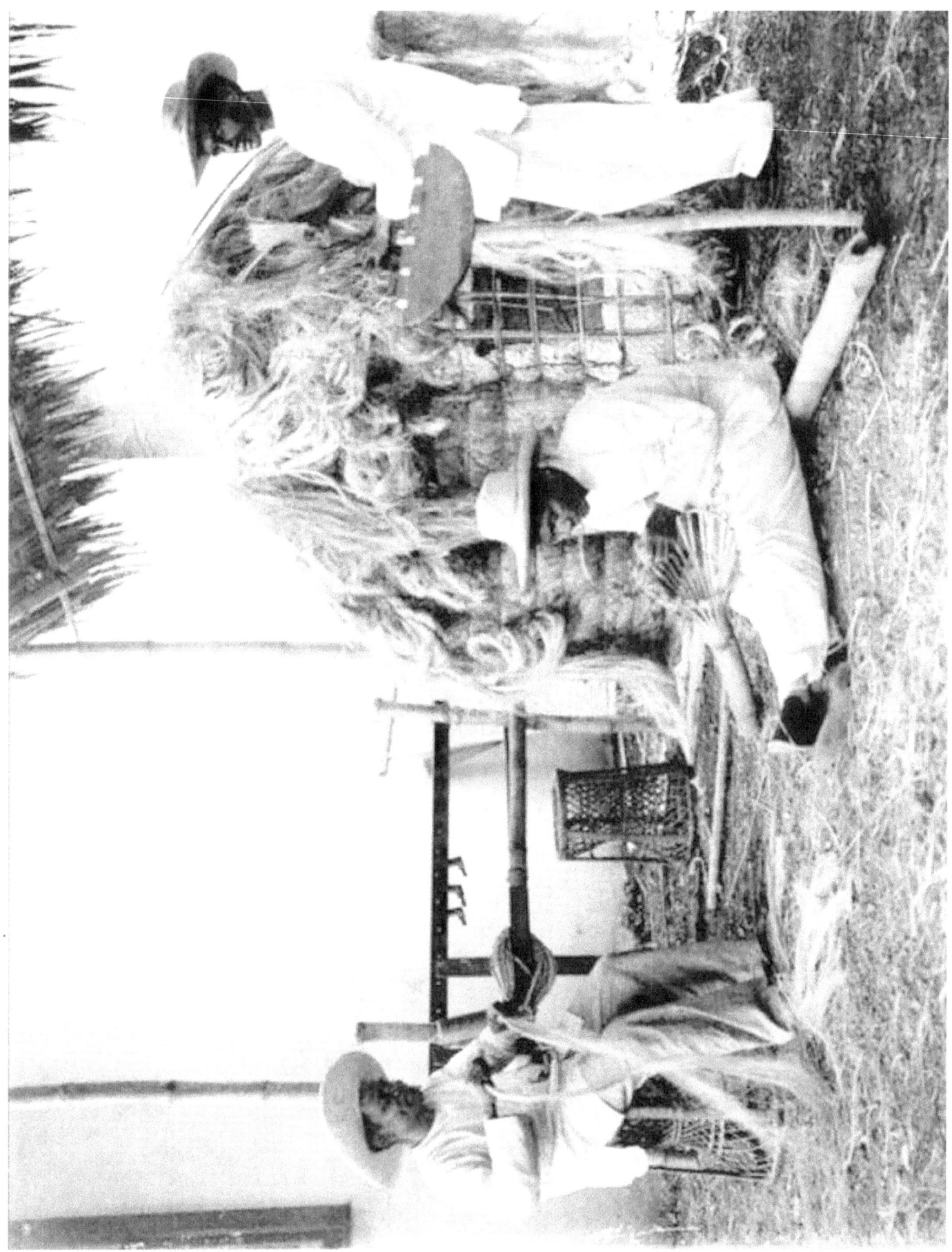

Abaca Fiber manual processing, early 1900s pic

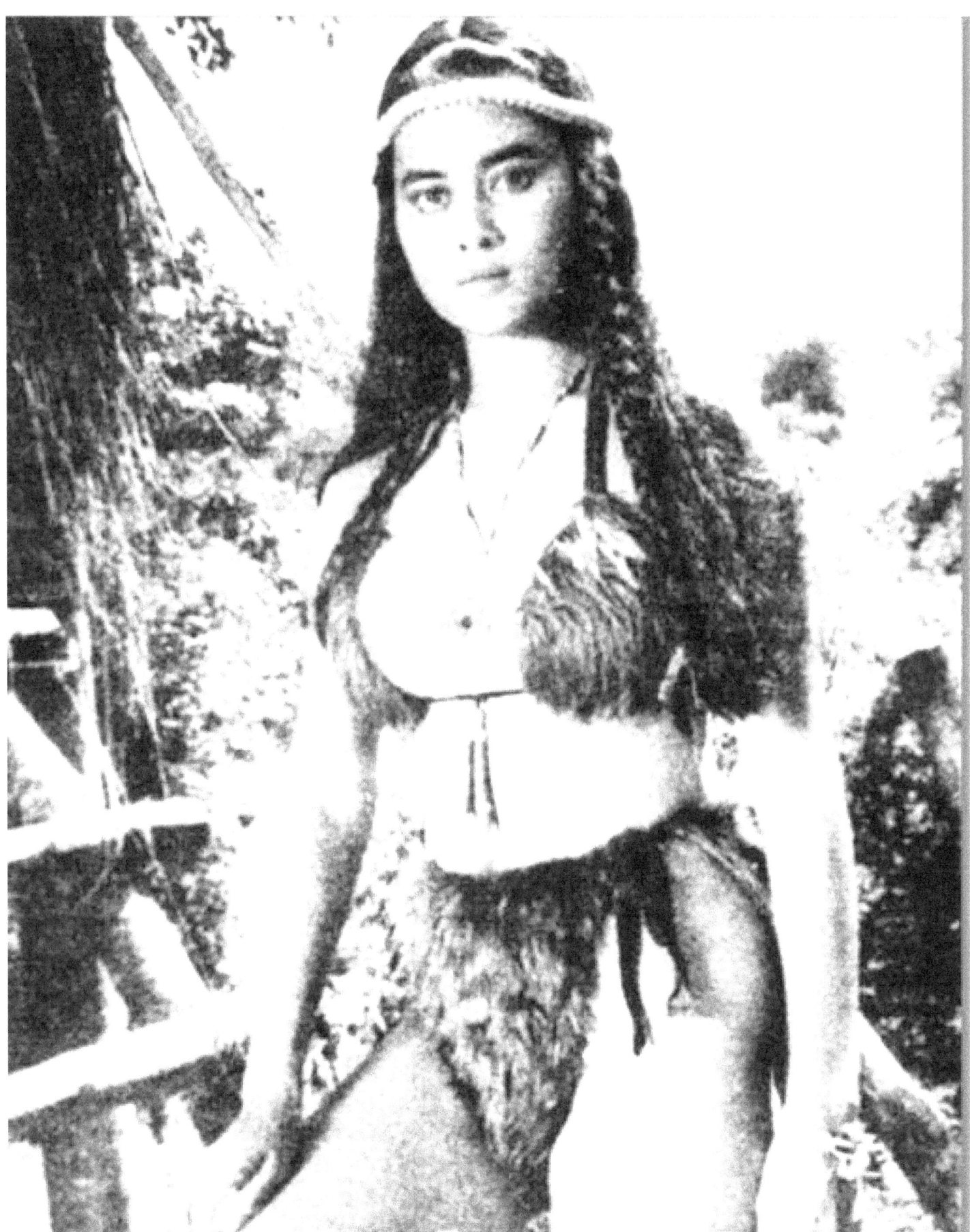

Elizabeth Oropesa, famous movie action star, 60-70s

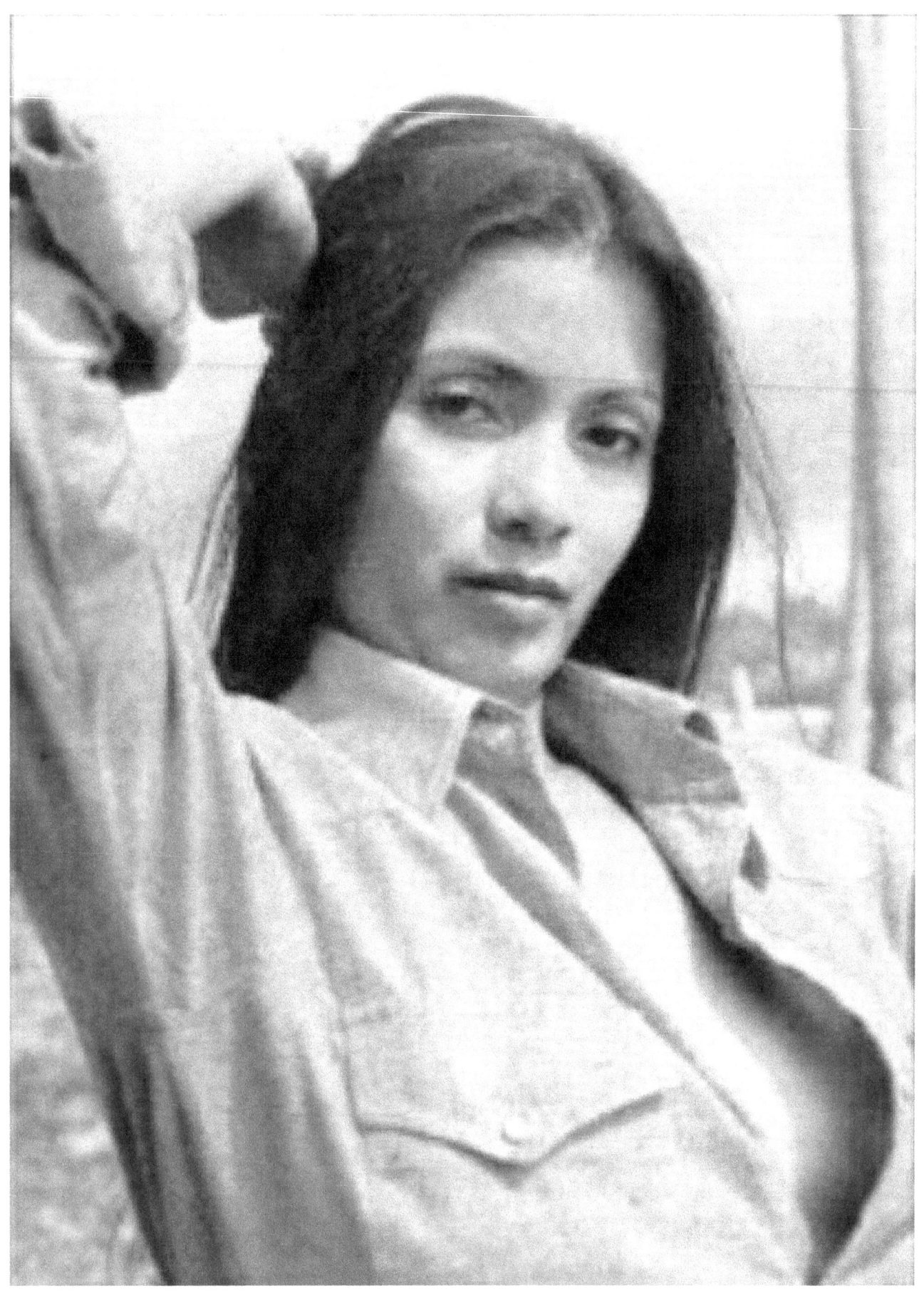

Daria, famous movie star, 70s-80s

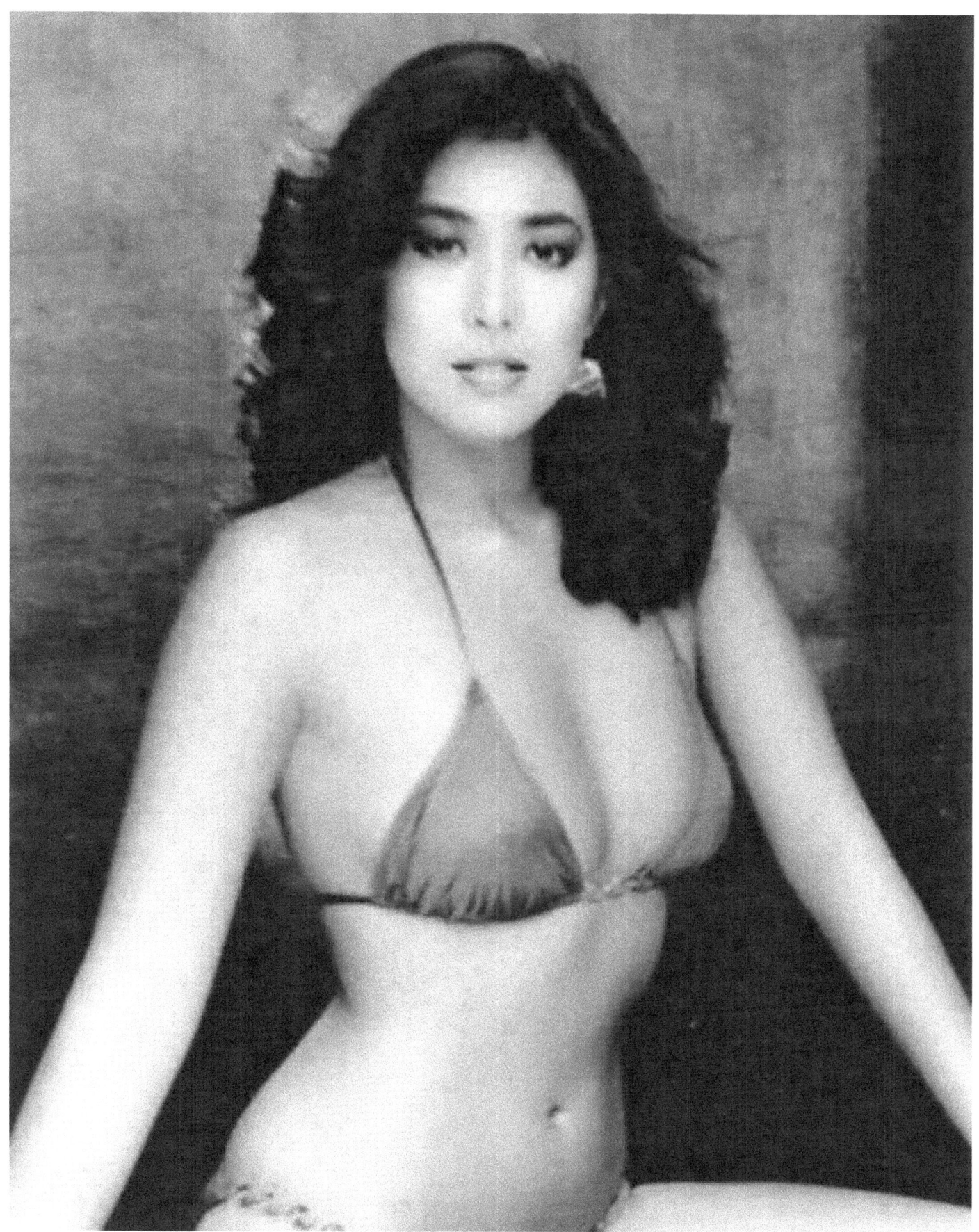

Vivian Velez, famous movie star, 70s-80s

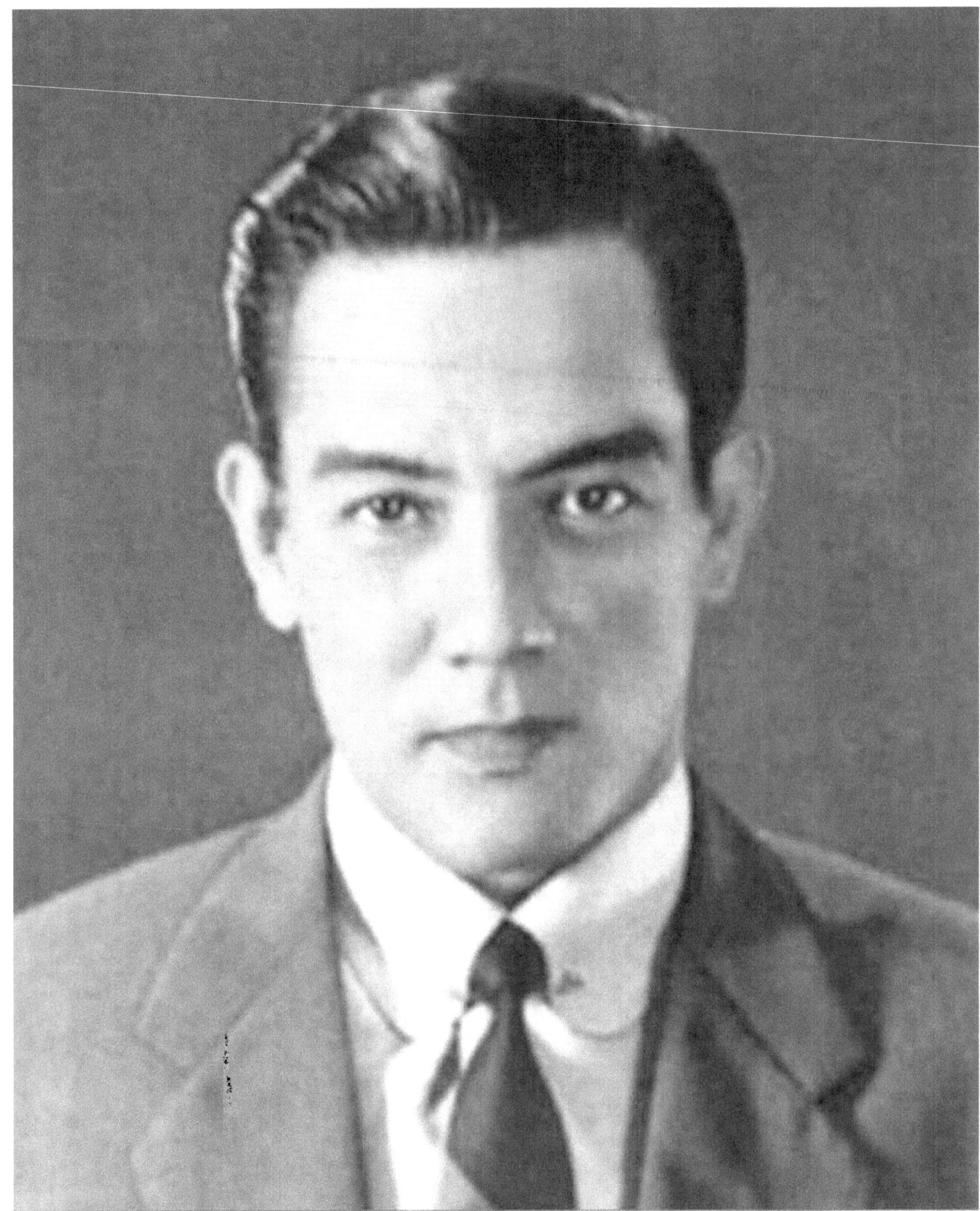

Leopoldo Salcedo, One-time king of Phl movies, 40s-90s

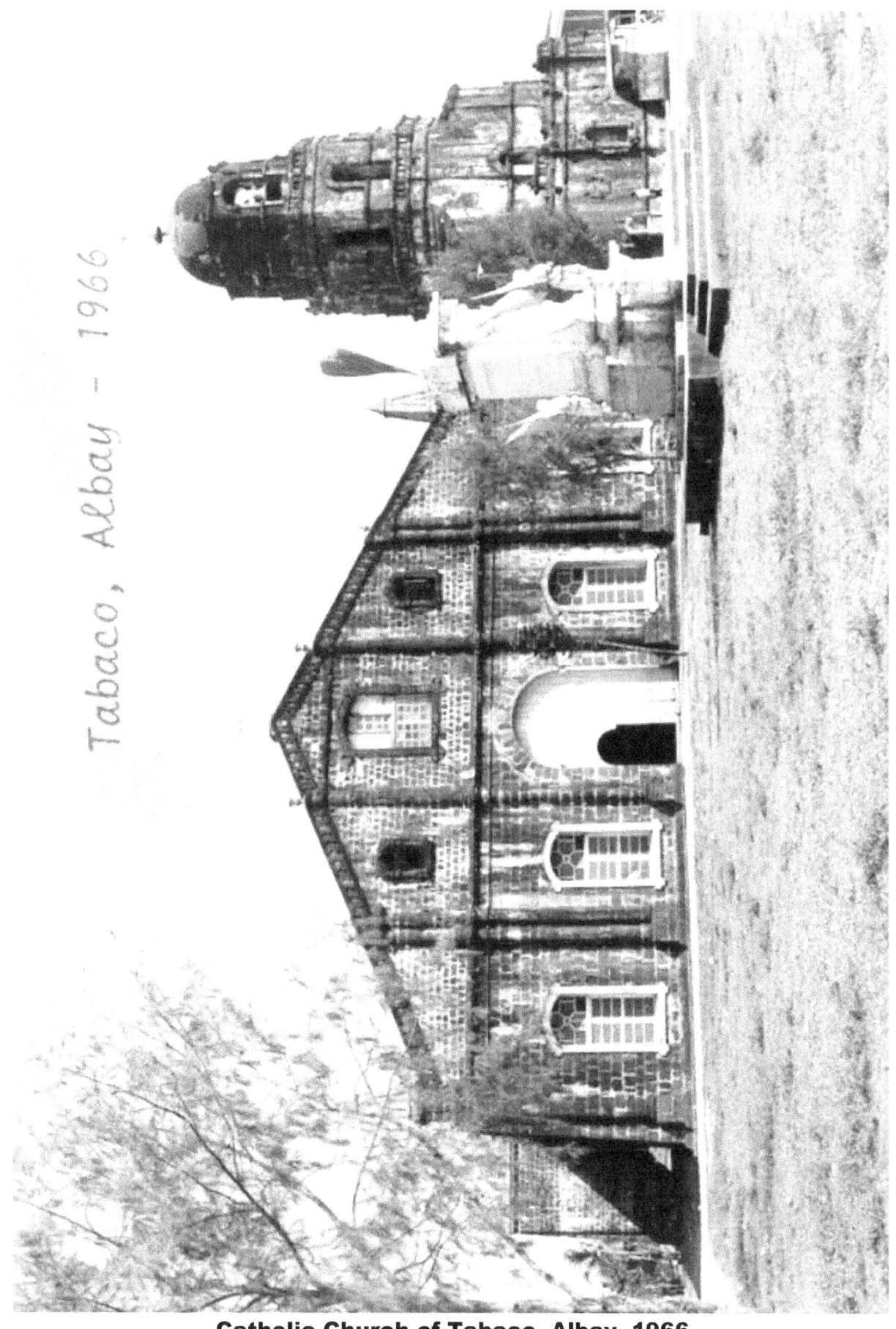

Catholic Church of Tabaco, Albay, 1966

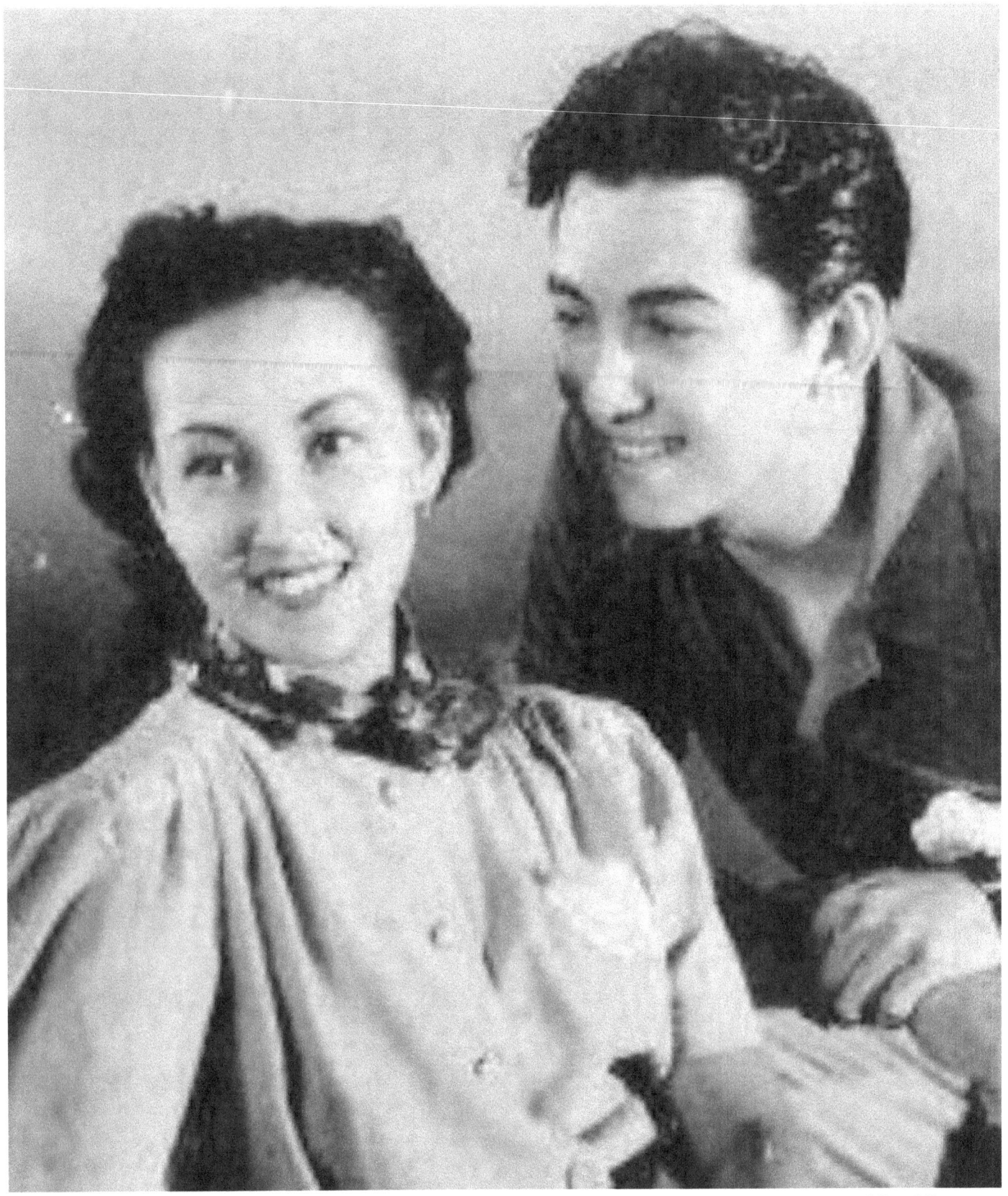
Carmen Rosales & Rogelio dela Rosa, famous movie stars love-team, 40s-60s

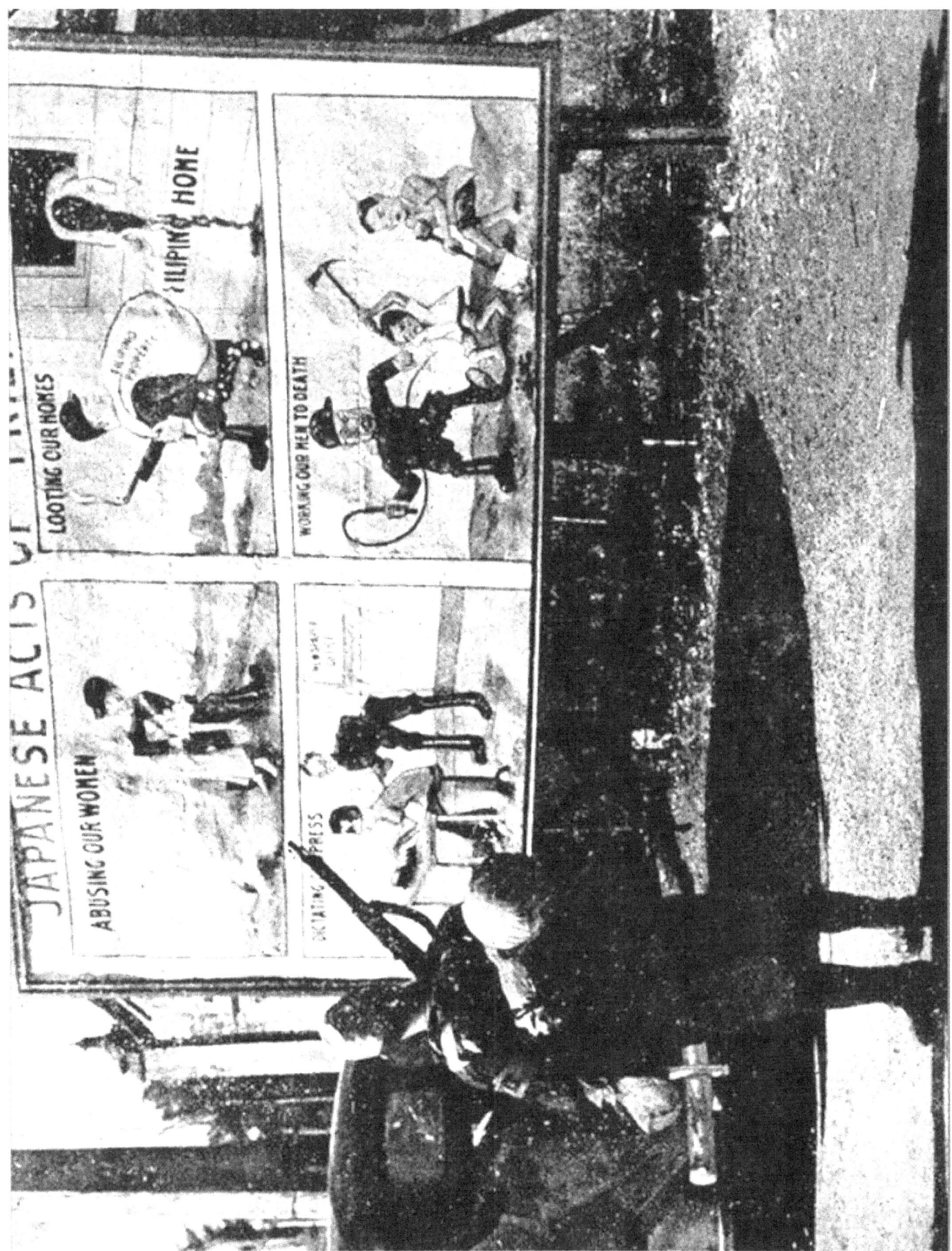
Unusual Anti-Japanese Billboard during Japanese time in Phl, WWII, 40s

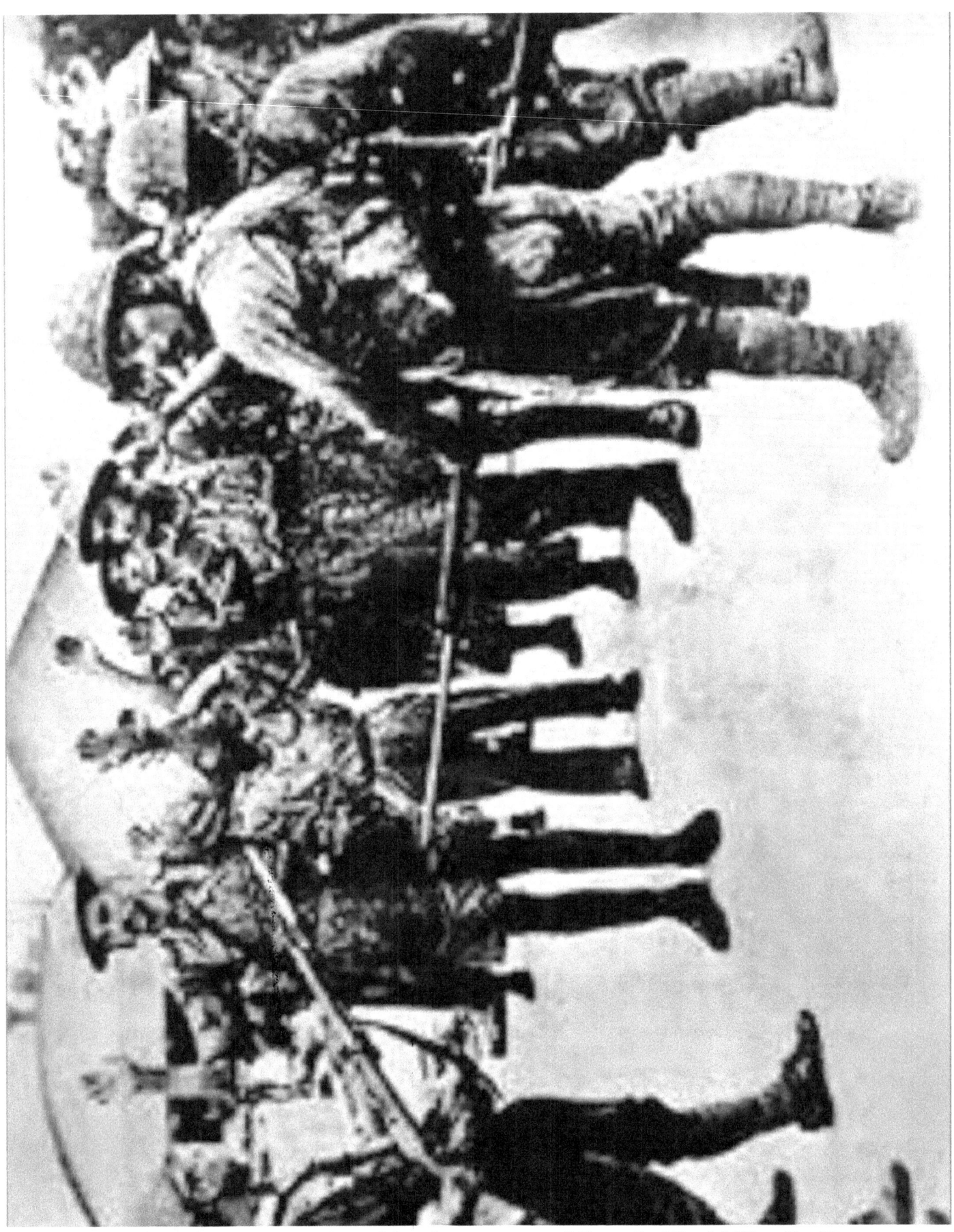

American Soldiers captured by Japanese soldiers in World War II, 40s

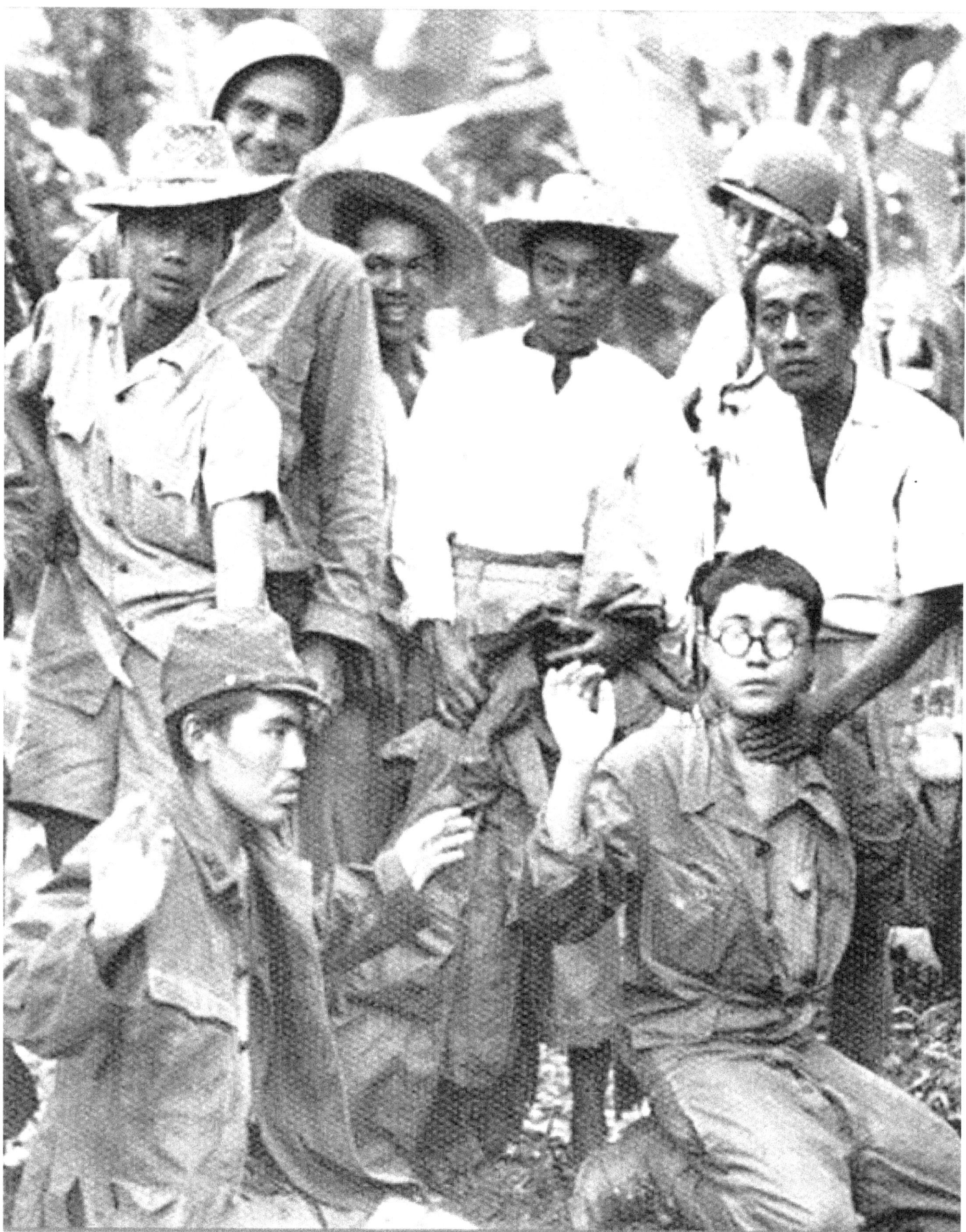
Captured Japanese soldiers by Filipino guerrillas in Phl in WWII, 40s

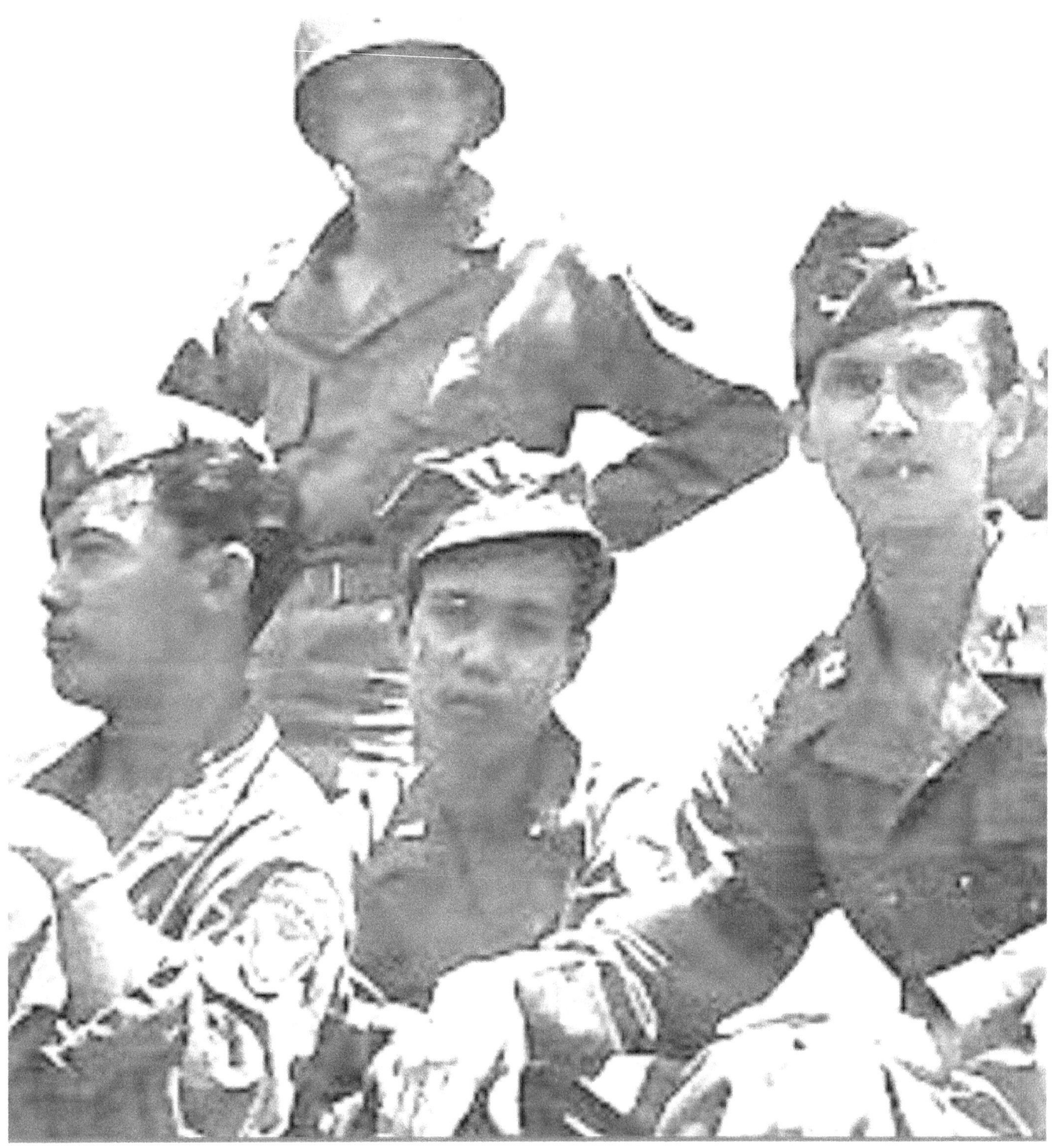

Combined Filipino and American soldiers in WWII in Phl, 40s

This book can be displayed as coffee table book for family and guests. Each picture can be cut and framed, by buying extra copies. This book is suitable for libraries and schools in Philippines and USA. It is ideal reference material for study of history and celebrities. It is suitable as gift for any occasion. It's a collector's item. Heirs of those shown in pictures may want to own this book for their own families. Pictures are arranged in no particular order. Browse at random.

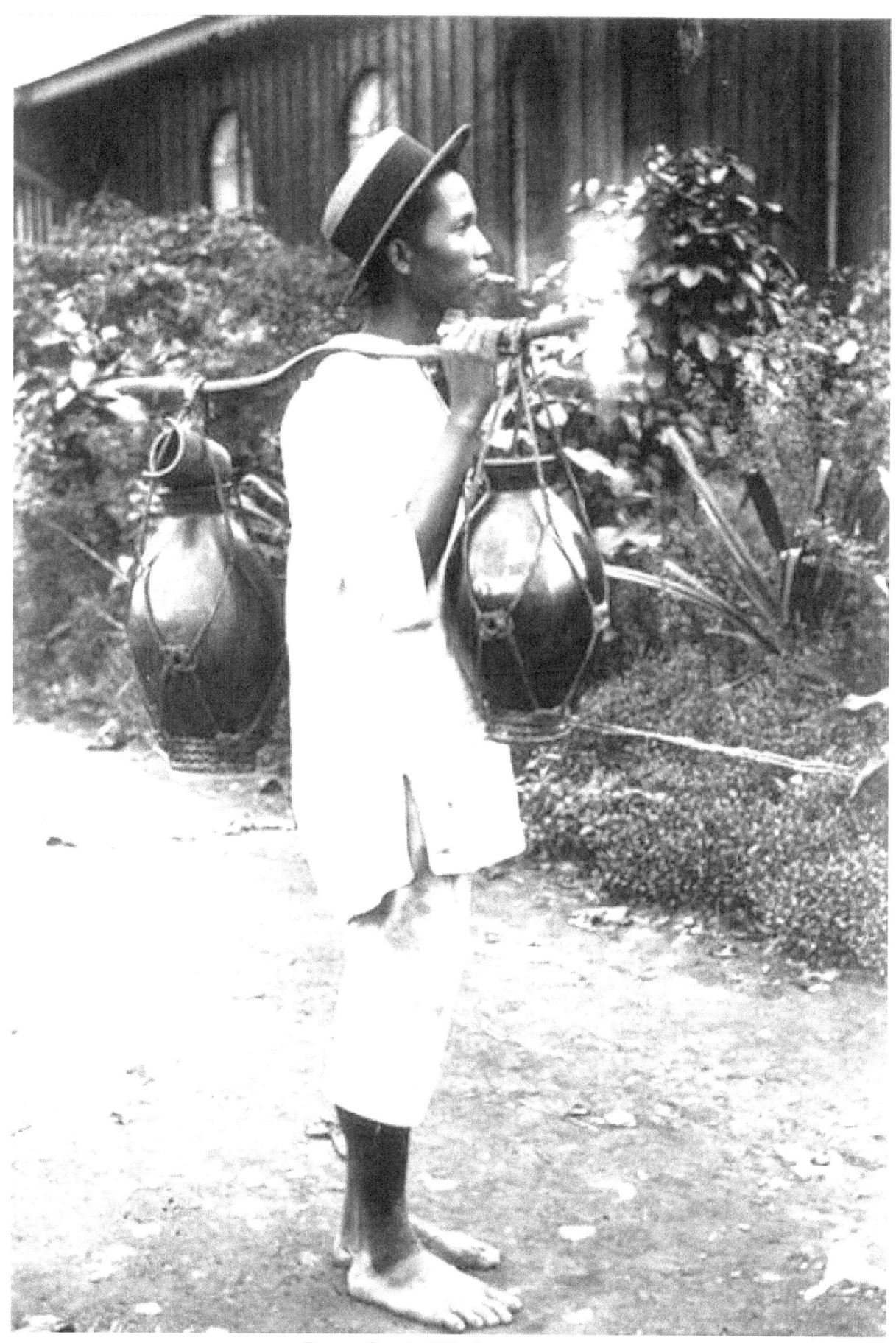

Bare-foot Filipino vendor

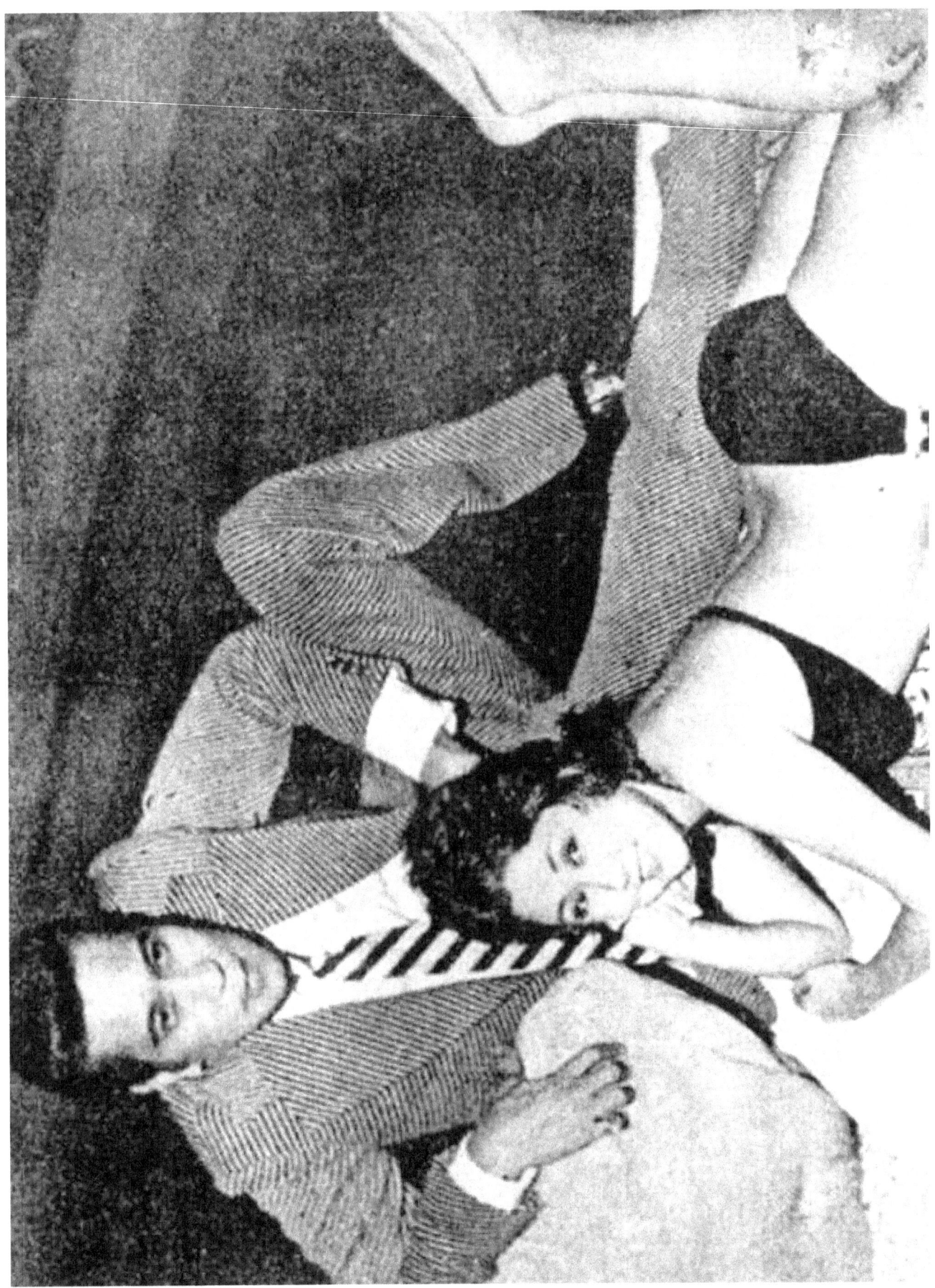

Eddie Rodriguez and Vilma Santos, movie stars 70s-80s

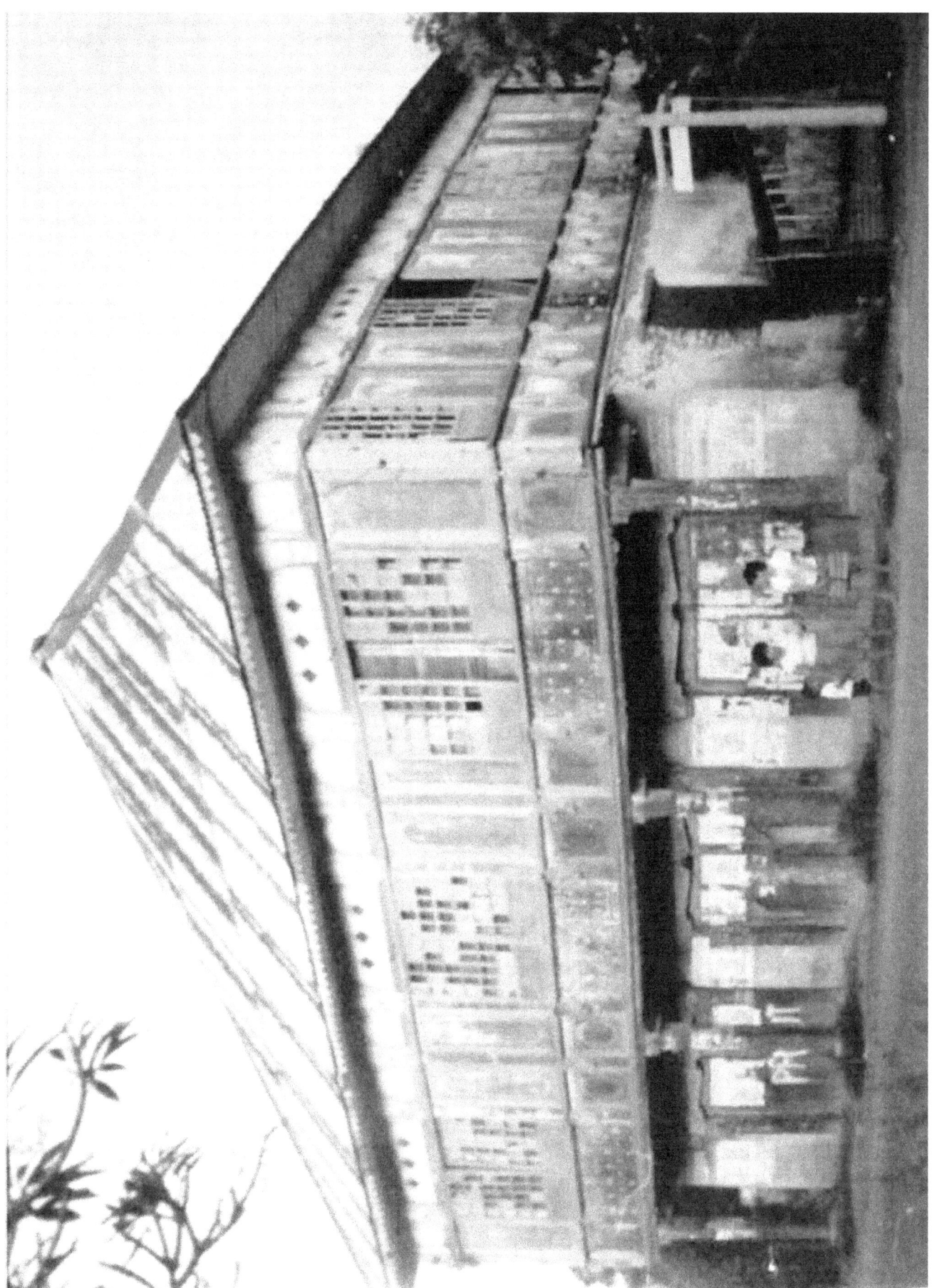

Typical Spanish Mansion, or "bahay castile" -19th century, landmark in towns

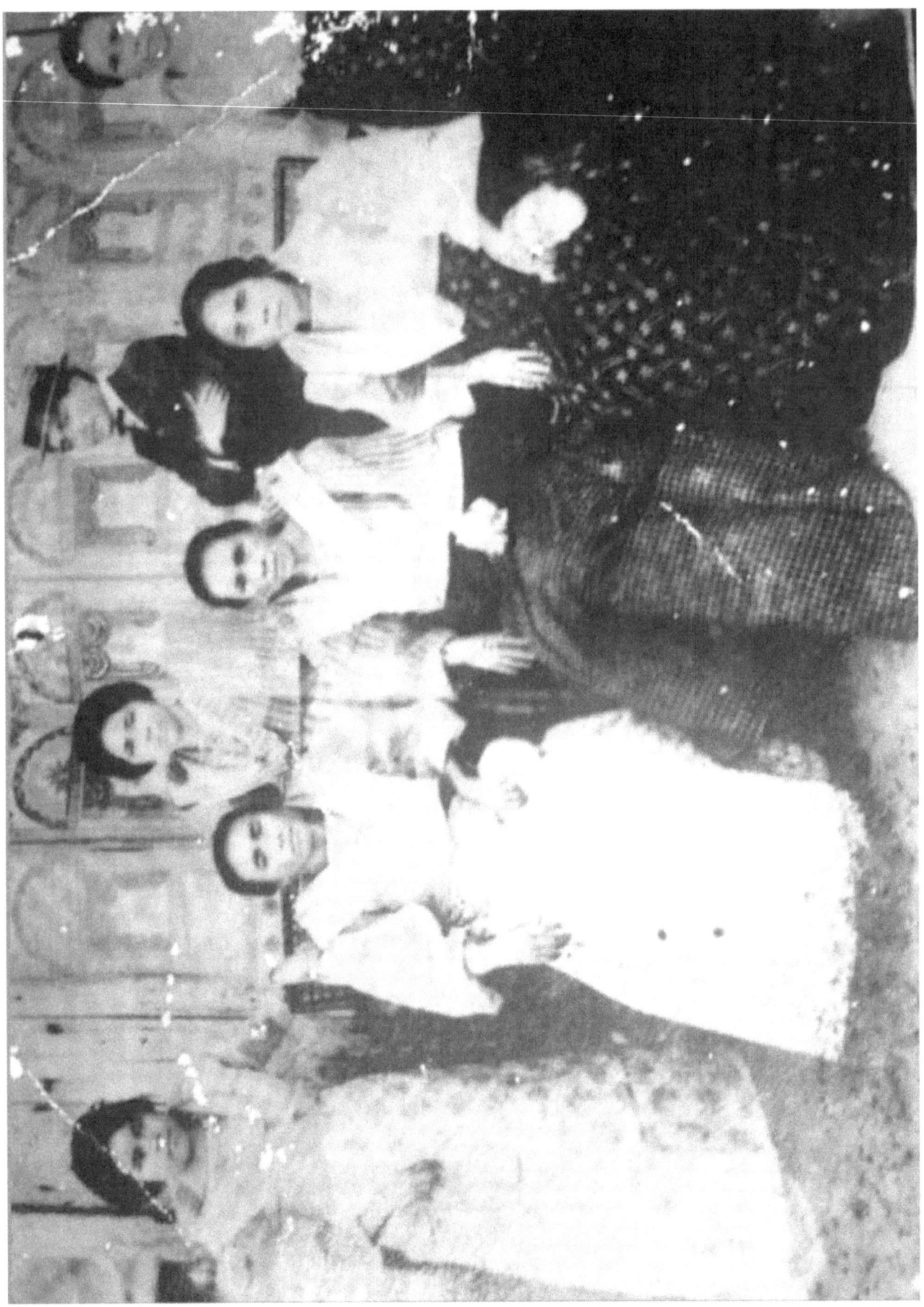

Typical Filipino formal attire in the early 1900s (Jamito clan of Talisay CN)

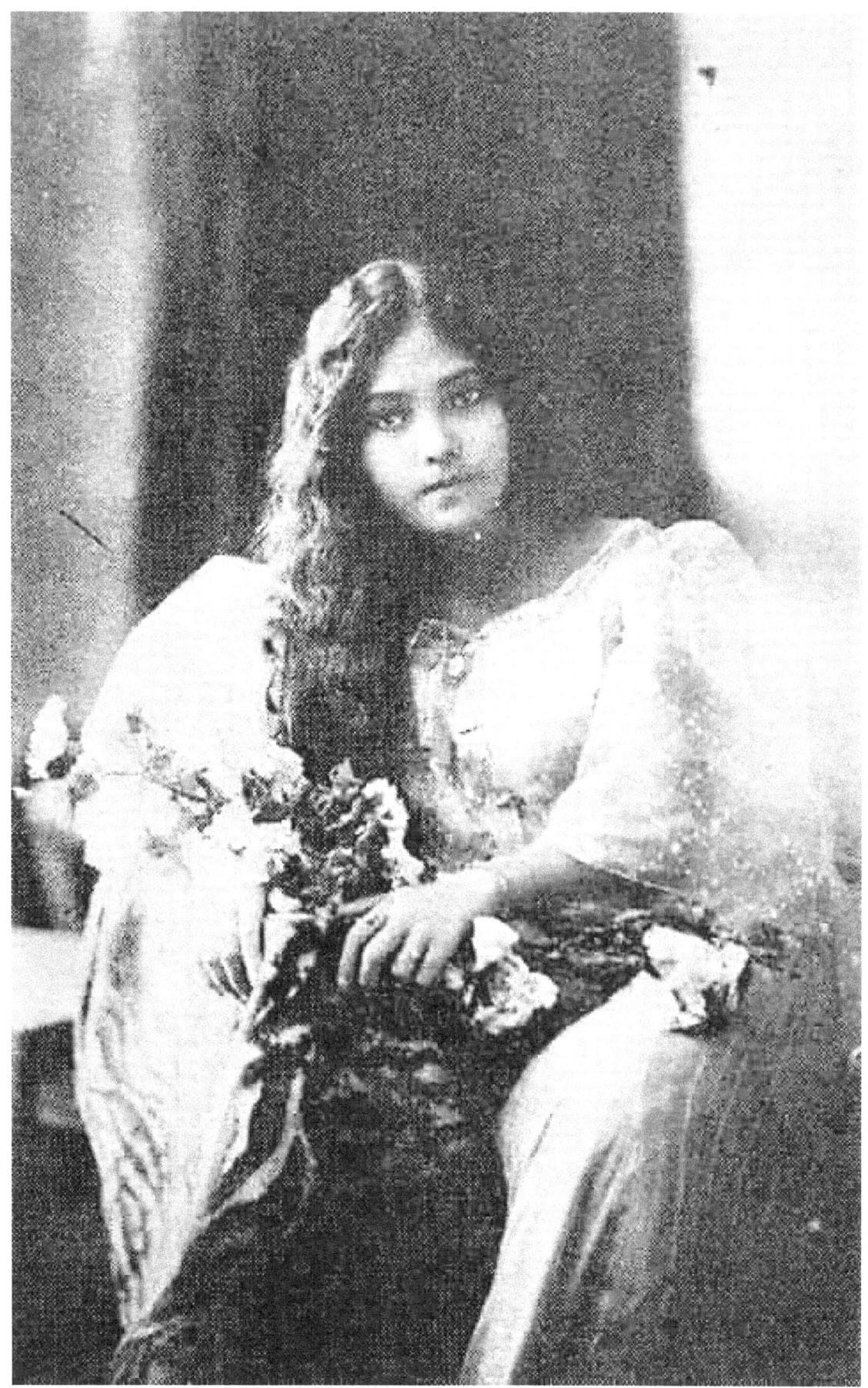

Typical Mestiza, from mix parentage of Spanish-Filipino, 1900s

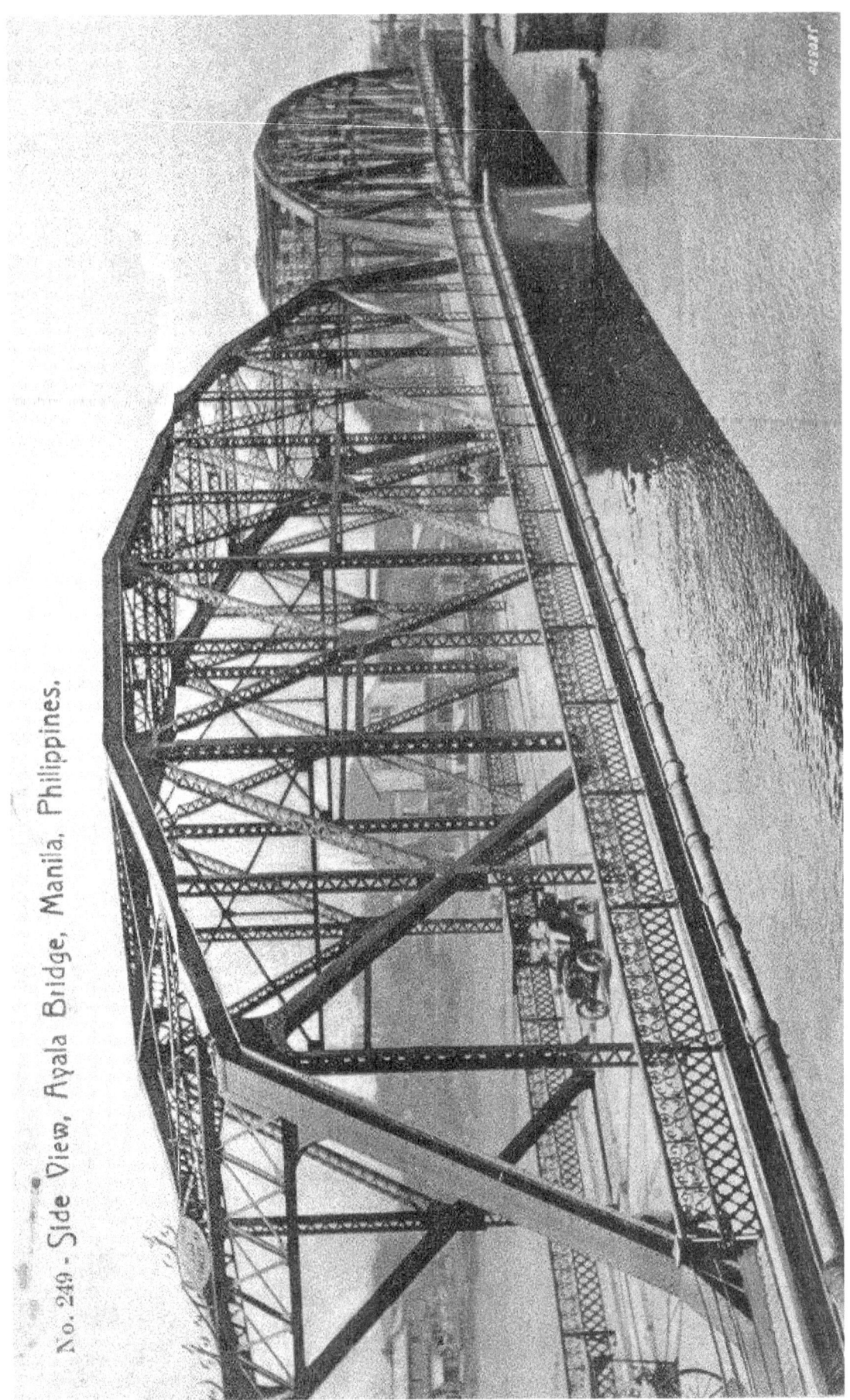

Ayala Bridge, 1900s (Note vintage T-Ford car)

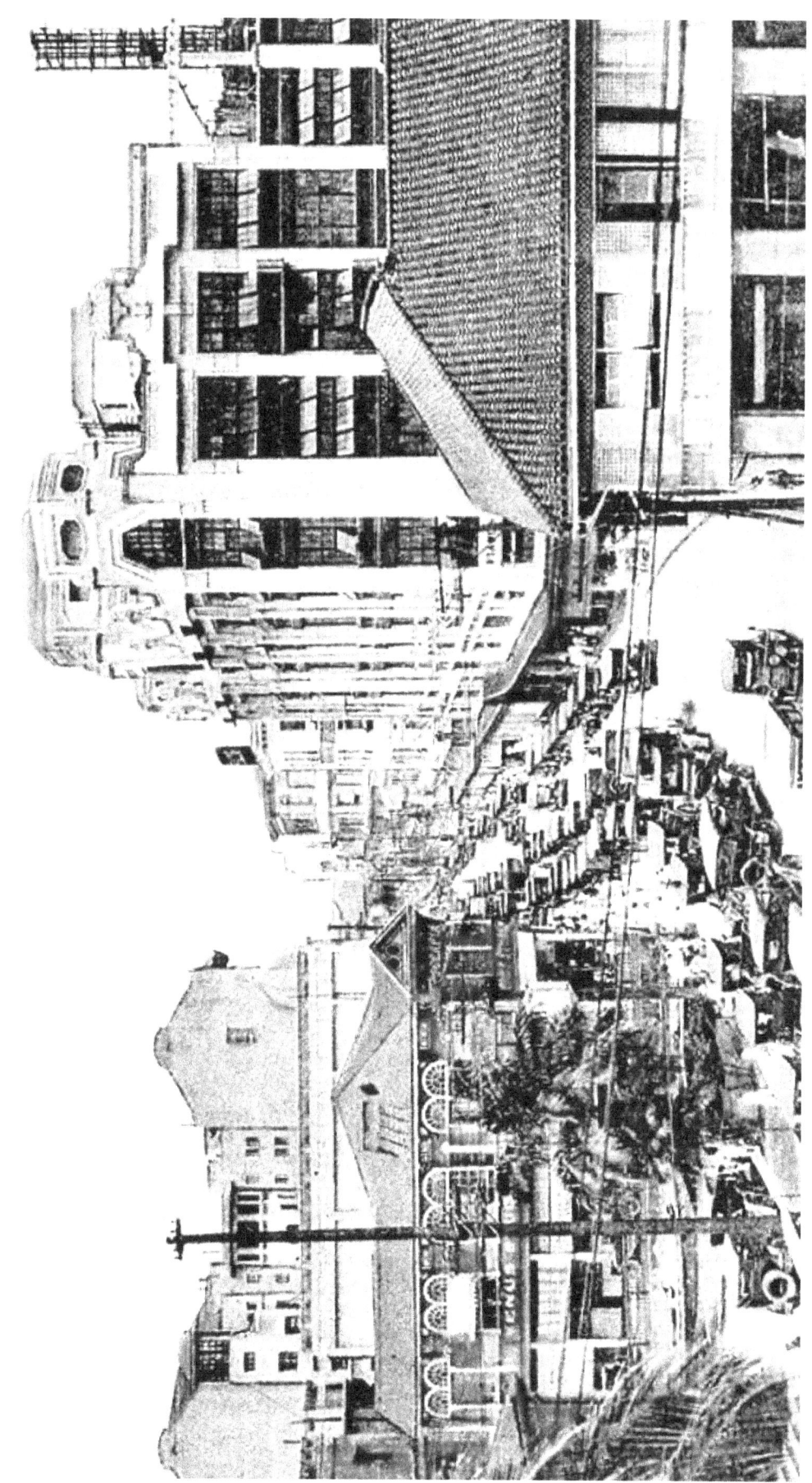

Escolta — Main St. in Manila

Escolta, 1900s-1930s (Note T-Ford Cars)

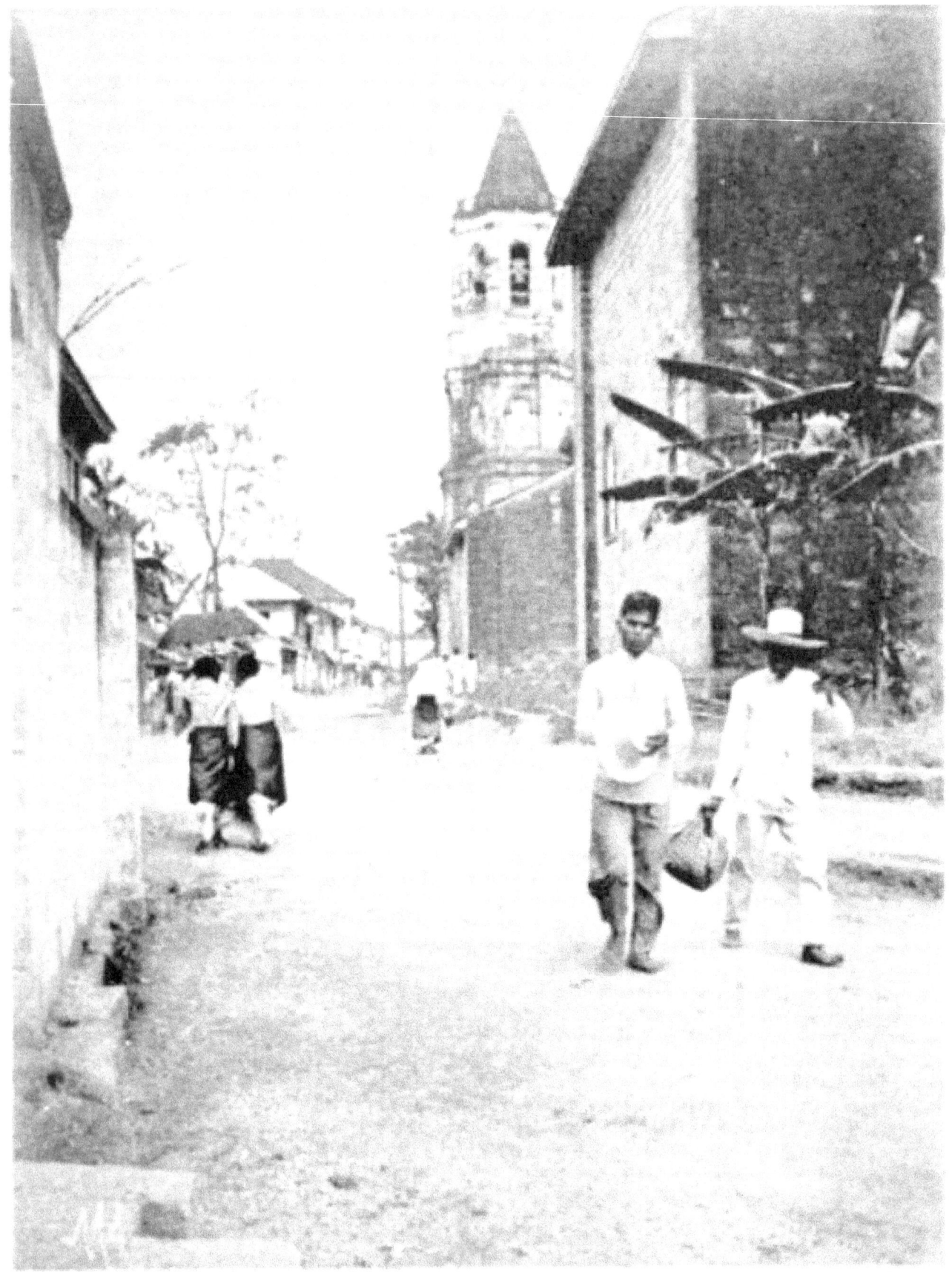

UNA CALLE DE MALOLOS (BULACAN-FILIPINAS)
Main Street, Malolos Bulacan, 1900s

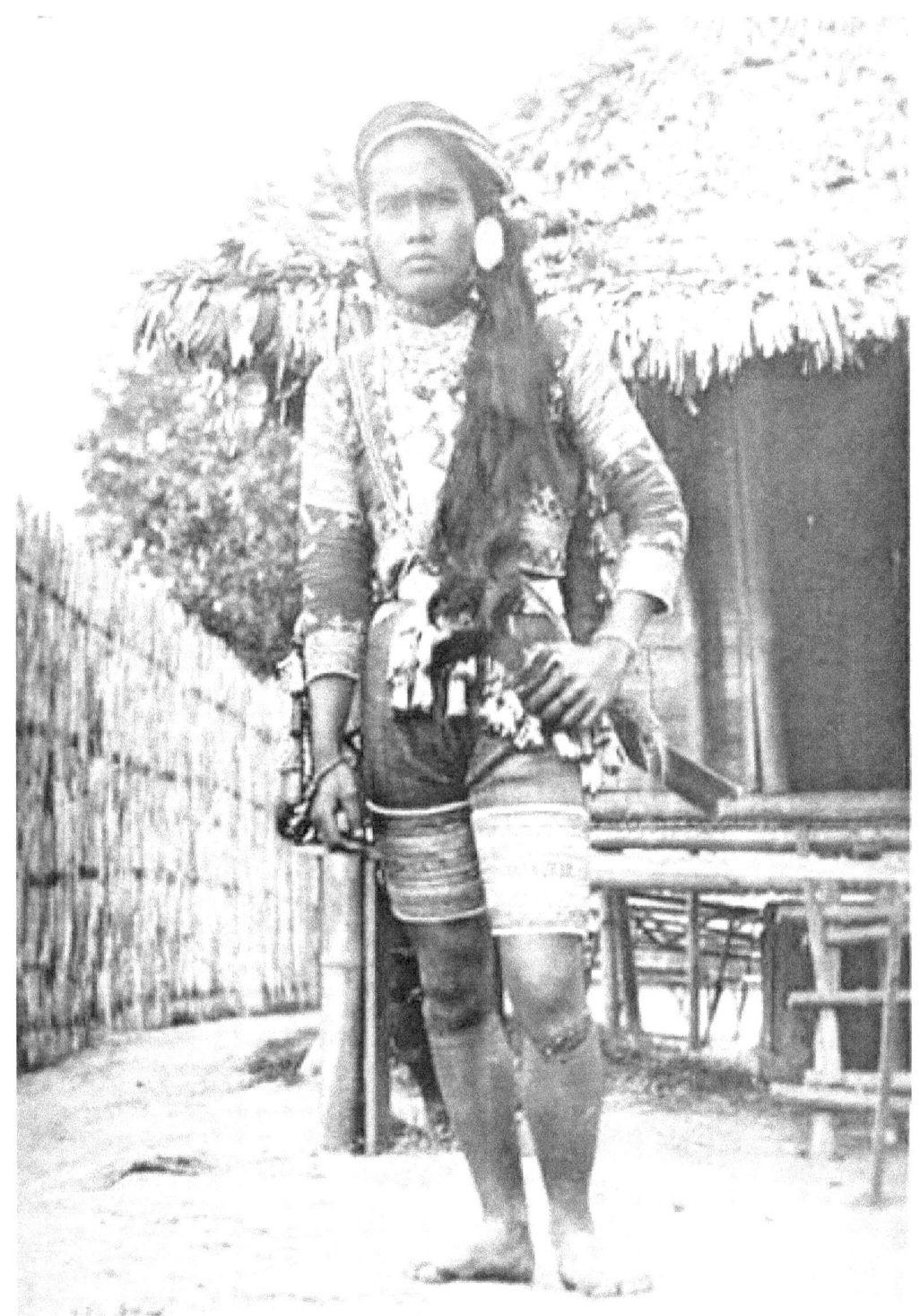

Datto Bulon, chief of the Bagobo, dressed in warrior attire. Philippine Reservation, 1904 Louisiana Purchase Exposition. Datu Bulon, the 19-year old chief of the Bagobo Tribe, was admired for his handsome physique and elaborately ornamented costume in the 1904 American World Fair entitled, Louisiana Purchase Exposition in Saint Louis, Missouri. The 47 acres of land display was dubbed as the largest and the finest colonial exhibit" with over 1,100 native Filipinos including Negritos, Igorot, Moros, Bagobos, Tagalogs and Visayans over the Philippine Exhibition participated as live exhibits. Photograph by: Gerhard Sisters, 1904 * New York Public Library Digital Collection

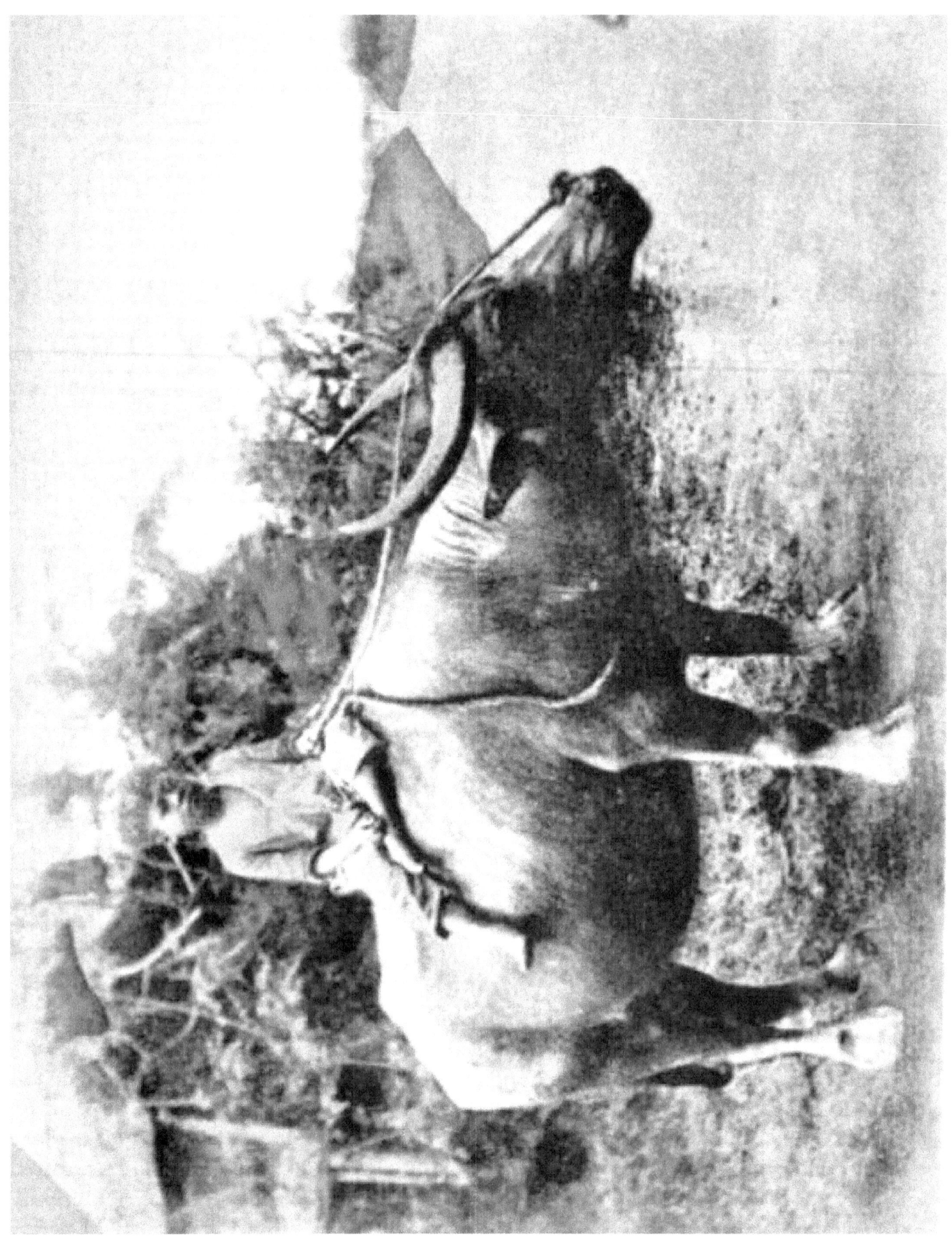

Typical large carabao, water buffalo, (beast of burden), 1900s

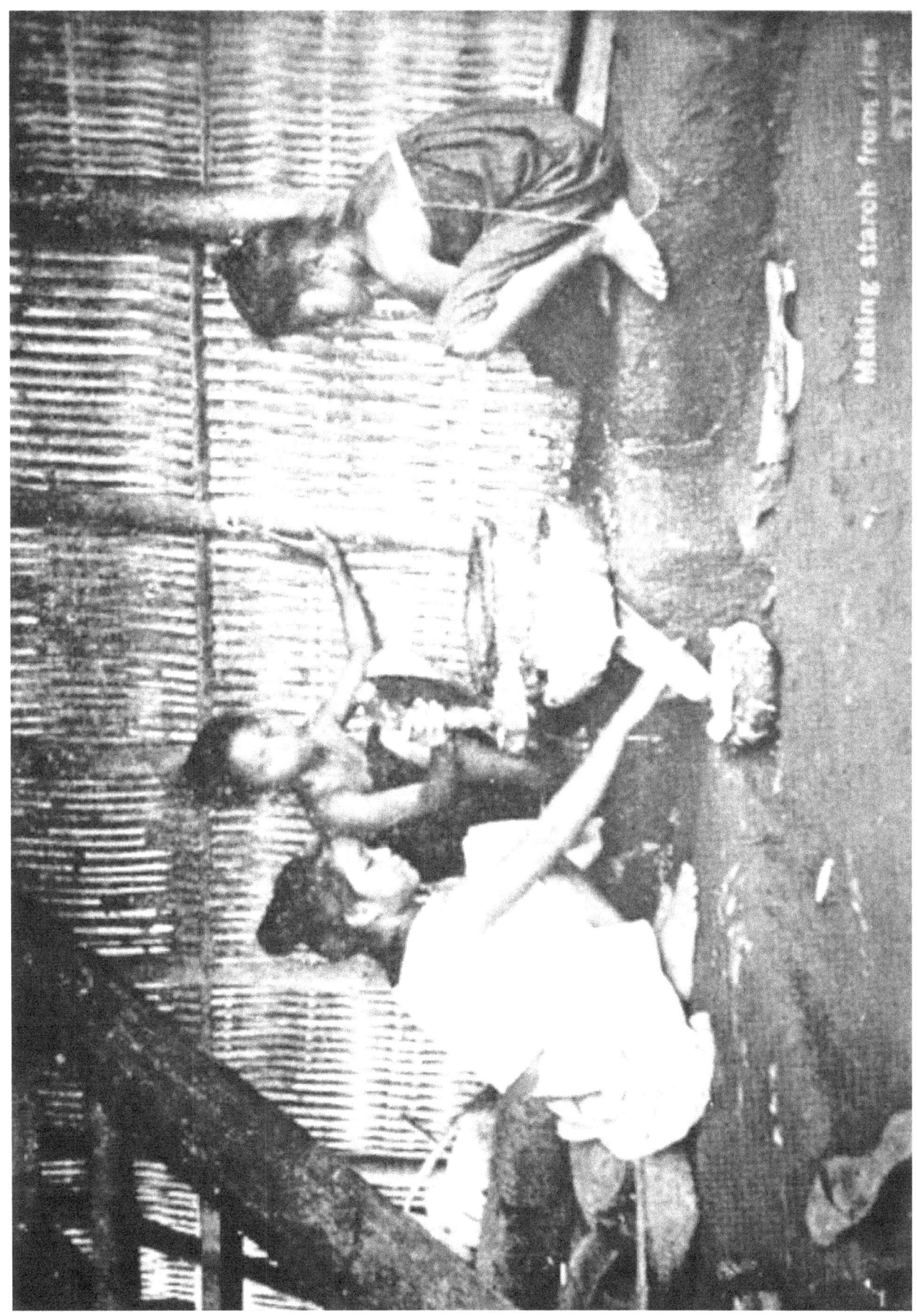

Crude starch making (presumably from cassava), 1900s

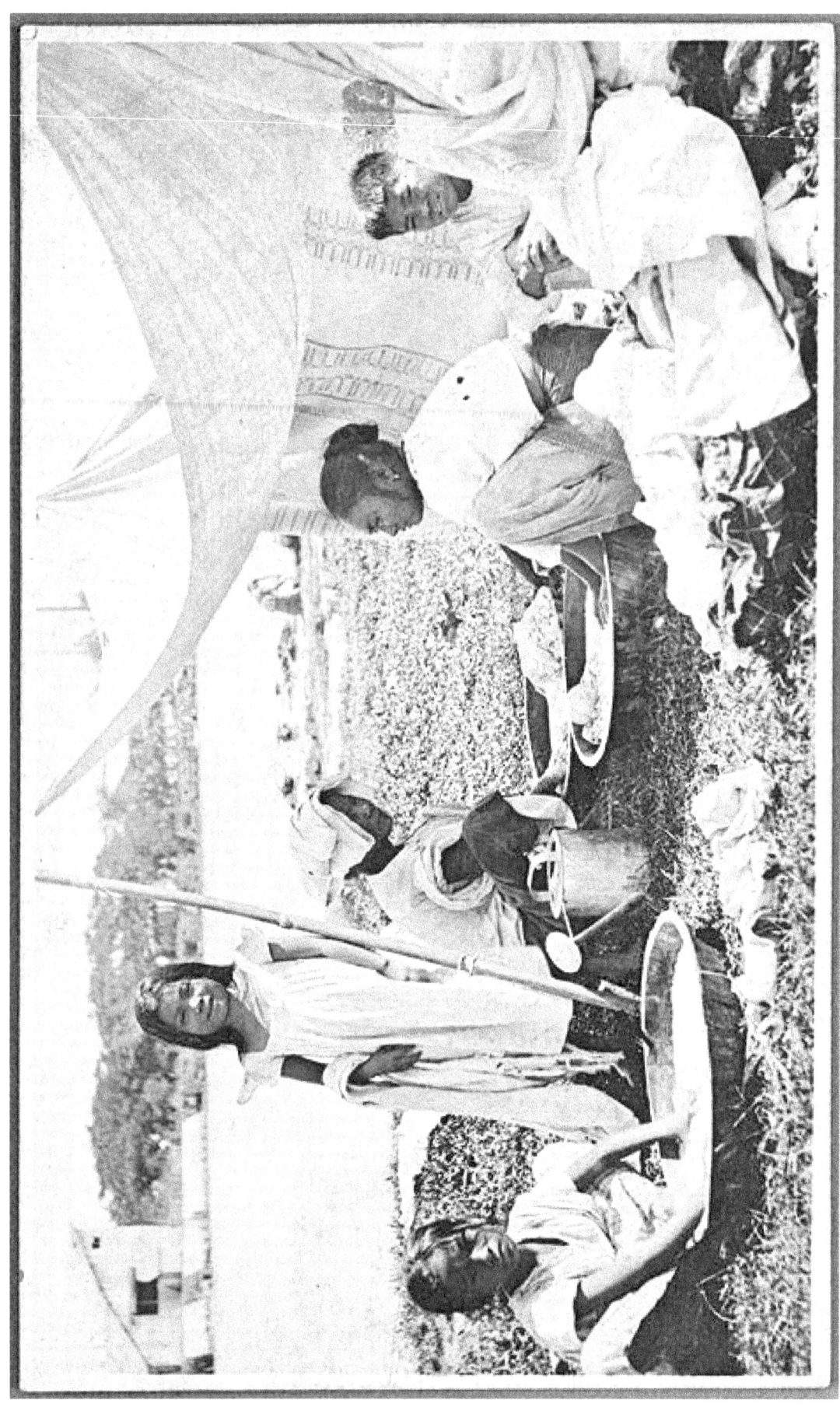

Typical washing clothes on the river, early 1900s

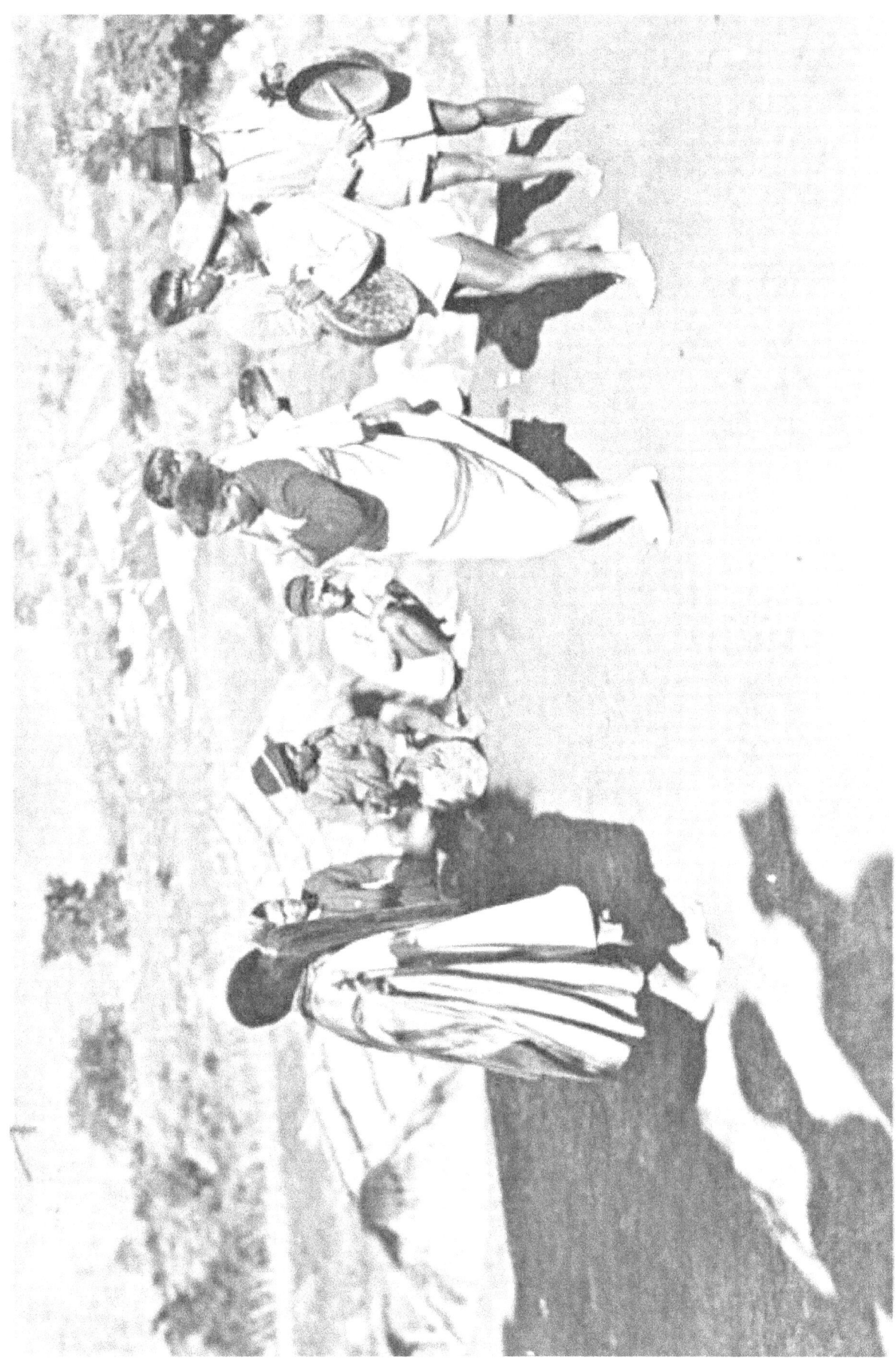

Mountain people, Kalinga Dancers (note coats with bare legs)

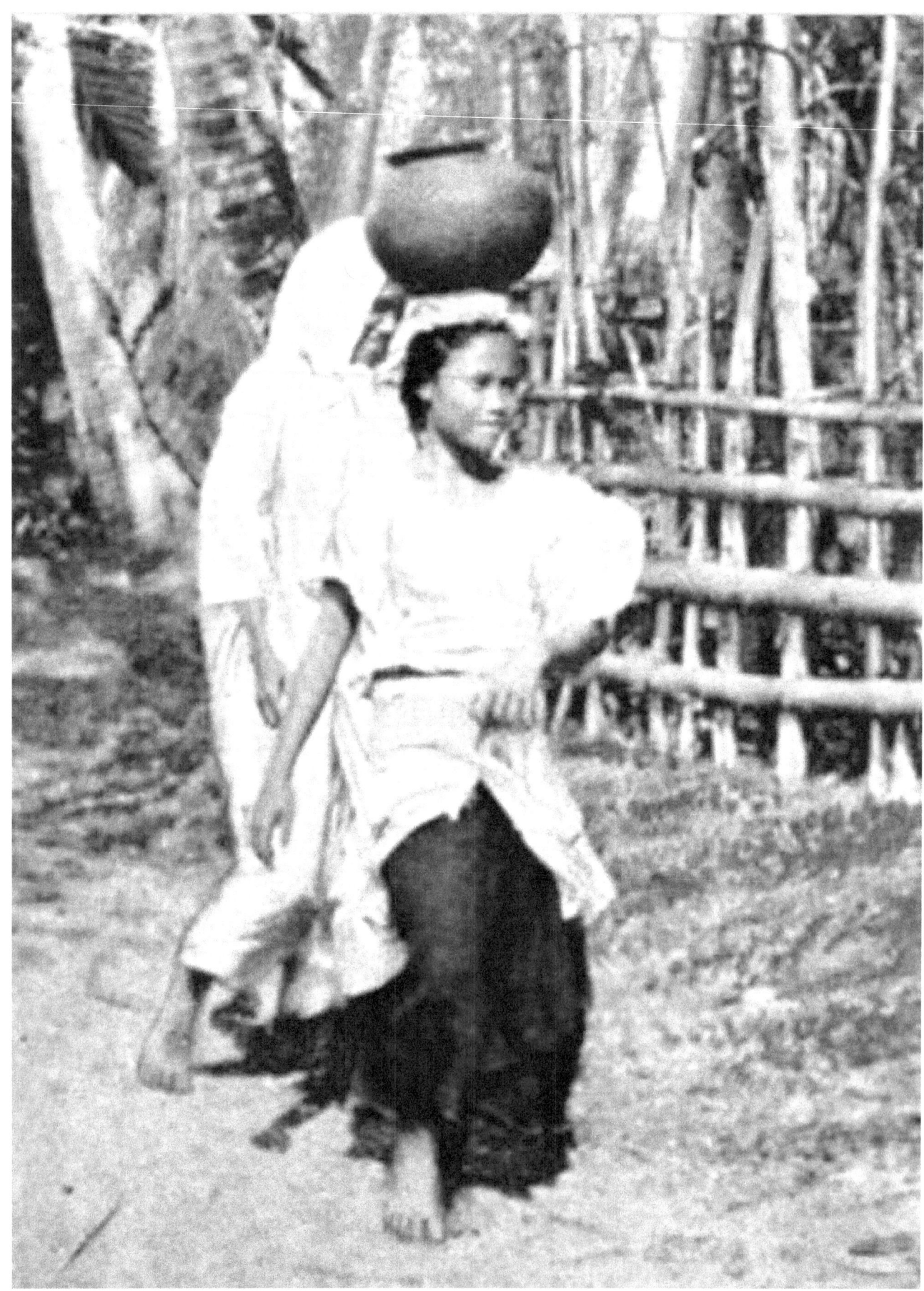
Typical rural native women, 1900s-1950s

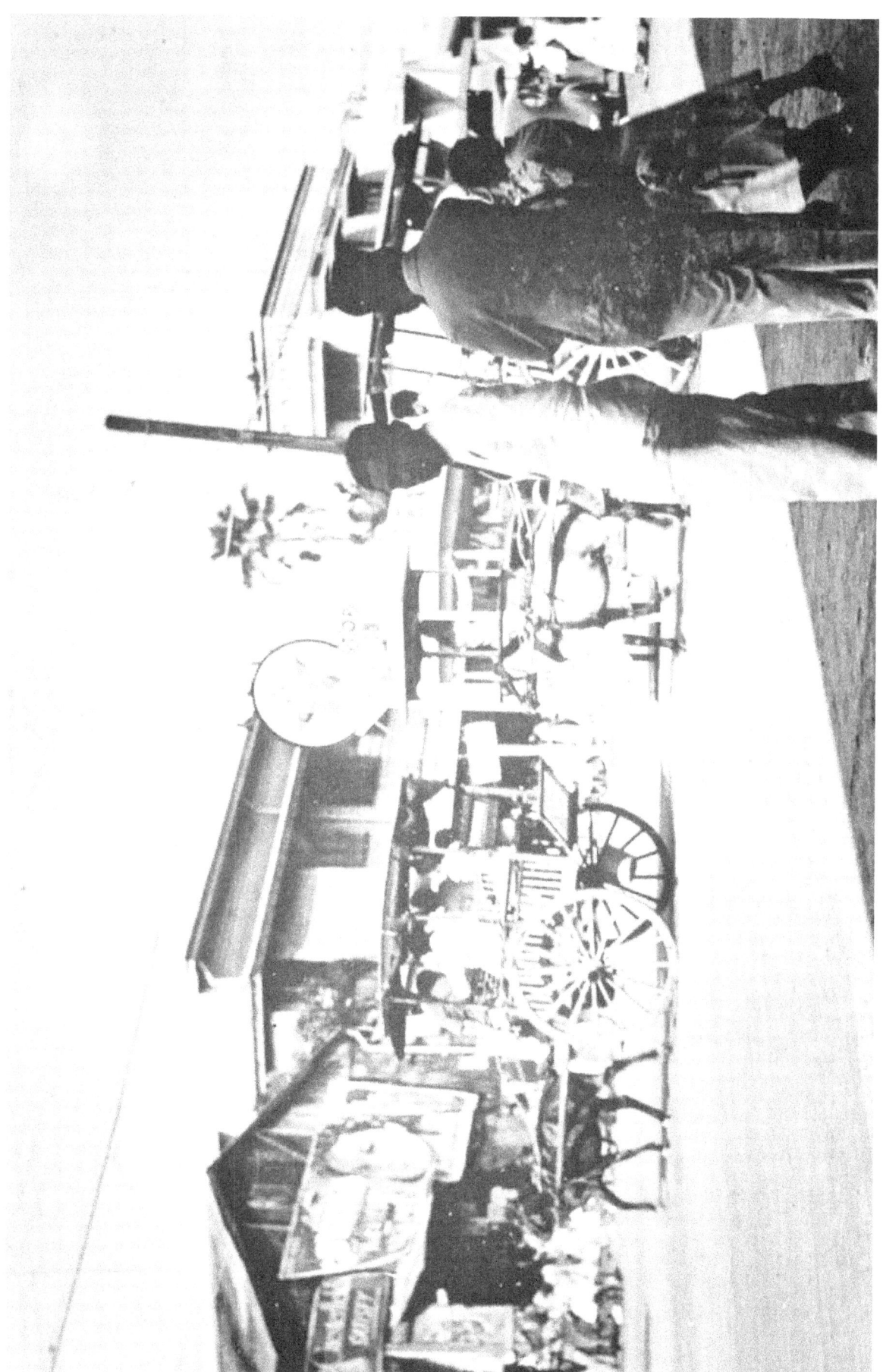

Typical side street in Manila, 1940s-1950s, calesas allowed yet

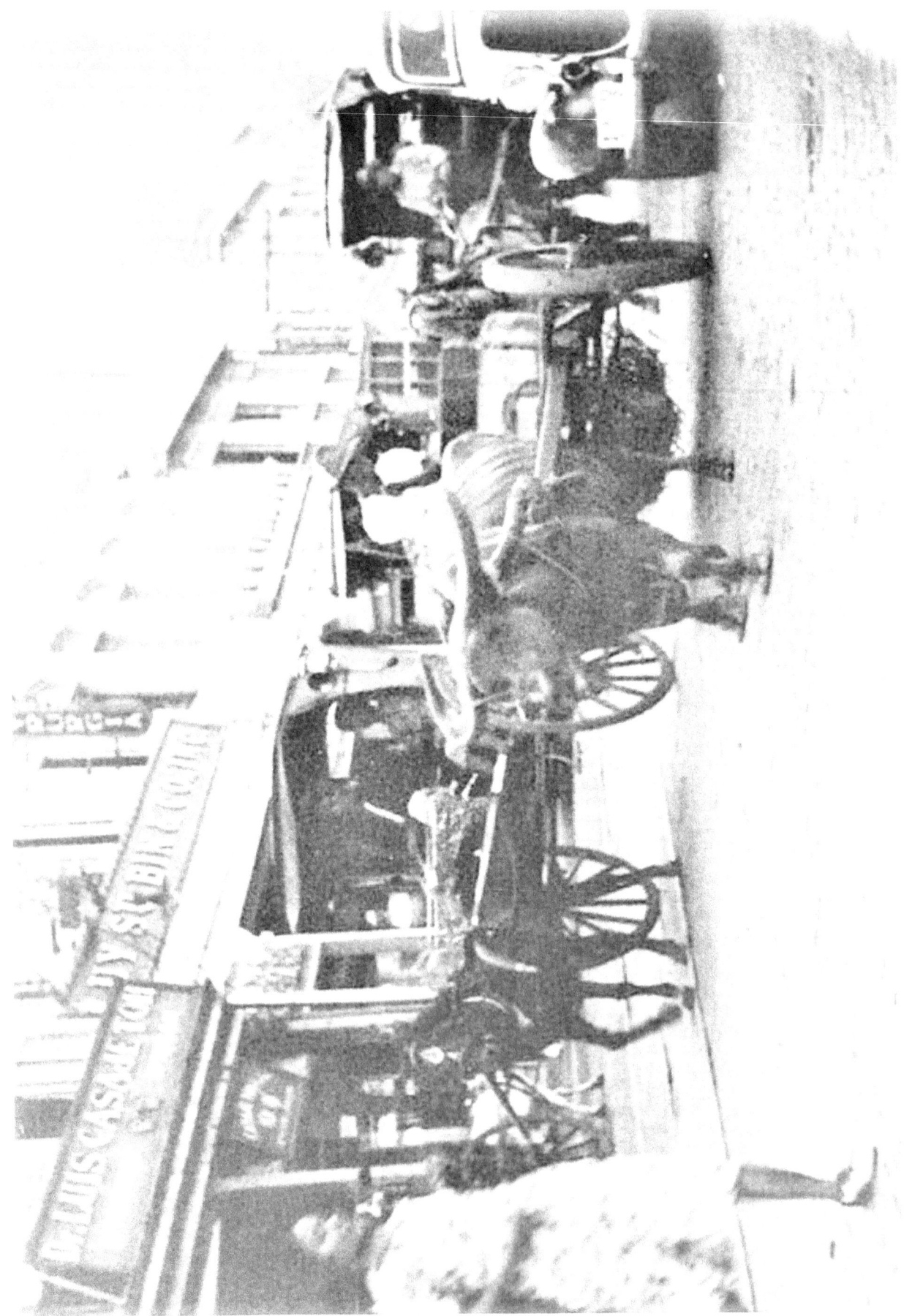
Typical Binondo street in Manila, when carabao carts yet allowed, 1930

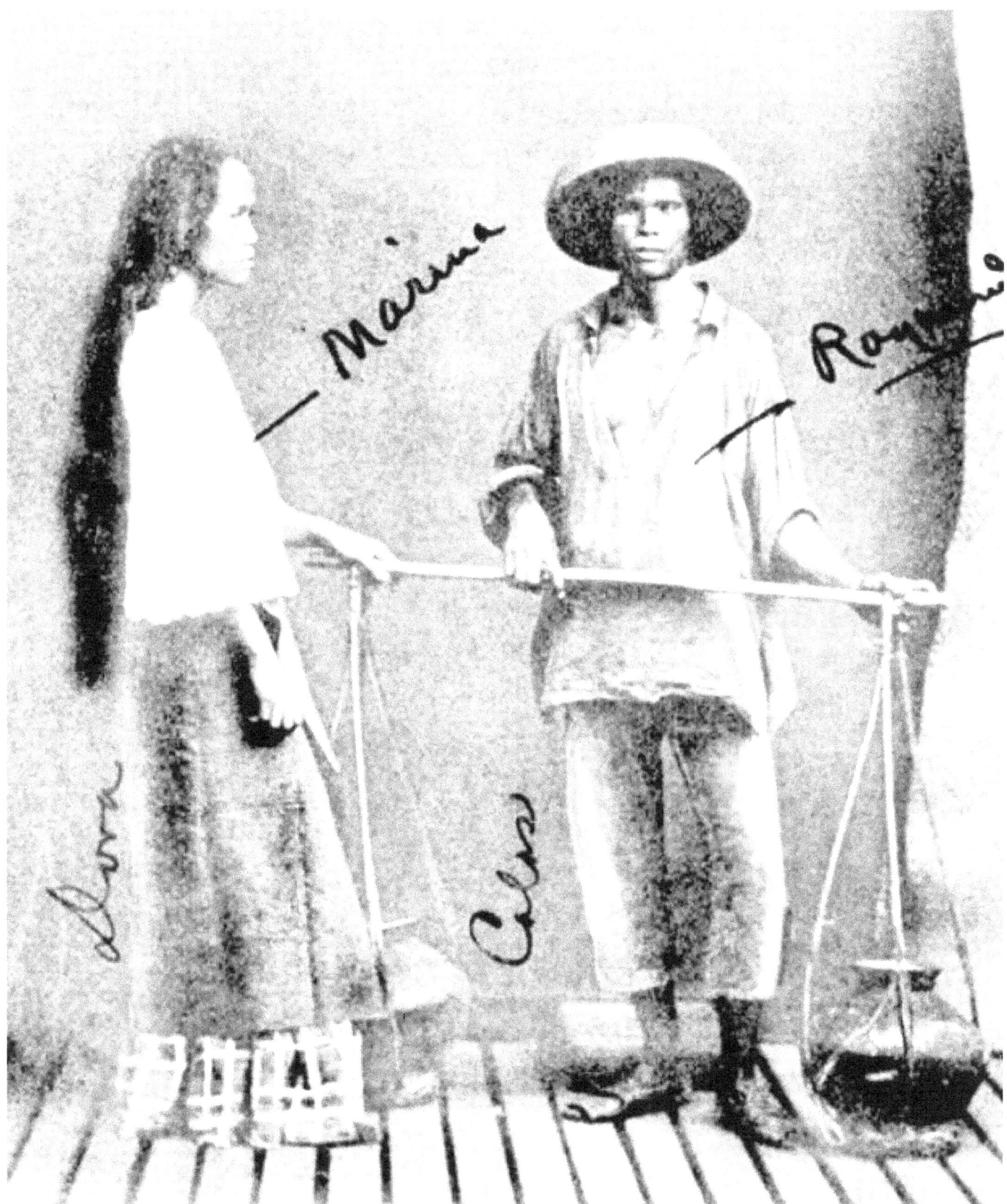

Oil Peddlers, Manila, Philippines, 1898 or before. This illustration was labeled "Peddlers of Oil Industry. These are to be met with on nearly every street corner. Oil being much used in cooking." In another book of the time it is labeled as "A water-carrier and customer"

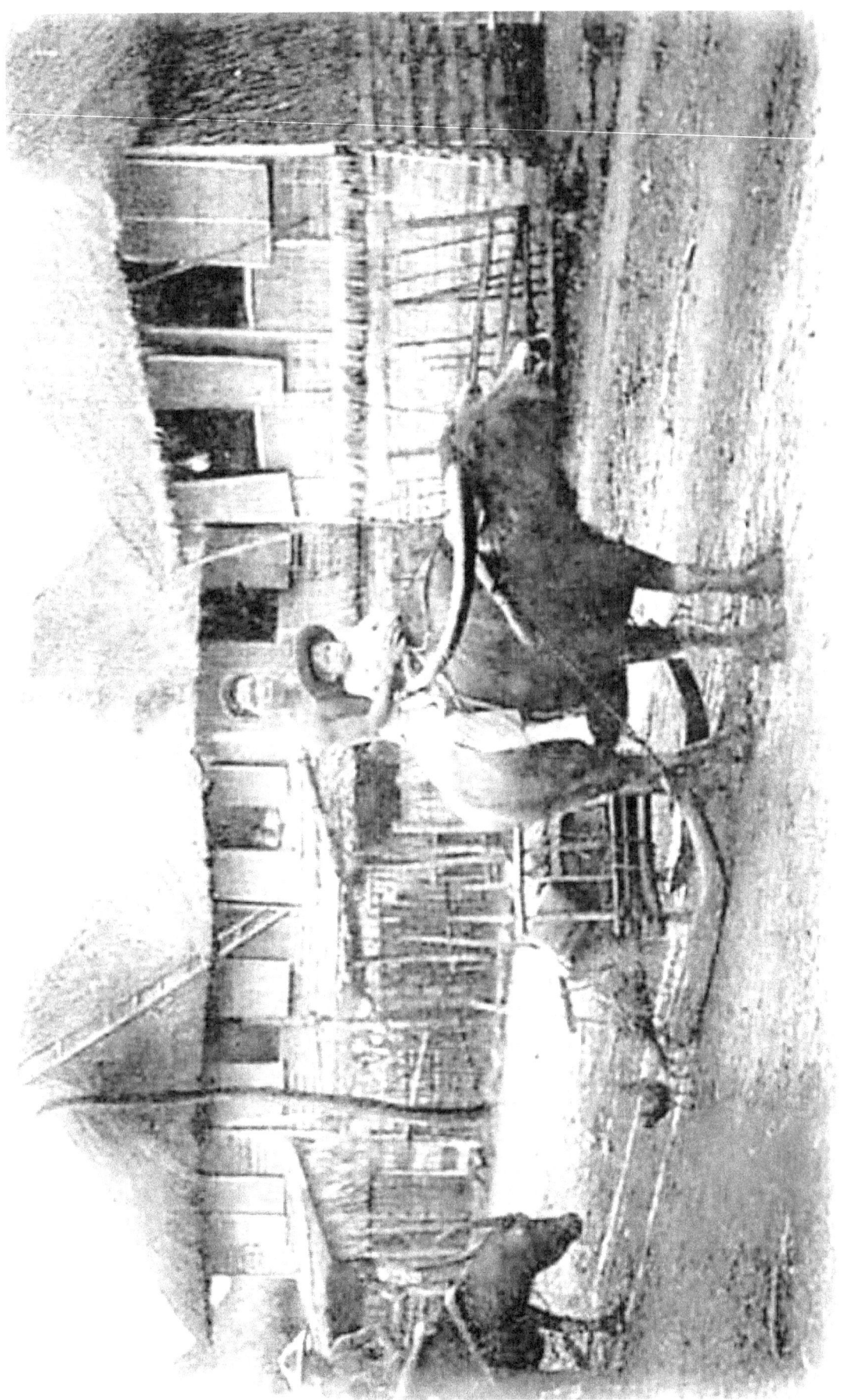

Carabao Sleigh (no wheels), another transport mode, many centuries

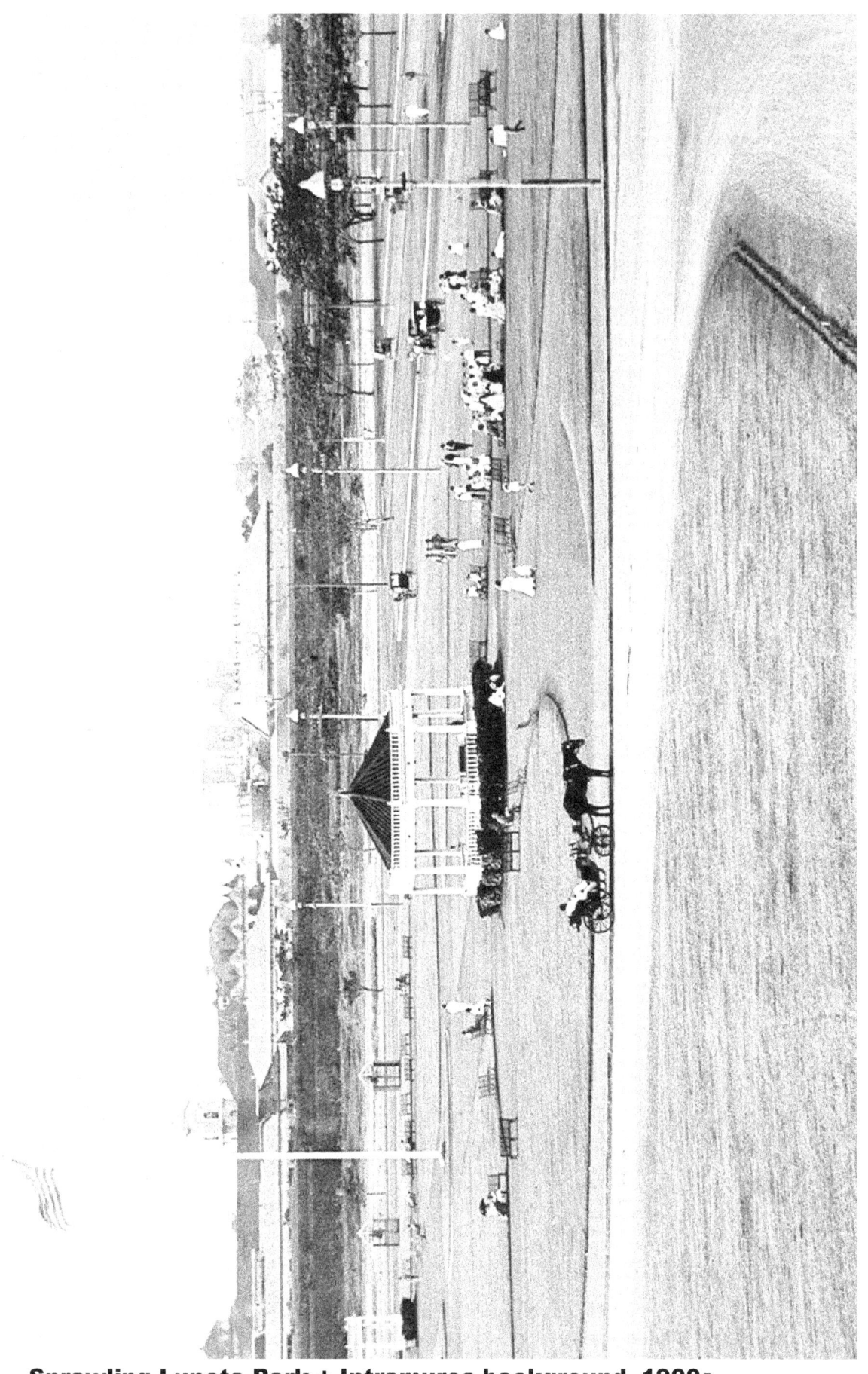

Sprawling Luneta Park + Intramuros background, 1900s

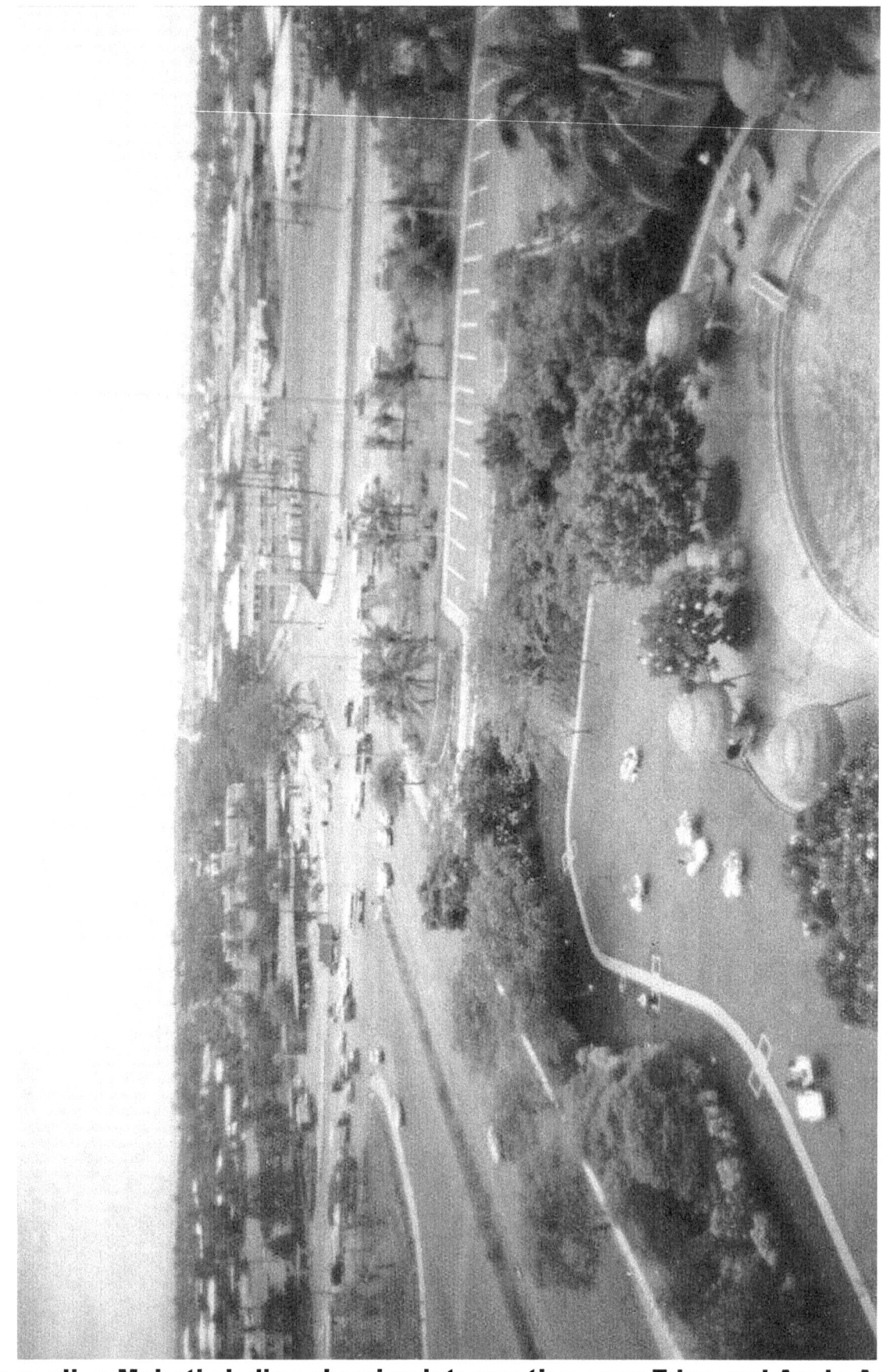

Sprawling Makati skyline showing intersection near Edsa and Ayala Ave. Camera shot from Intercon Hotel, 1970 (no high rise bluidings. yet)

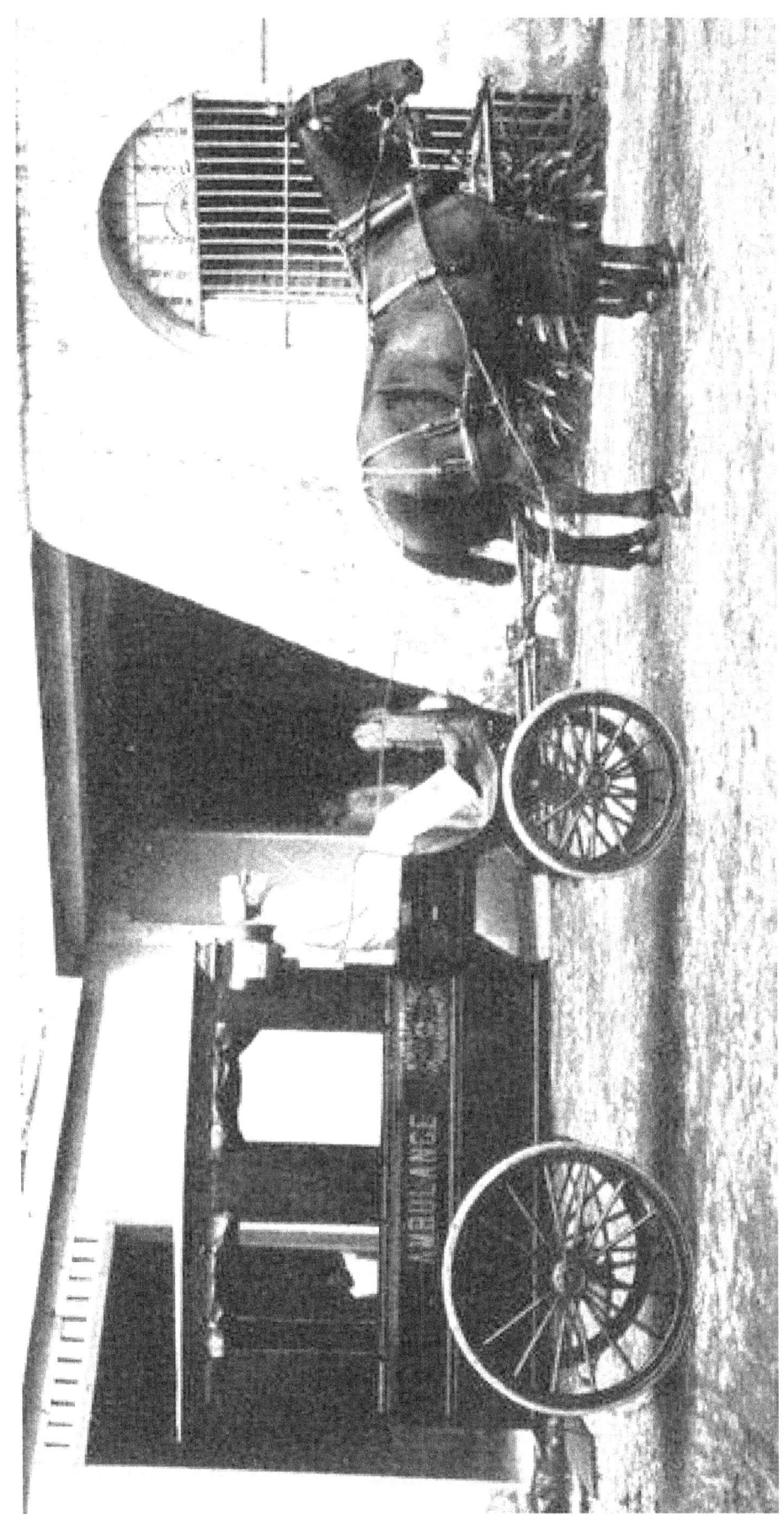

Horse-drawn Ambulance, circa 1900s

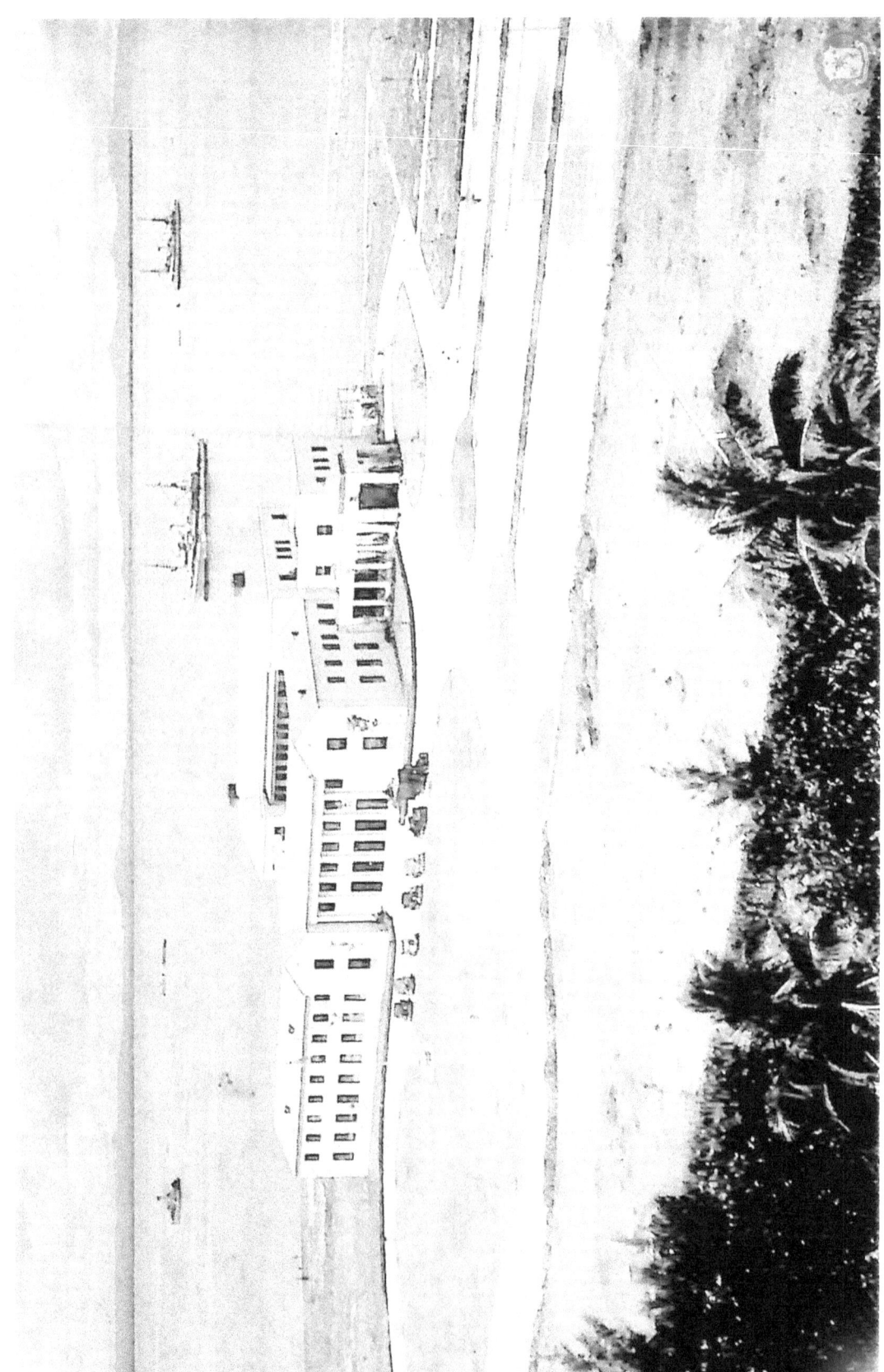

Beside palm-fringed Dewey Boulevard, overlooking Manila Bay, is the new residence of Francis B. Sayre, American High Commissioner to the Commonwealth. (Photo from Philippines Magazine, Volume I Number 1 - December 1940) * Presidential Museum and Library

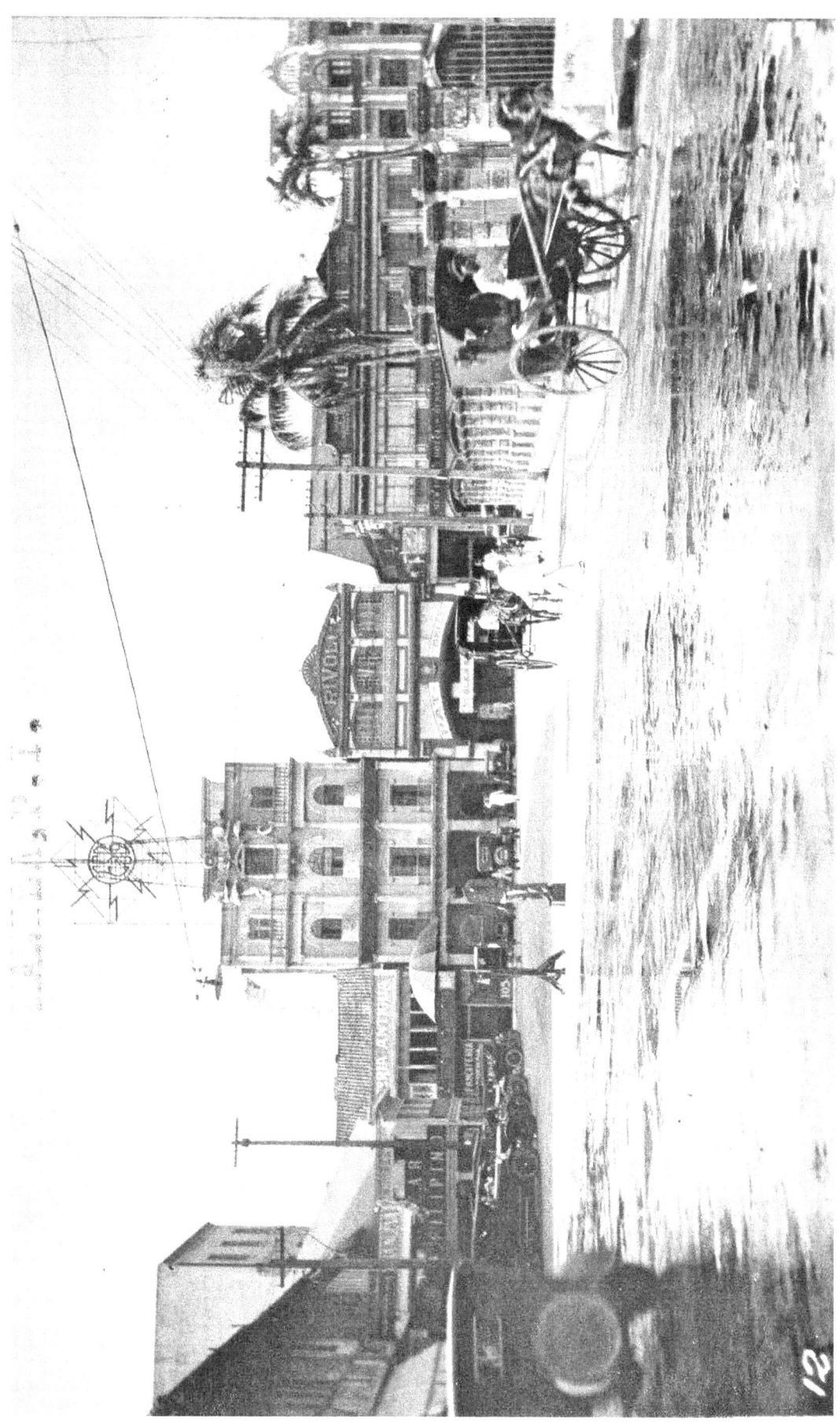

Plaza Sta. Cruz, Manila, 1920

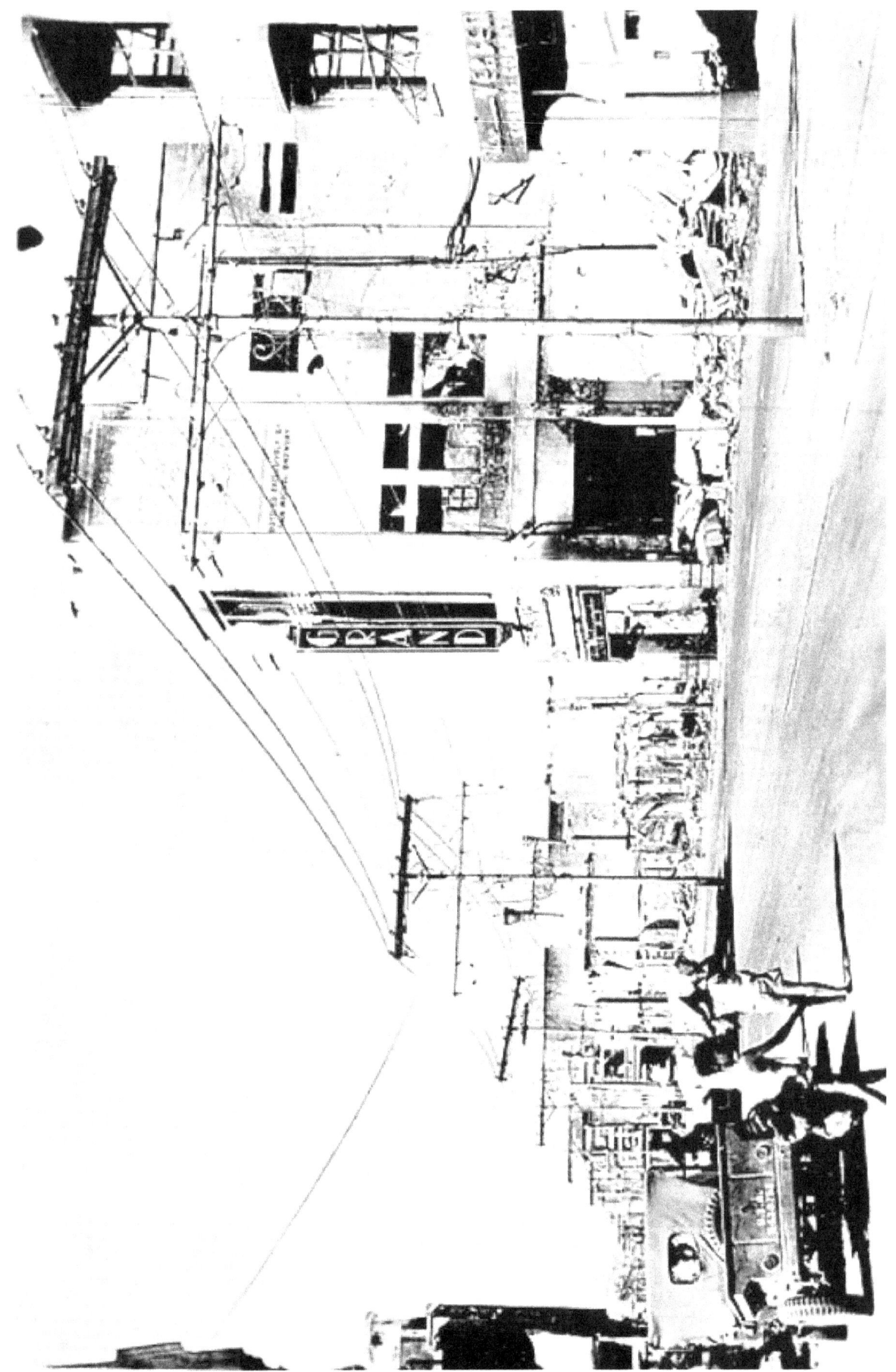

Rizal Ave, 1945, war devastation still visible (note US jeep)

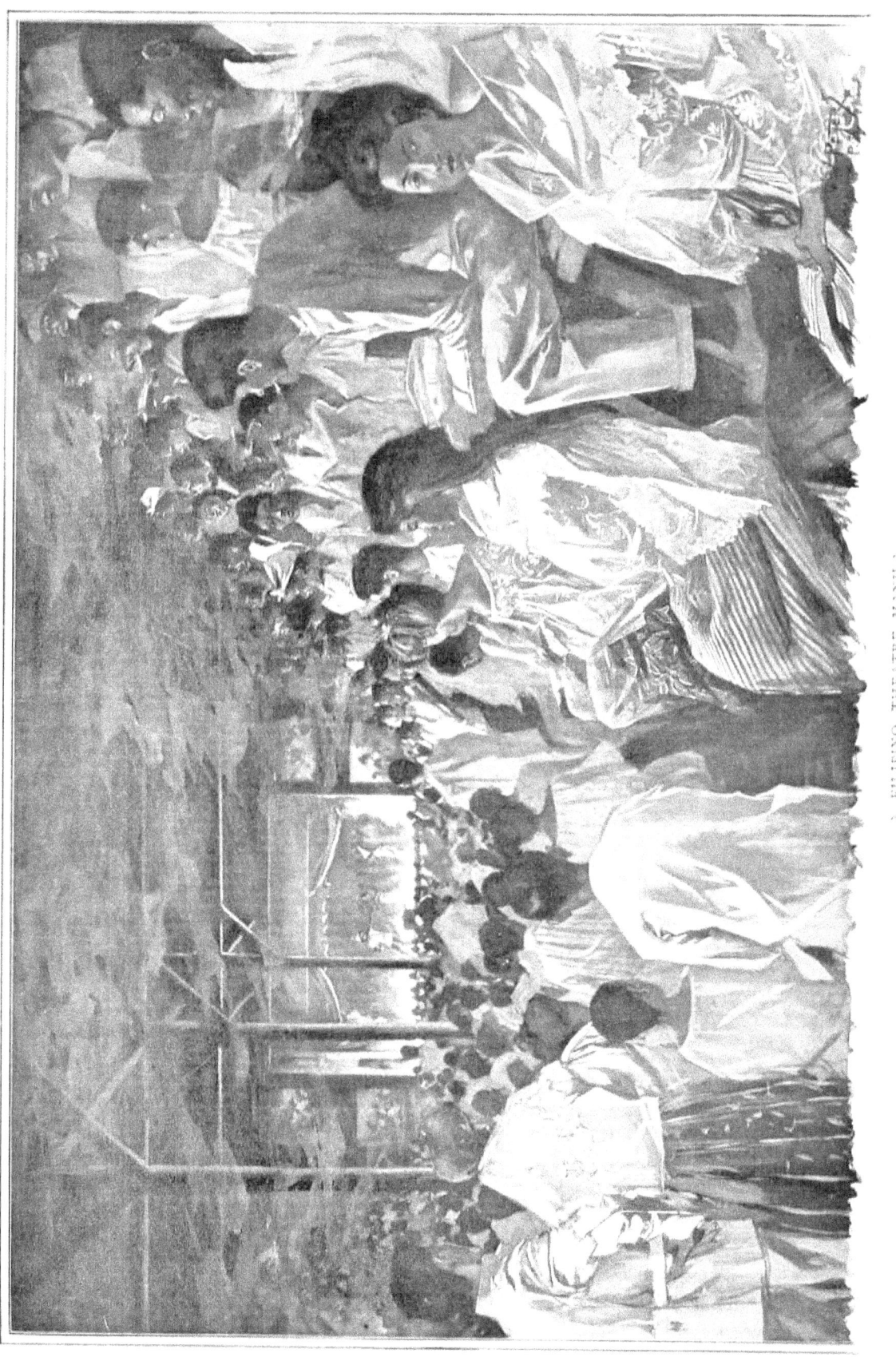

A Filipino Theatre with stage shows in early 1900s

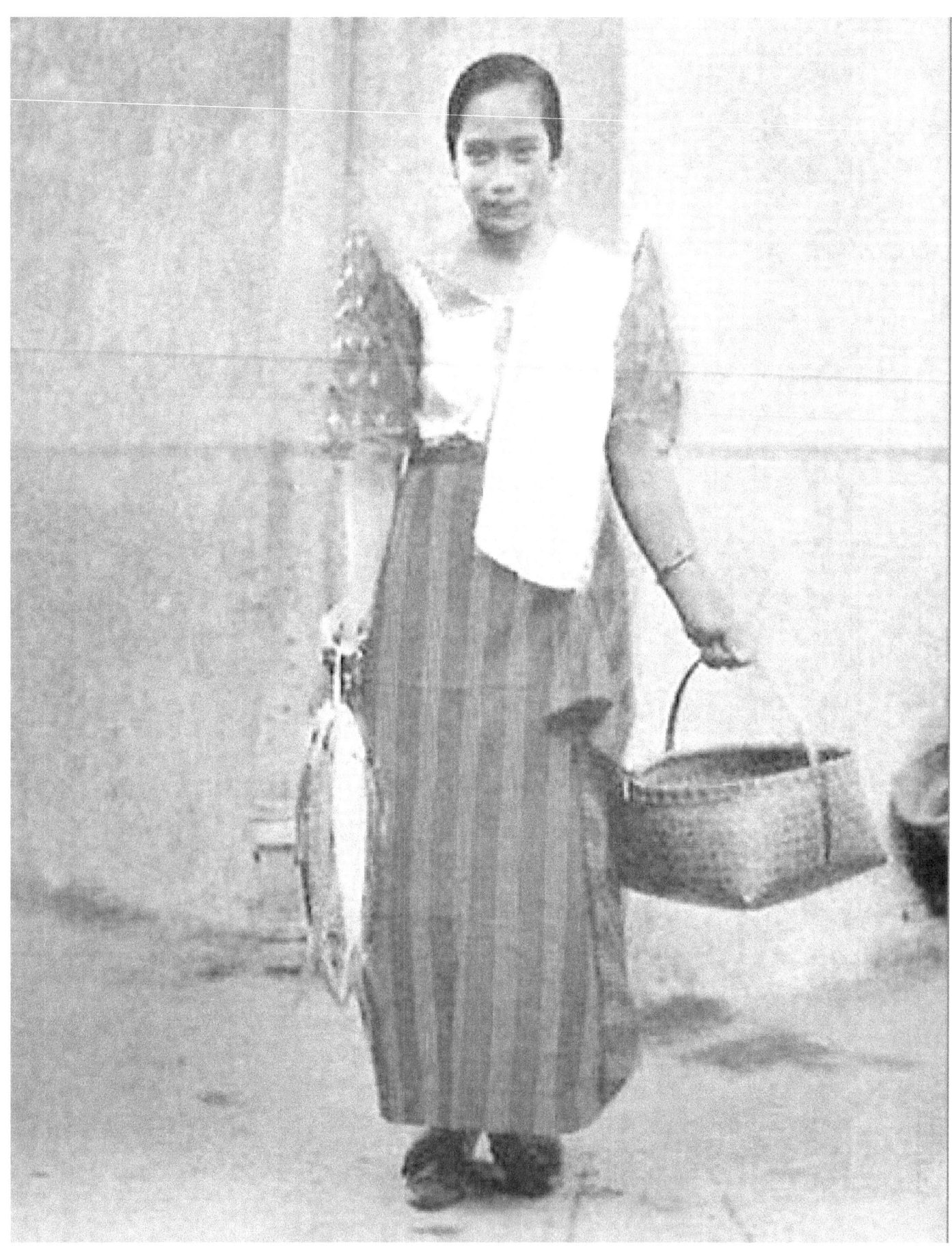

Filipina lady done marketing typical day, 1900s

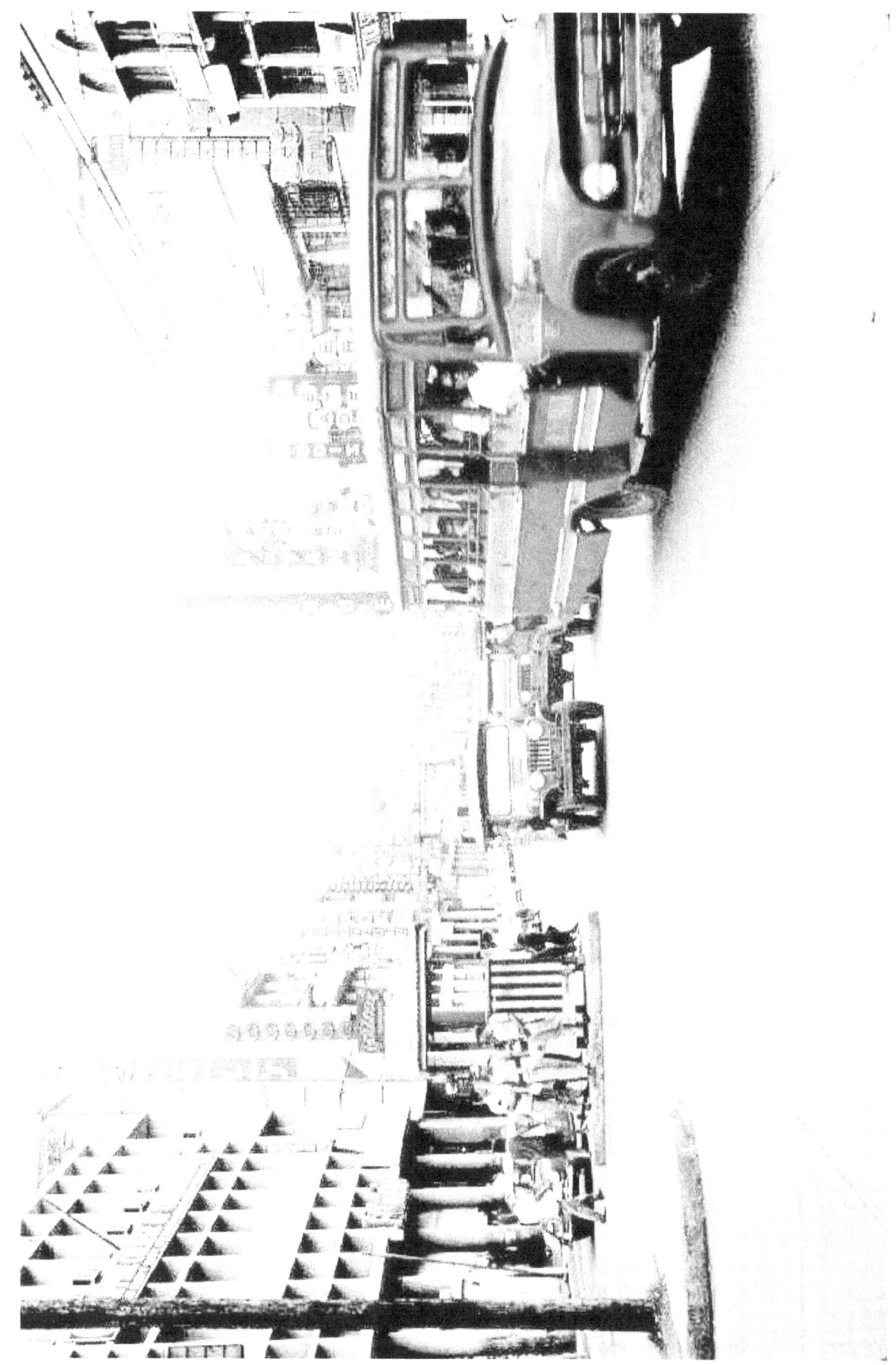

Rizal Avenue, 1960. Note jitneys and old bus

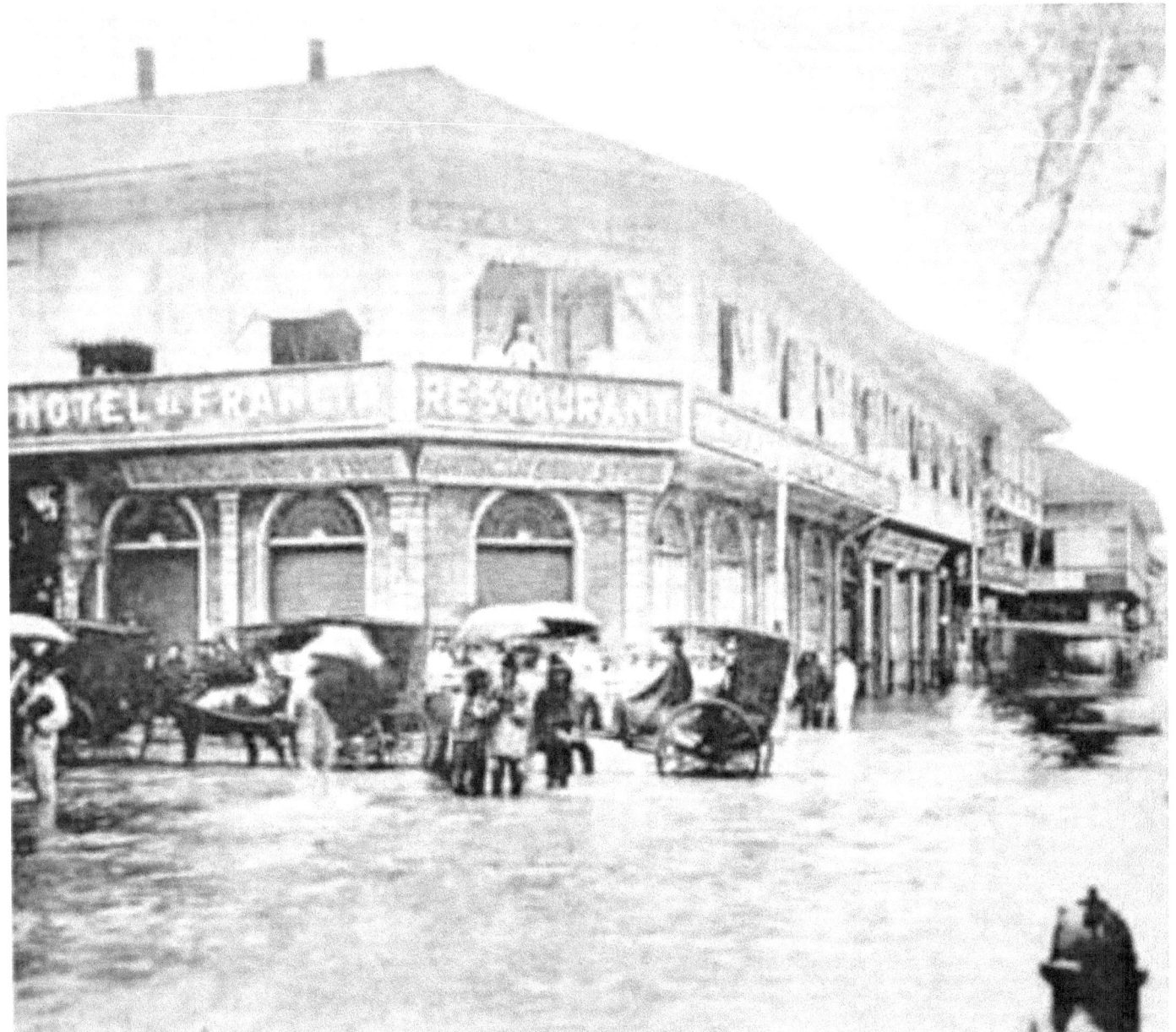

Escolta – Grand Hotel + Francia Restaurant – Fooded Manila, early 1900s

WELCOME! Thank you for viewing these heritage or nostalgic pictures of individuals, places and events in the history of our beloved country, The Philippines. They say, a picture is worth a thousand words. More info about the person/event can easily be searched in the internet. These old pictures are available in prints, galleries, museums, magazines, and other forms of media. We record them as archives in this format for posterity.

This book can be displayed as coffee table book for family and guests. Each picture can be cut and framed, by buying extra copies. This book is suitable for libraries and schools in Philippines and USA. It is ideal reference material for study of history and celebrities. It is suitable as gift for any occasion. It's a collector's item. Heirs of those shown in pictures may want to own this book for their own families. Pictures are arranged in no particular order. Browse at random.

Most pictures are courtesy of Philippines My Philippines facebook website, but some were derived from various sources, like Museums, Wikipedia and historical websites.

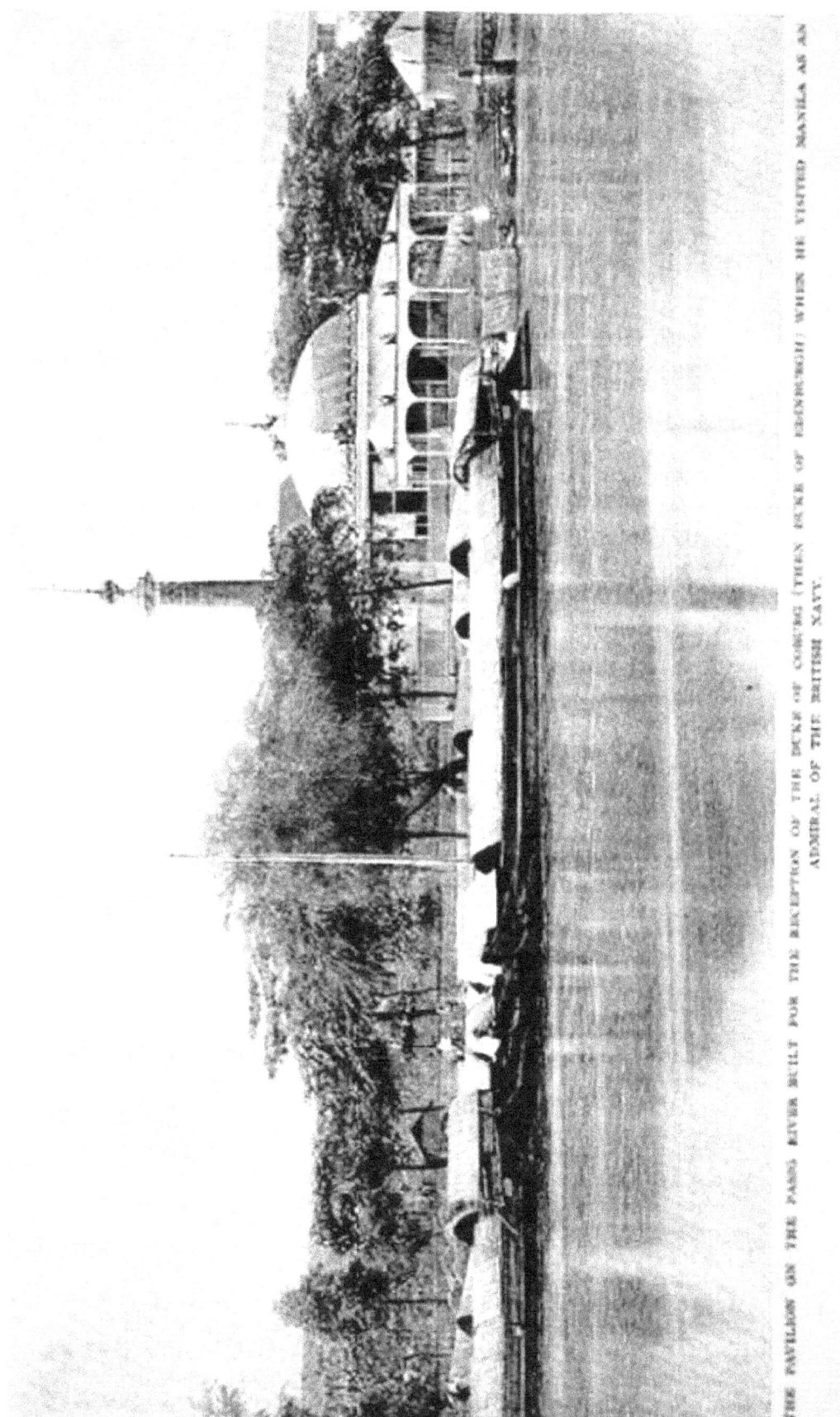

Pavilion On Pasig River Built for Reception Duke of Coburg When he Visited Manila. 1898. He a royal blood related to the House of Wales? May be related to Queen Elizabeth? So majestic and it has minaret.

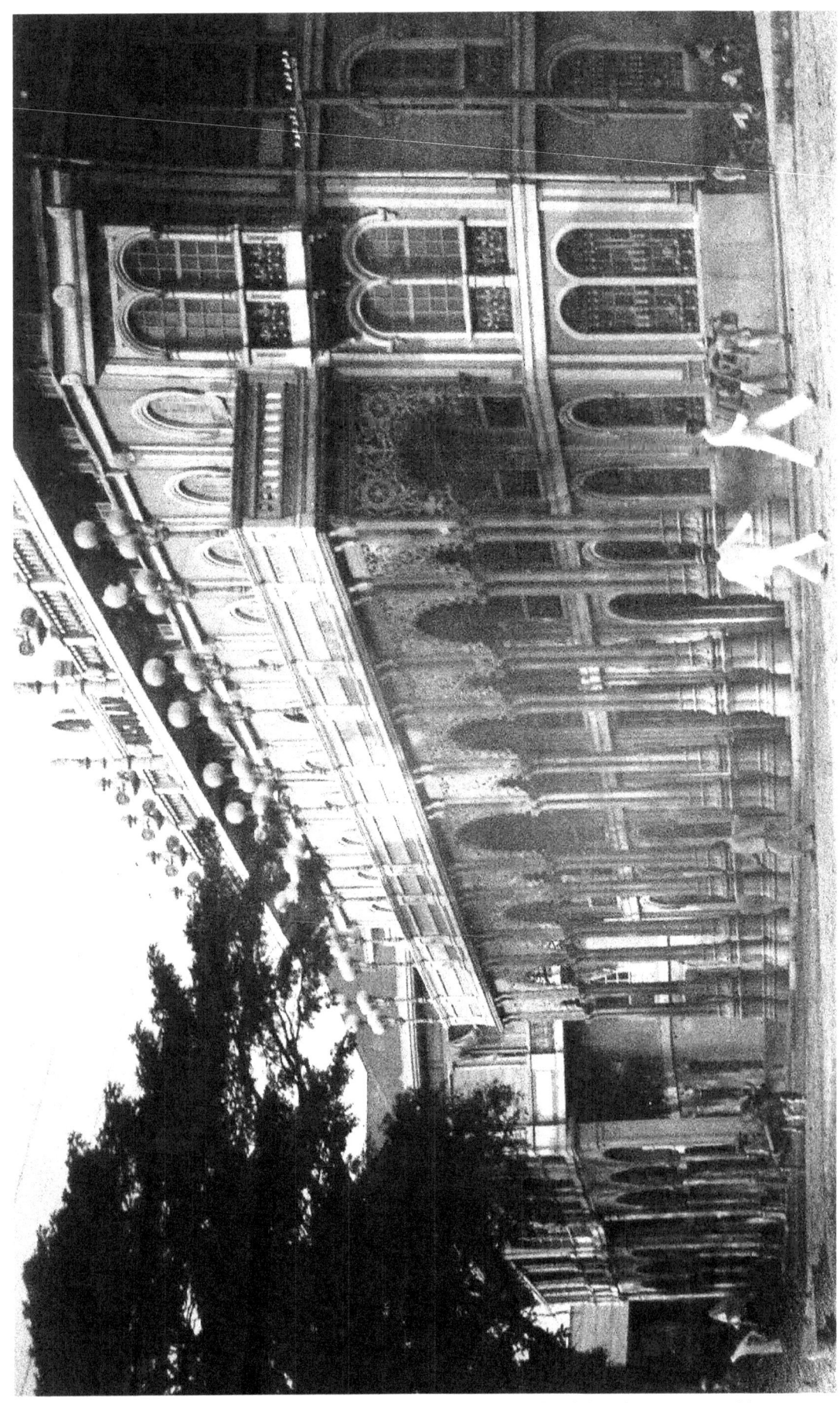

La Insular Cigar Factory in Manila, 1900s (location?)

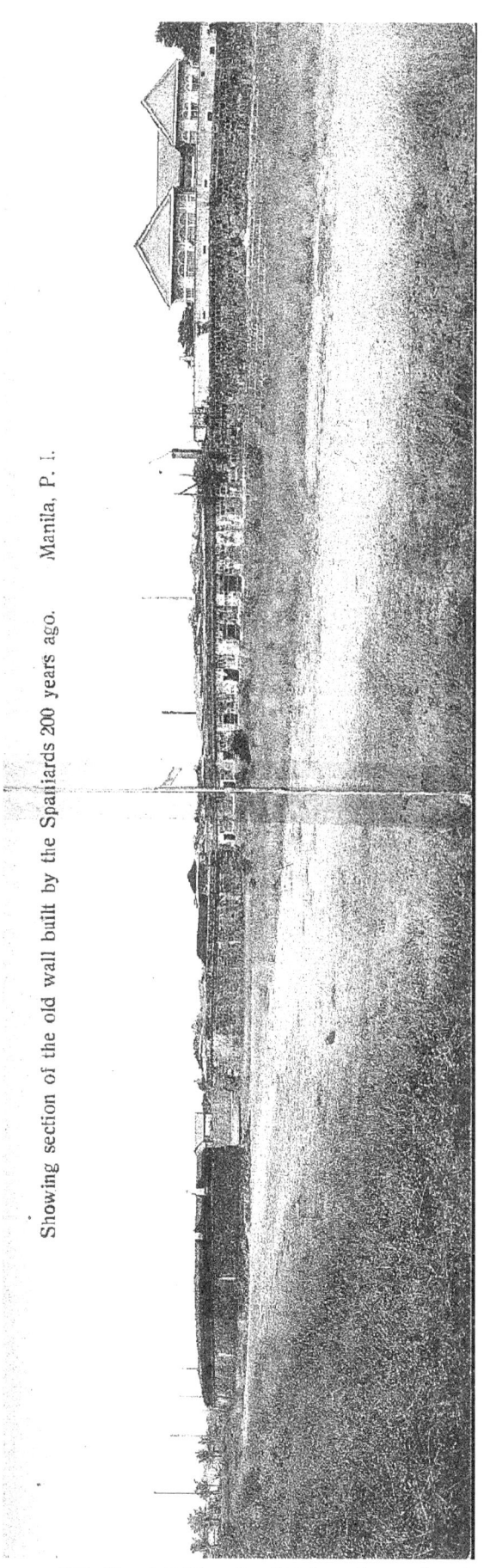

Intramuros or Walled City, built by Spaniards in 1800s

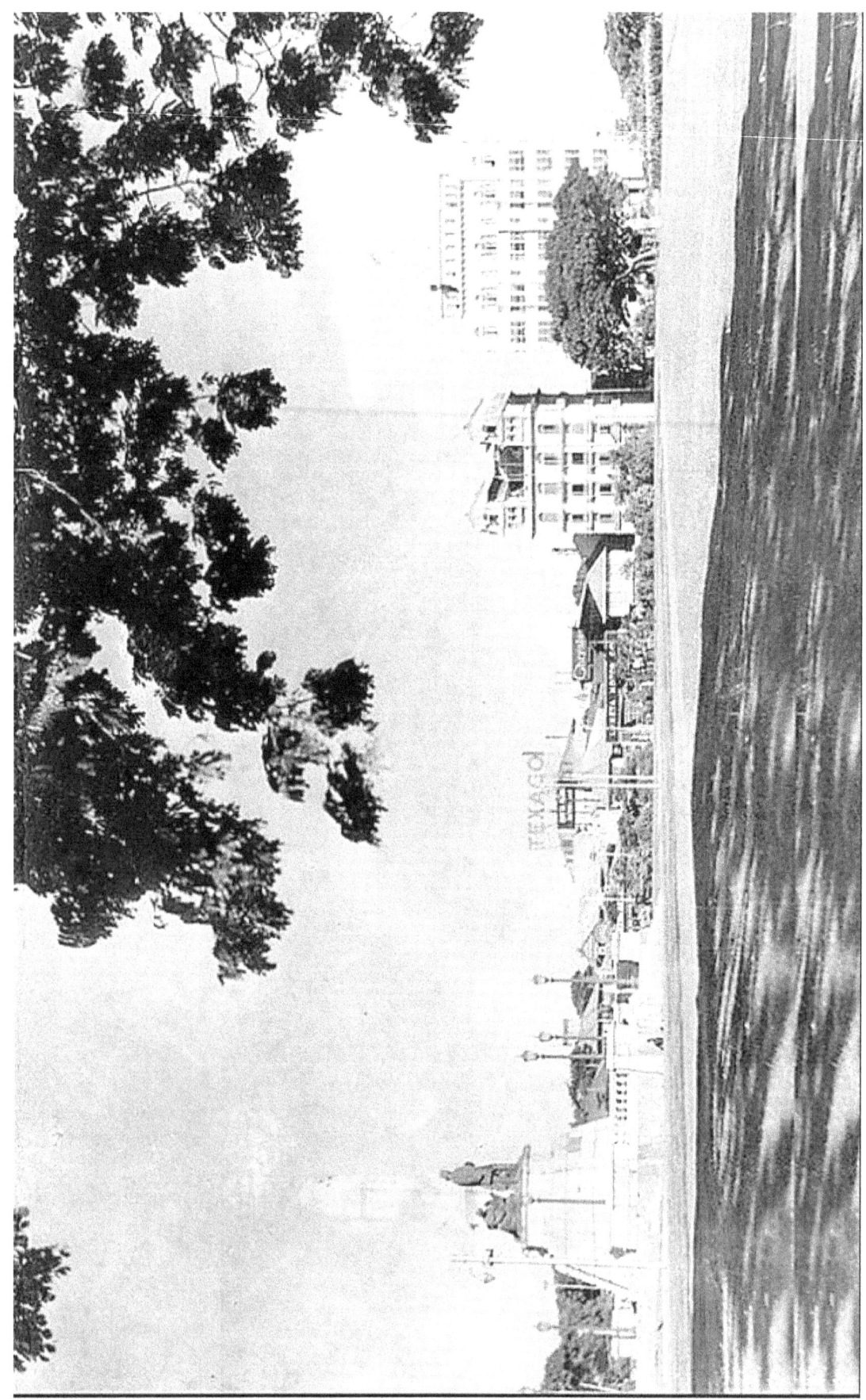

Luneta Park (Rizal Park), Manila... Texaco. Chrysler. Luneta Motor Co. Luneta Hotel. Those brand names are still very much in business. 1930s-40s

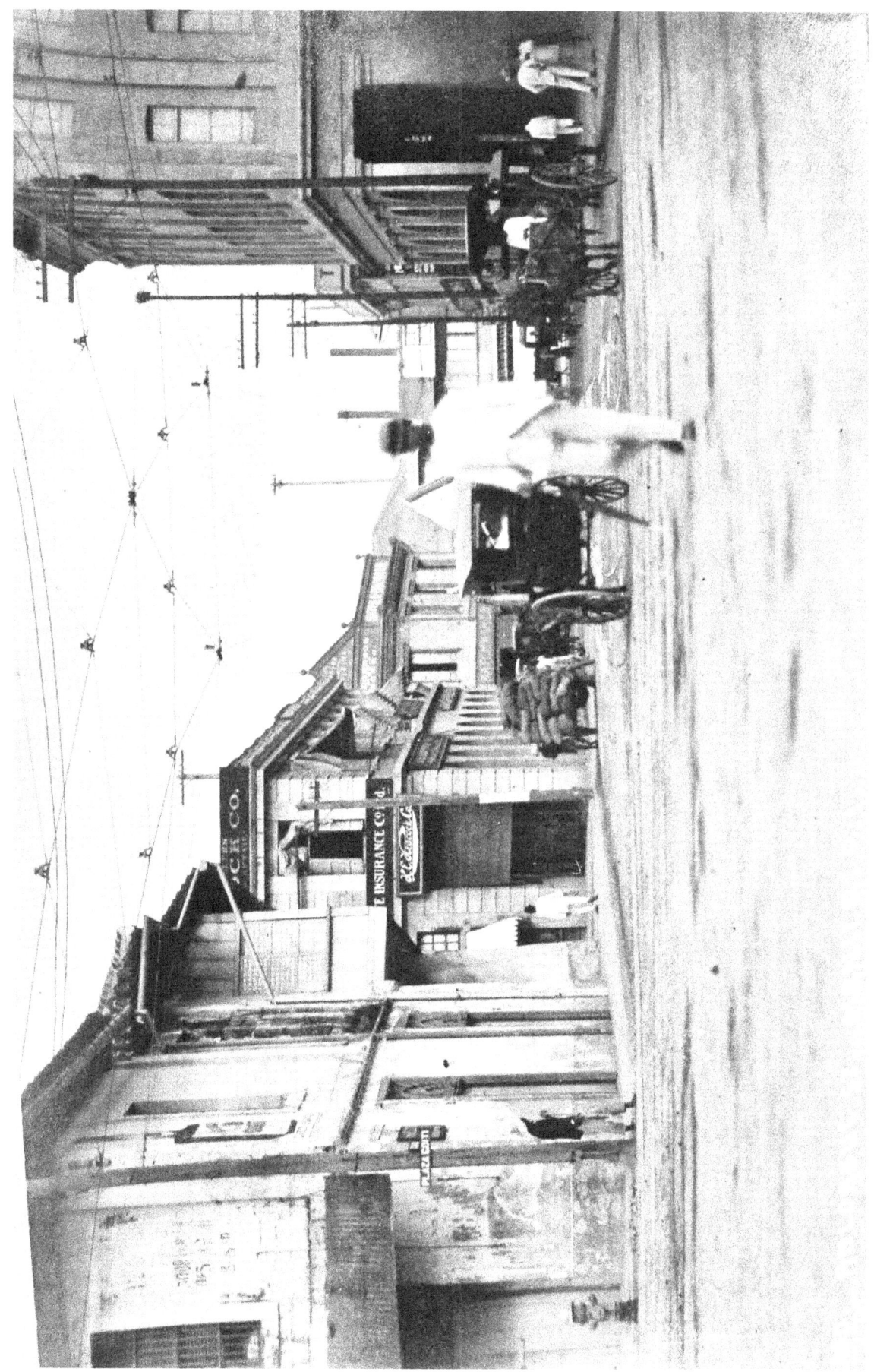

Echague St. Manila, 1900

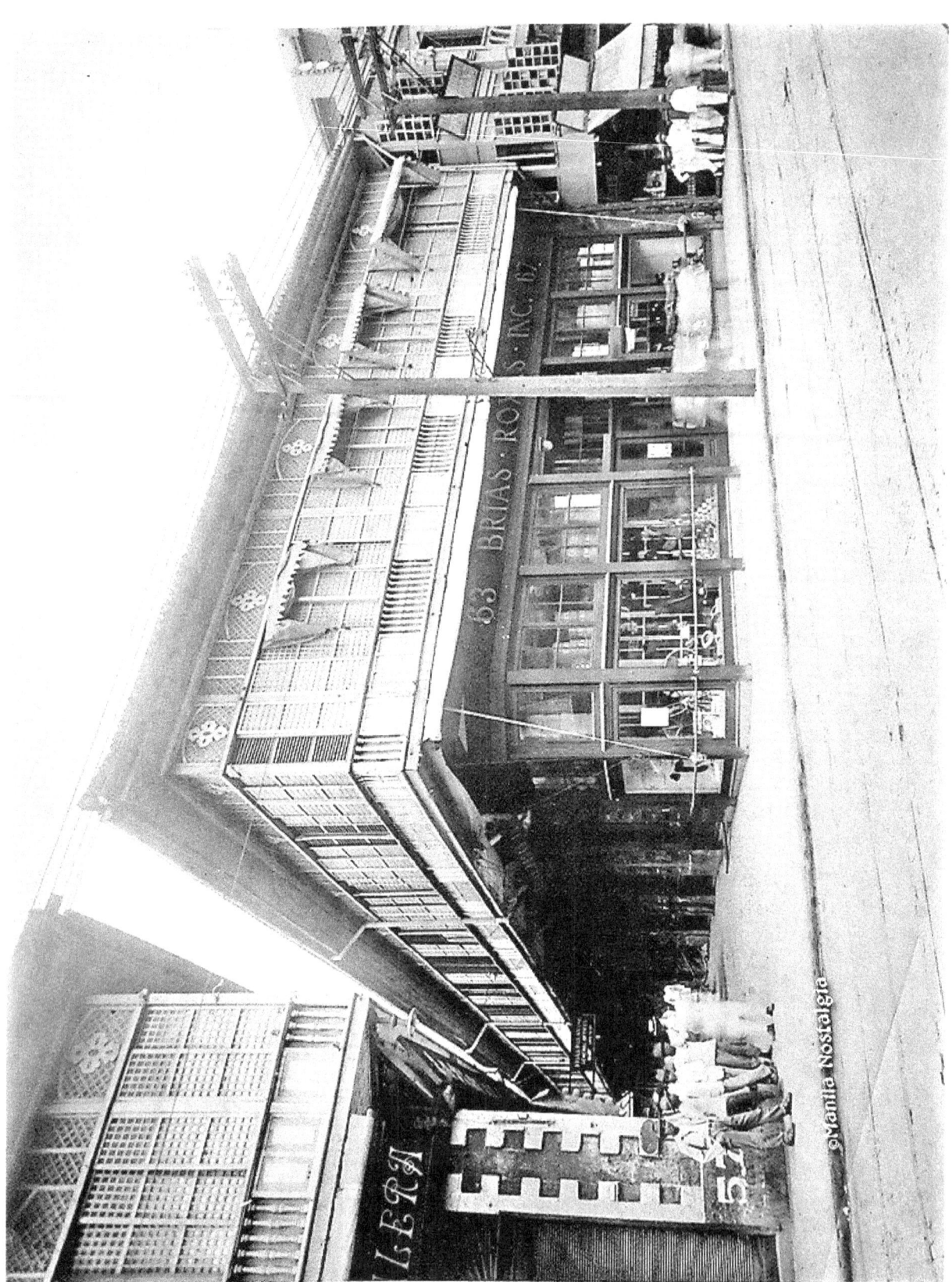

The newly remodeled Brias Roxas "Military Store" next to Pasaje de Paz was one of the most modern and largest department store of its day. Pasaje de Paz was an alley that extended from the Escolta past Calle San Vicente to Calle Dasmarinas. It was eliminated when the new Crystal Arcade was built. Note: to the right of the building was the Escolta Restaurant, also Known as M.Y.San. 1930s-40s

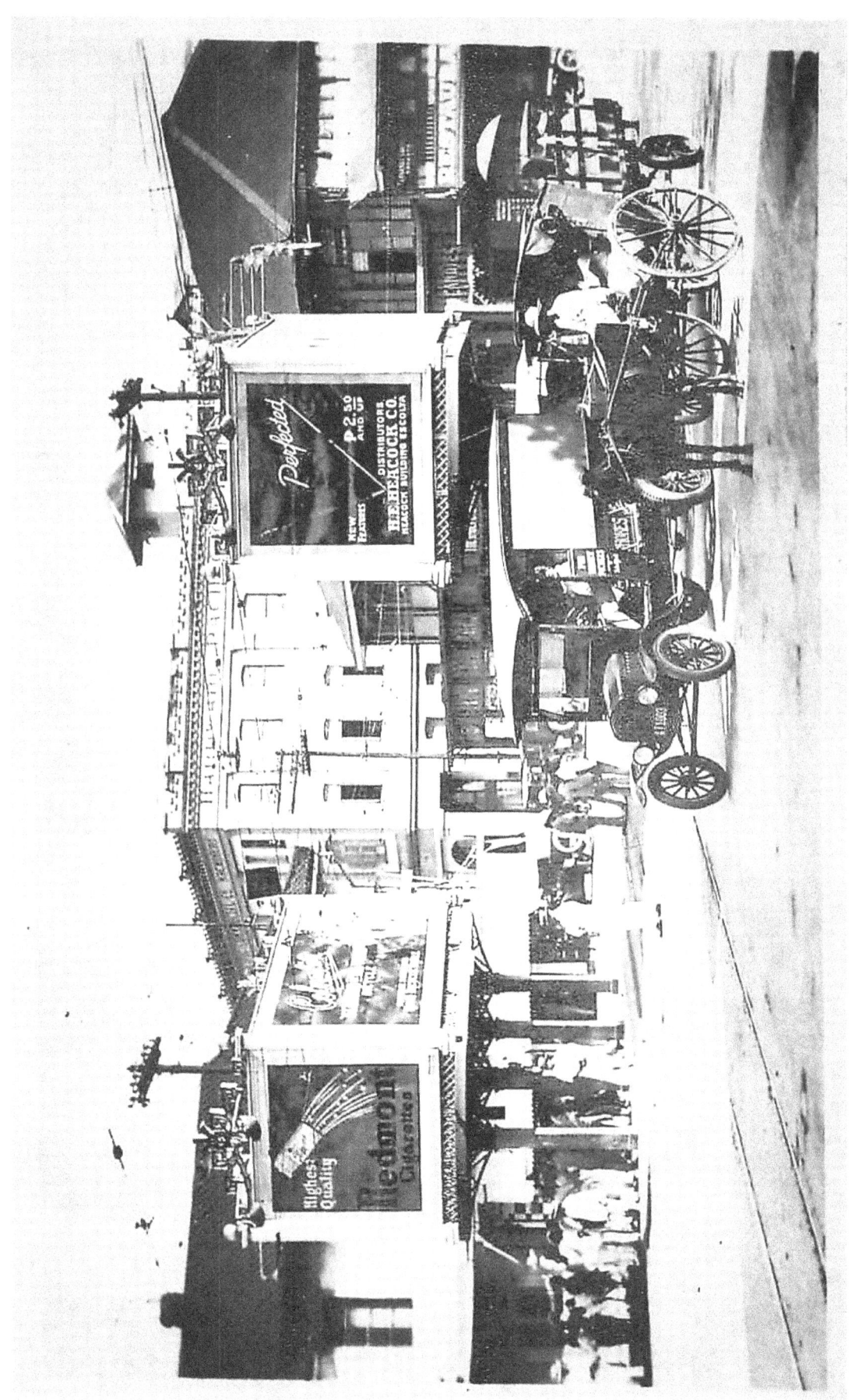
Plaza Goiti (now Lacson), 1925

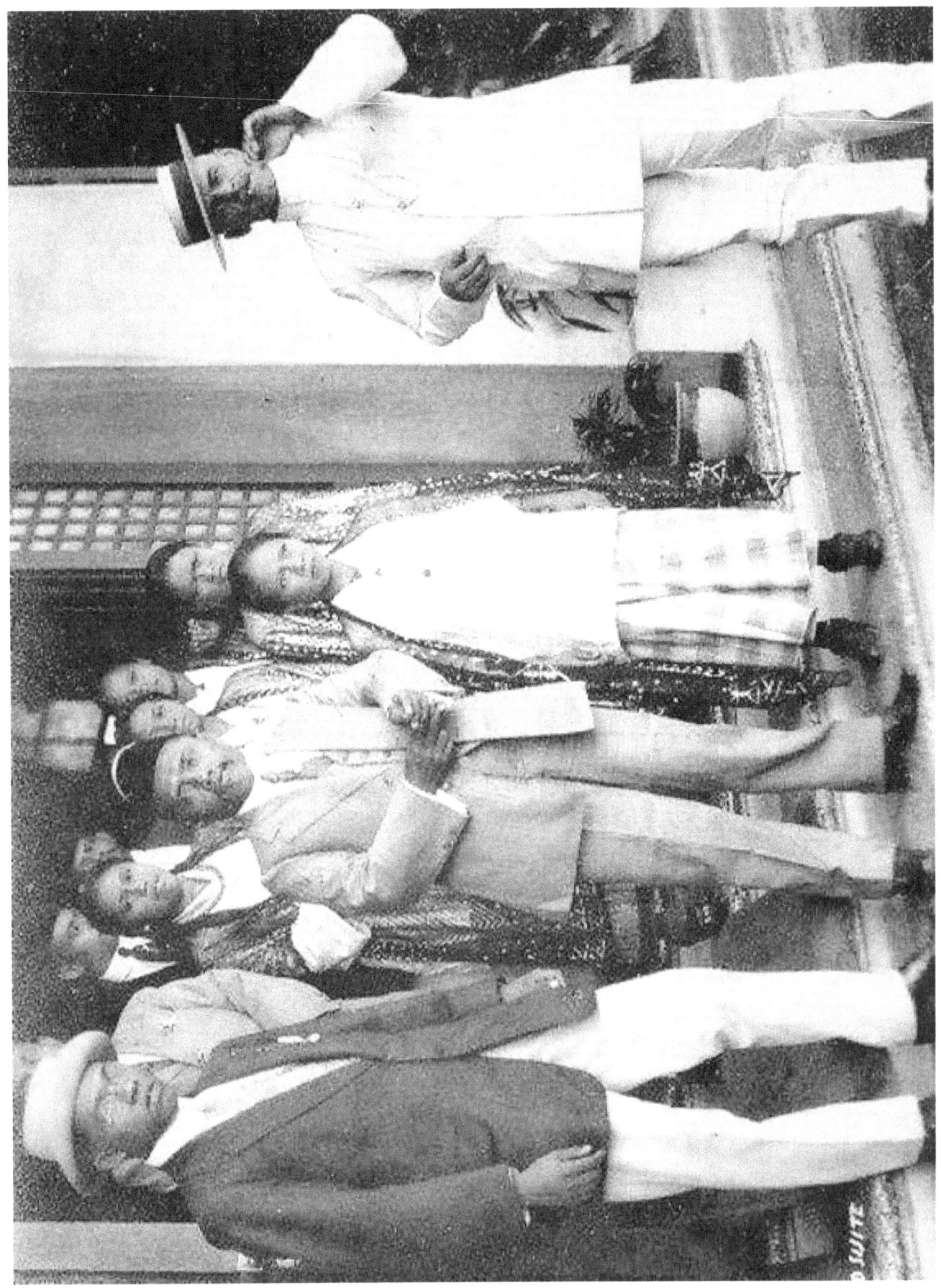
Sulu (Jolo) Sultan Jamalul Karamil + American – 1900

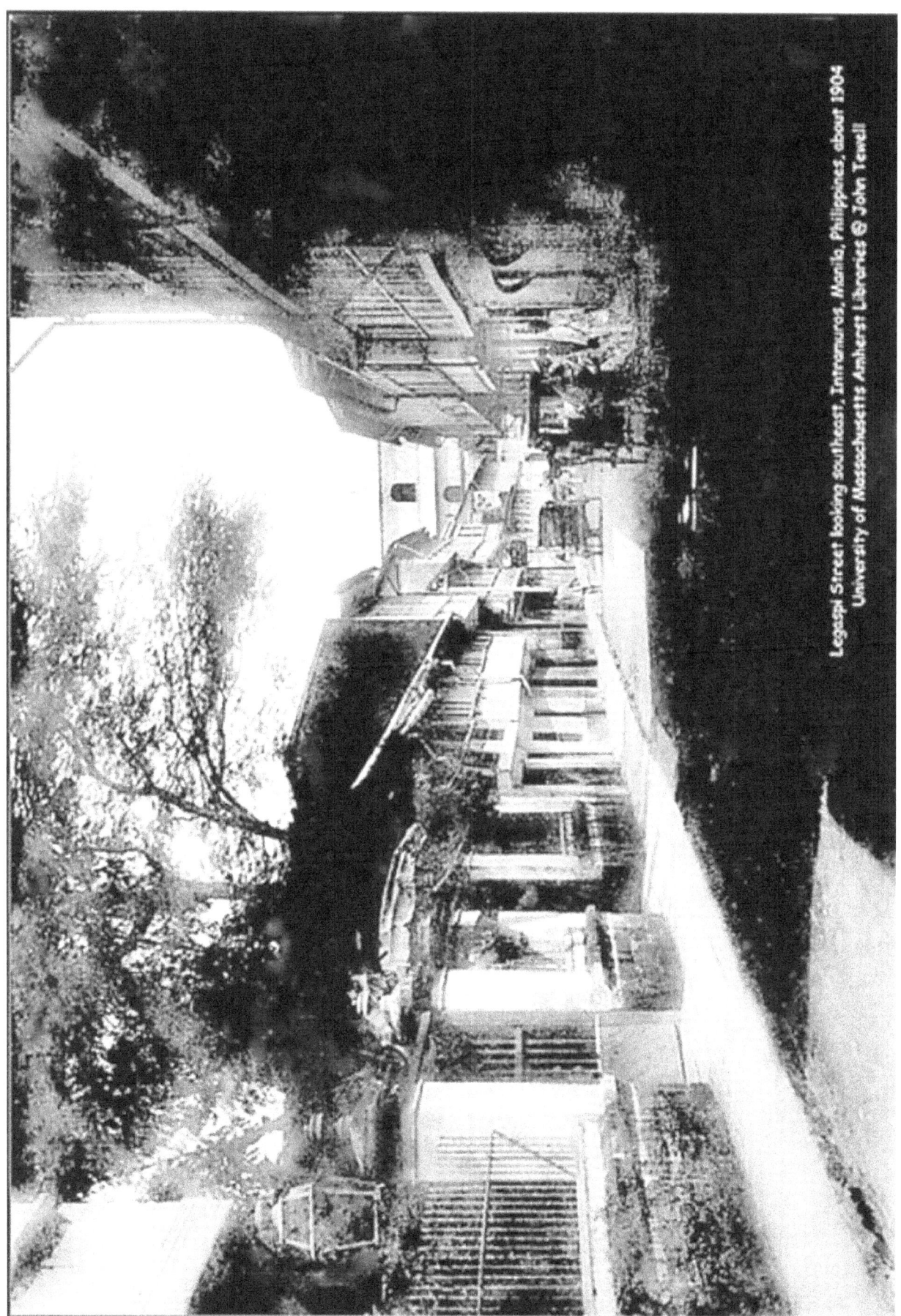

Inside Intramuros, Legaspi Street pleasant scene, 1904

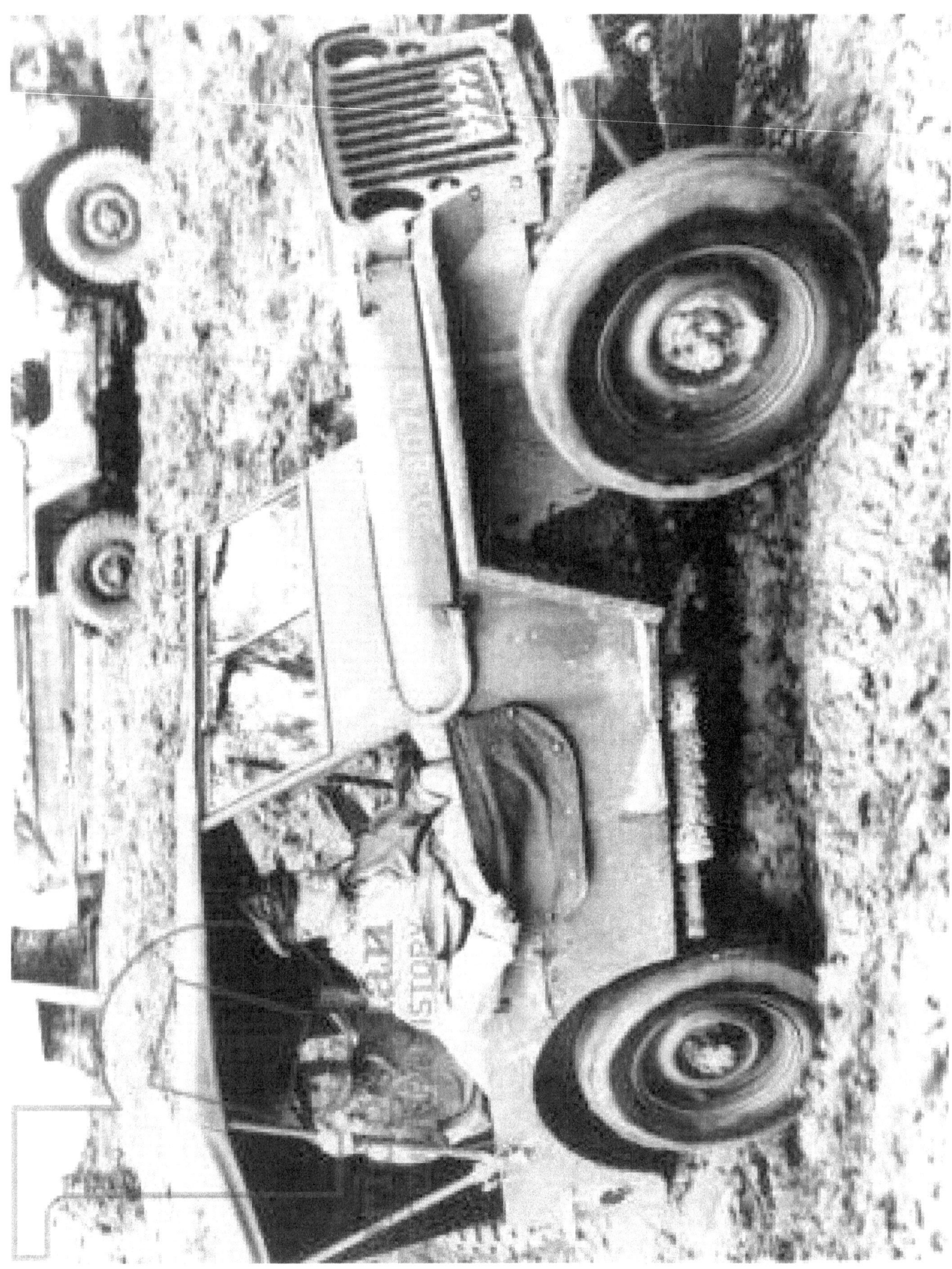

General Douglas MacArthur in a jeep in Leyte landing, 1945

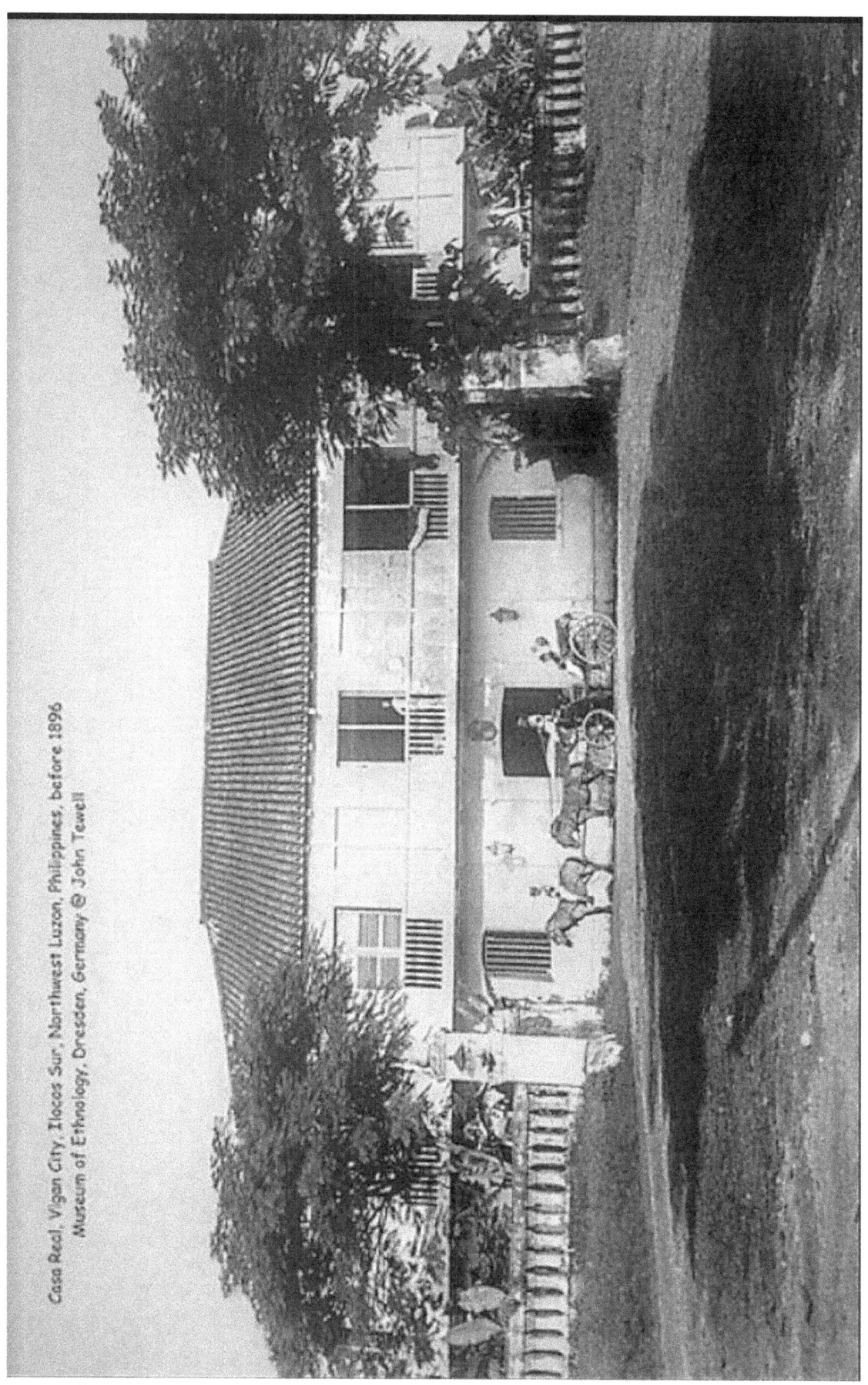

Spanish Mansion, Casa Real, Vigan City, Ilocos Sur, 1896

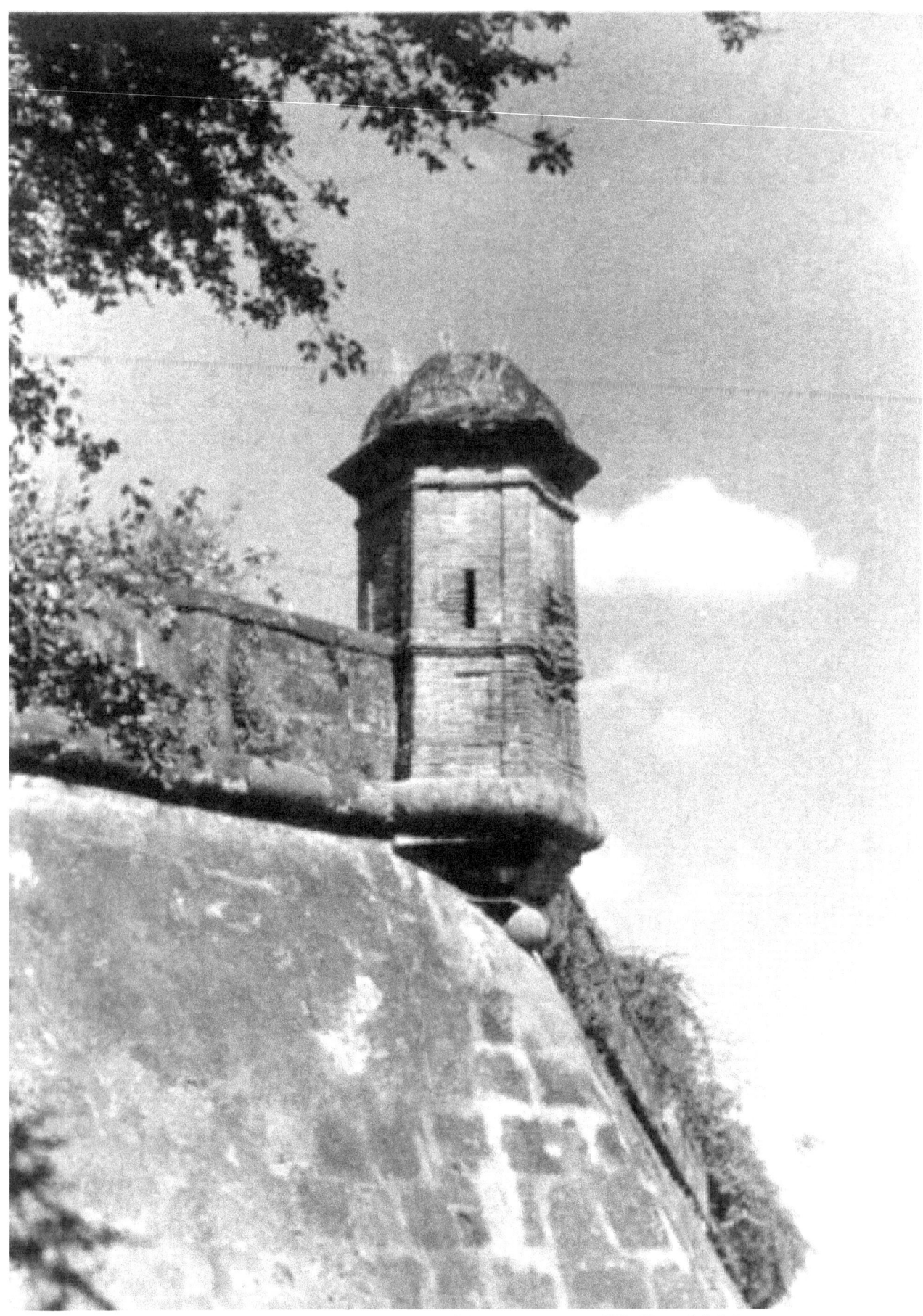

Watchtower, Corner of Intramuros Walls, 1900

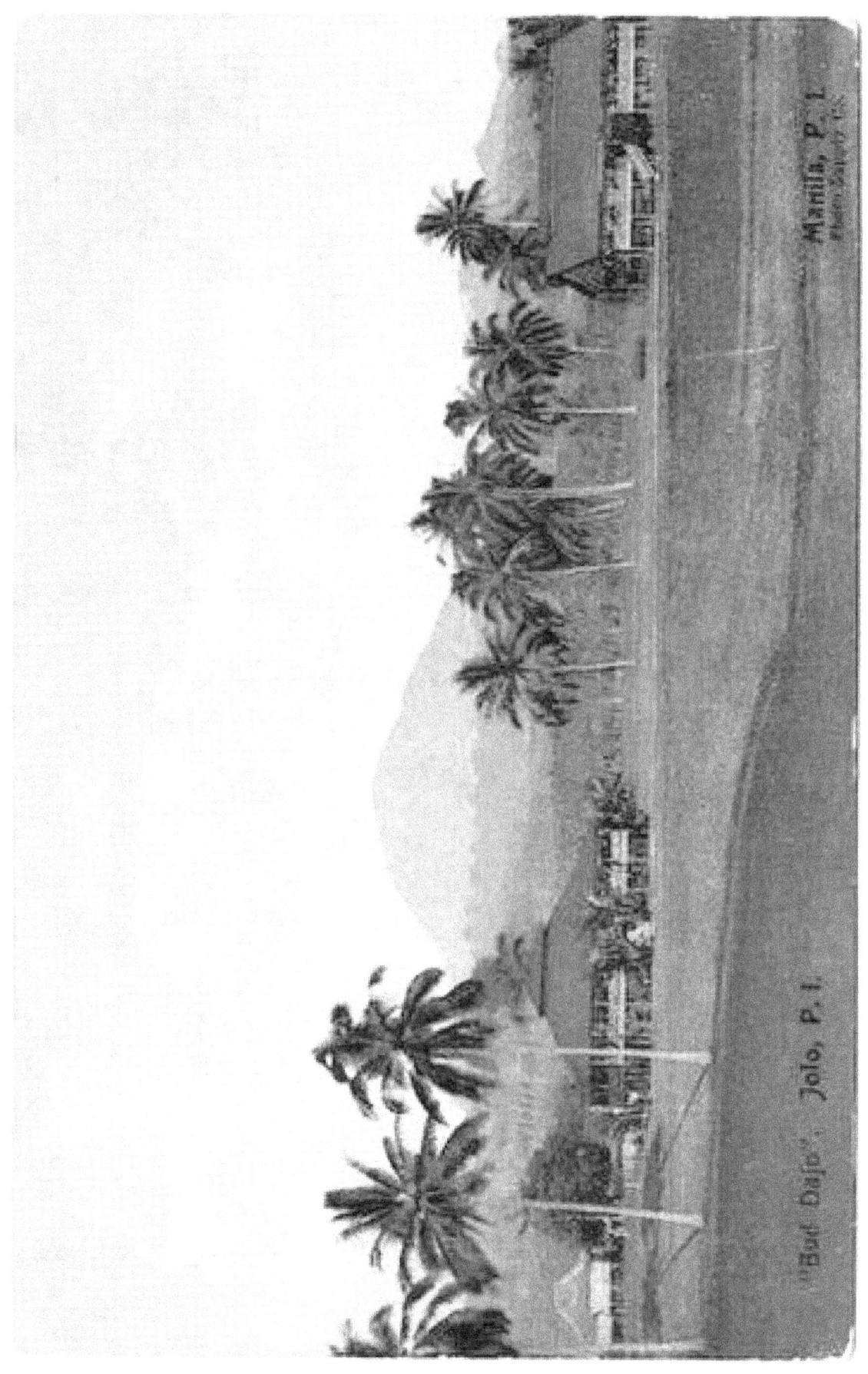

Bod Dajo, Jolo, 1900s

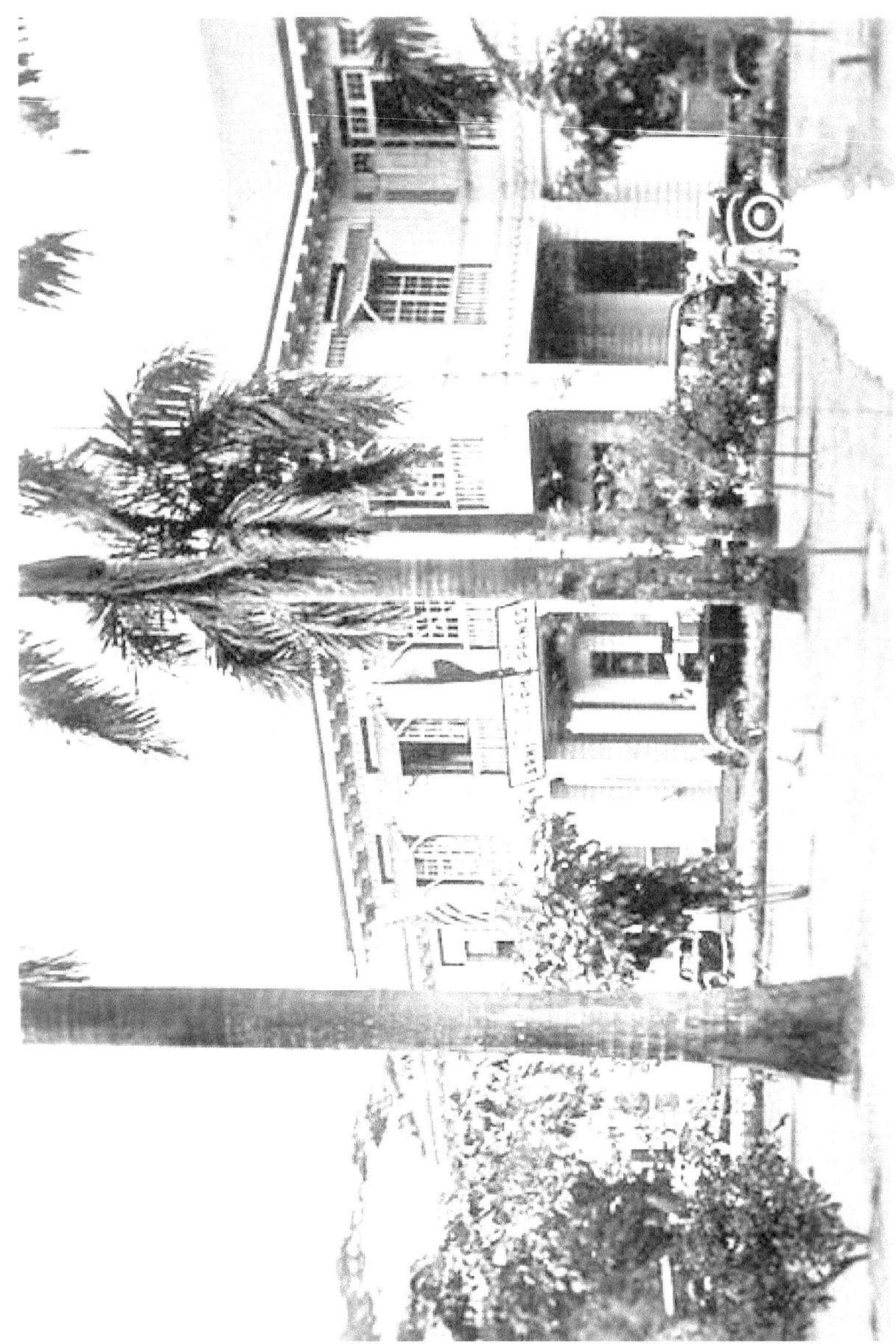

Army Headquarters, Manila, 1930s

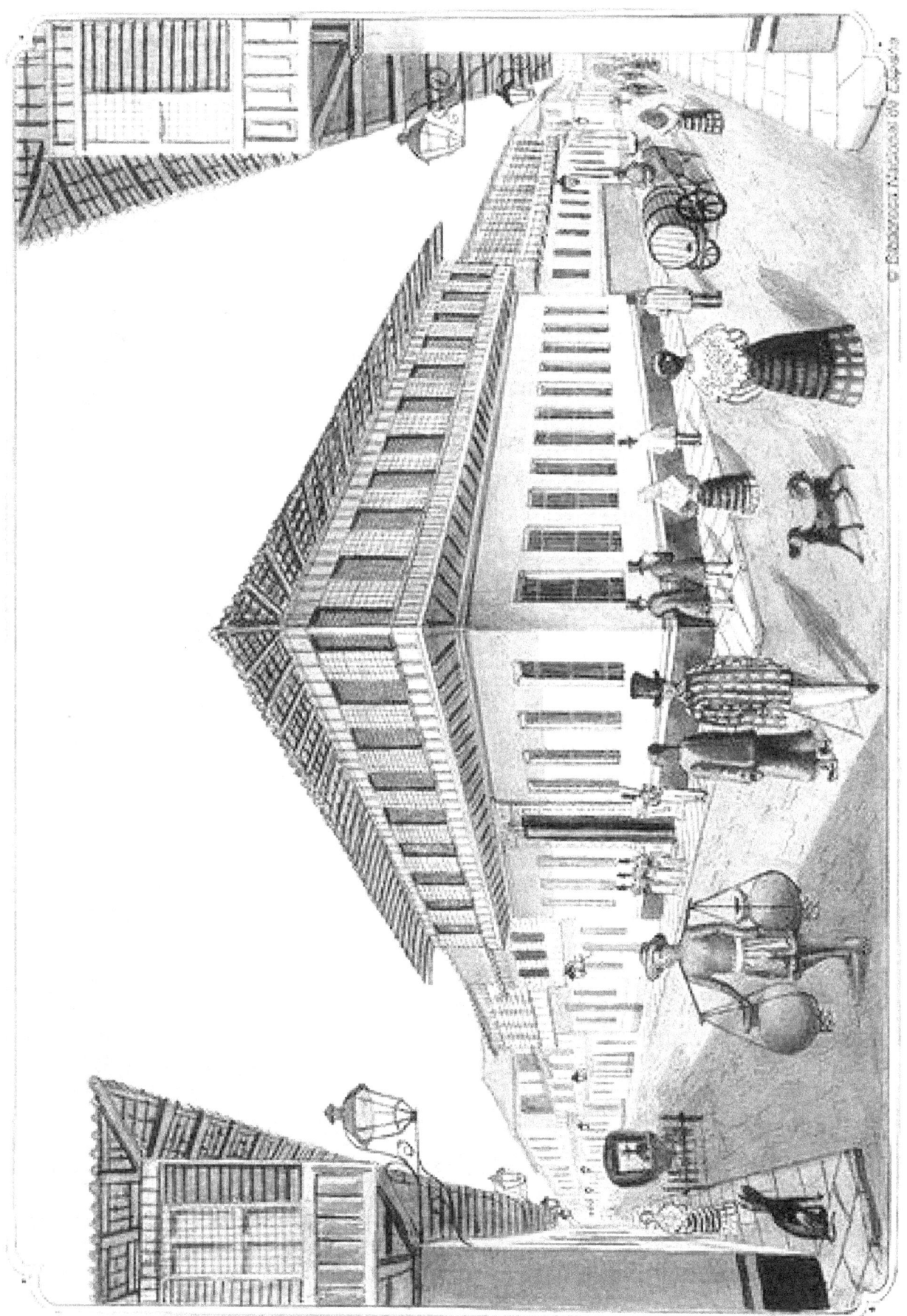

Sketch, Intendencia Casa, Intramuros, 1847

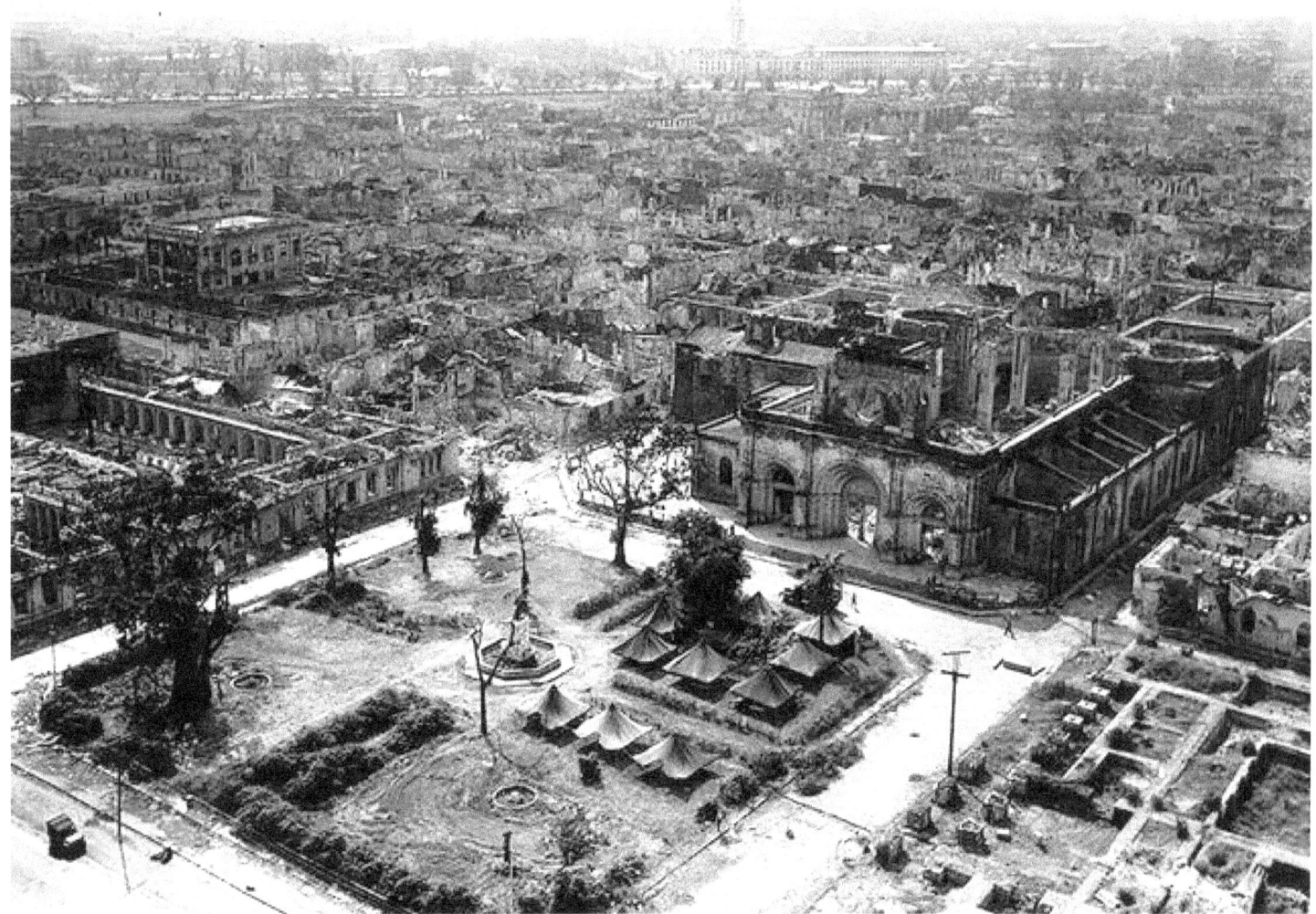

Manila in ruins immediately after WWII battle. Manila Cathedral skeleton still intact, Manila City Hall tower at far background is visible, Nearby scene mostly in Intrramuros, 1945 pic

WELCOME! Thank you for viewing these heritage or nostalgic pictures of individuals, places and events in the history of our beloved country, The Philippines. They say, a picture is worth a thousand words. More info about the person/event can easily be searched in the internet. These old pictures are available in prints, galleries, museums, magazines, and other forms of media. We record them as archives in this format for posterity.

This book can be displayed as coffee table book for family and guests. Each picture can be cut and framed, by buying extra copies. This book is suitable for libraries and schools in Philippines and USA. It is ideal reference material for study of history and celebrities. It is suitable as gift for any occasion. It's a collector's item. Heirs of those shown in pictures may want to own this book for their own families. Pictures are arranged in no particular order. Browse at random.

Most pictures are courtesy of Philippines My Philippines facebook website, but some were derived from various sources, like Museums, Wikipedia and historical websites.

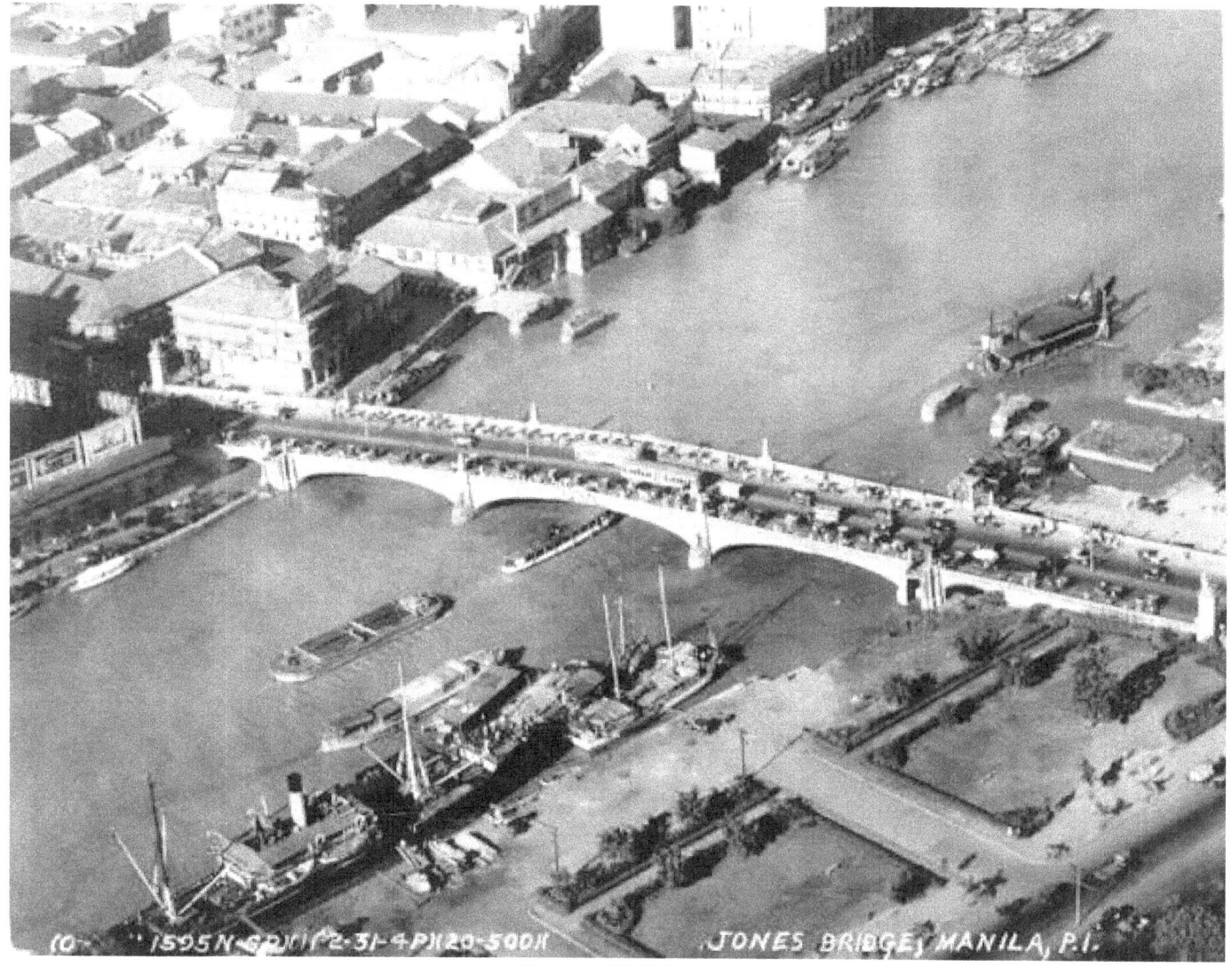

Jones Bridge

Aerial view of the Jones Bridge, c1920s. You can still see the foundations of the Puente de Espana just a few meters upriver from the Jones, ca. 1920's The William Atkinson Jones Memorial Bridge or more commonly known as the Jones Bridge is a bridge that connects the Binondo district on Calle Rosario (Q. Paredes St.) with Calle Padre Burgos (Padre Burgos St.) just outside the walls of Intramuros. The bridge honored former Virginia representative, William Atkinson Jones, the principal author of the Jones Law or the Philippine Autonomy Act of 1916.

* Nostalgia Filipinas (Note: Tranvia or tramway on bridge)

This book can be displayed as coffee table book for family and guests. Each picture can be cut and framed, by buying extra copies. This book is suitable for libraries and schools in Philippines and USA. It is ideal reference material for study of history and celebrities. It is suitable as gift for any occasion. It's a collector's item. Heirs of those shown in pictures may want to own this book for their own families. Pictures are arranged in no particular order. Browse at random.

Most pictures are courtesy of Philippines My Philippines facebook website, but some were derived from various sources, like Museums, Wikipedia and historical websites.

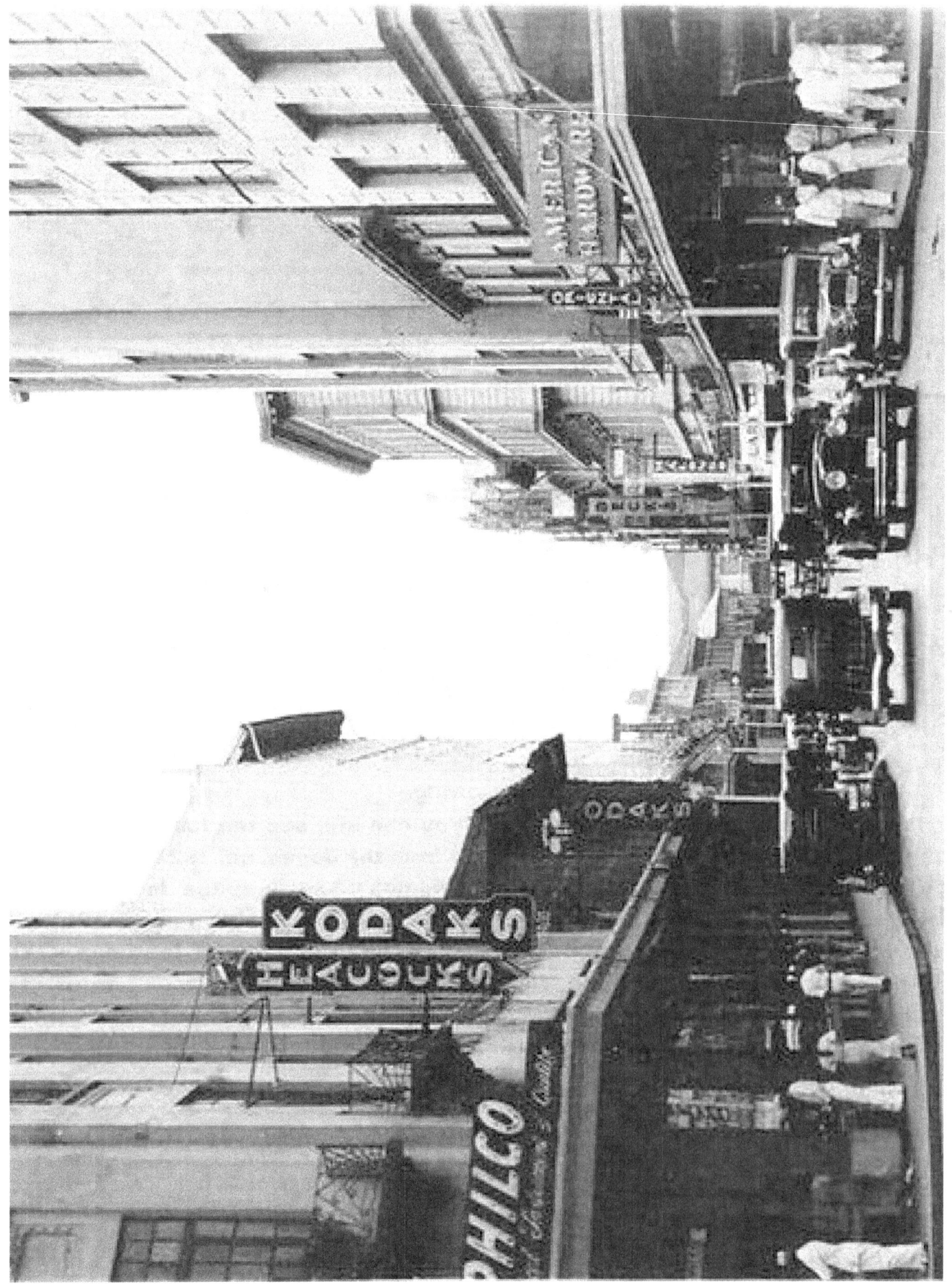

Escolta in glorious days, 1920s

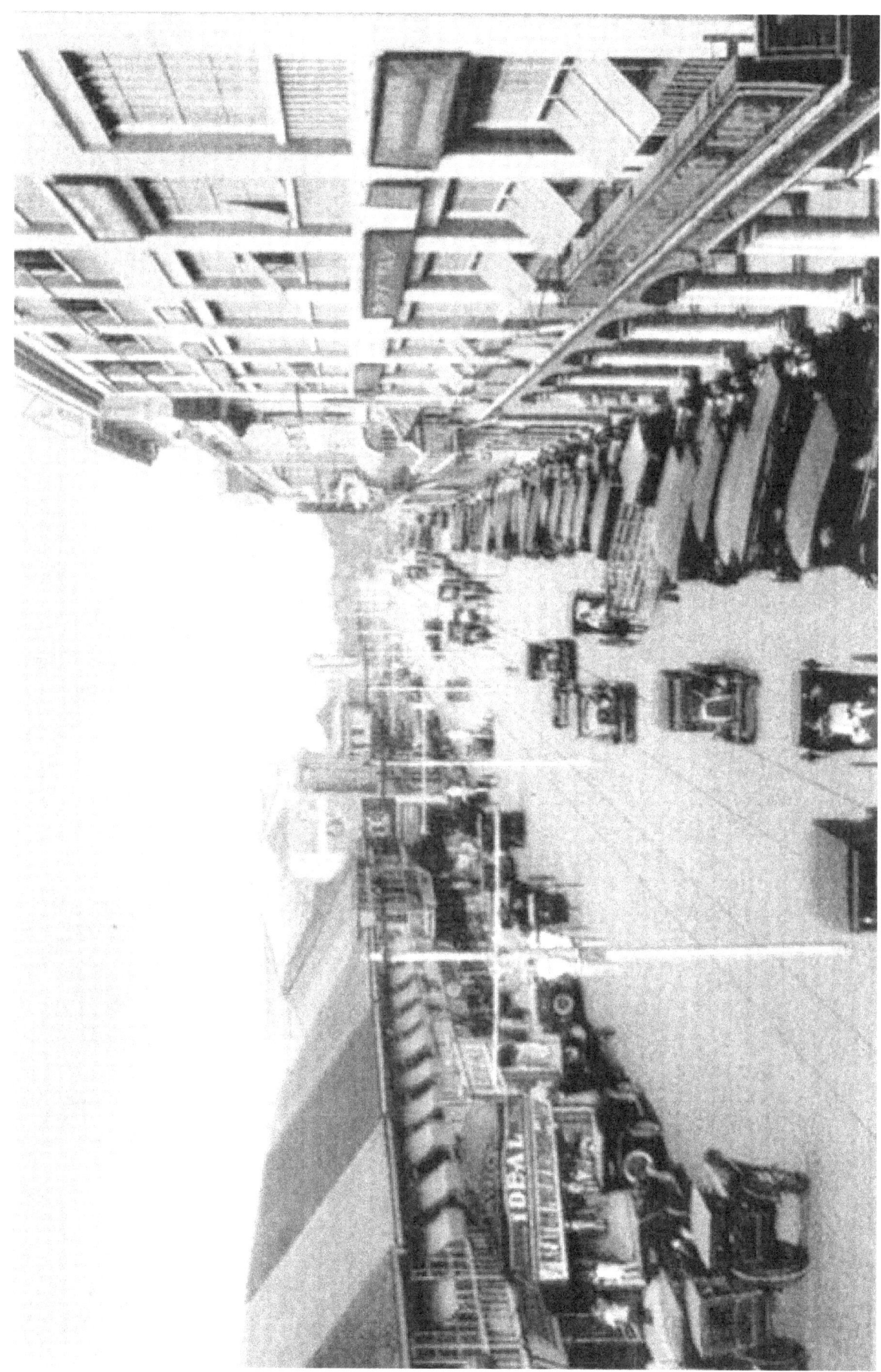

Rizal Avenue, 1931 (Note T-Ford cars)

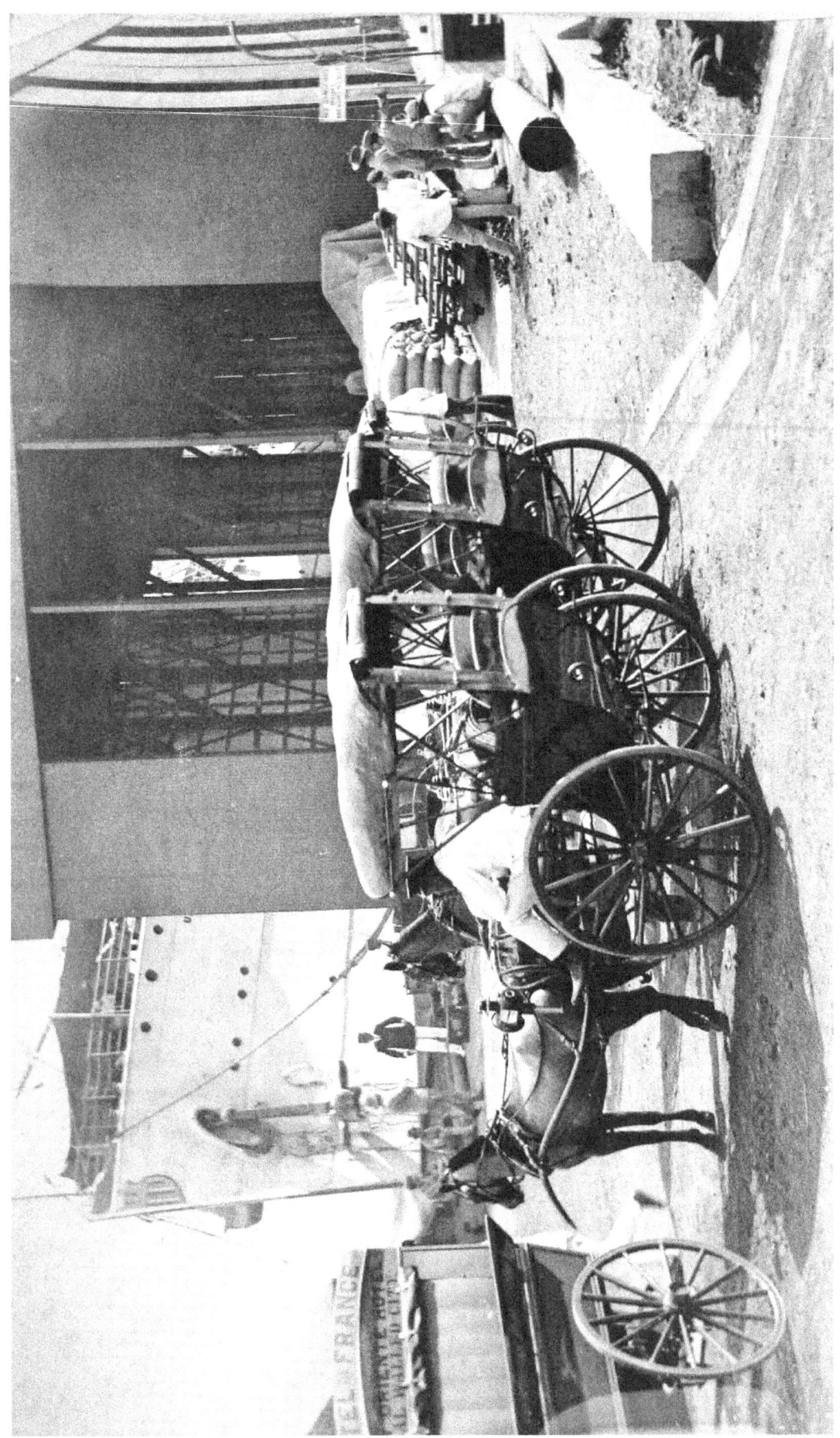
Manila Piers, 1910, at mouth of Pasig River

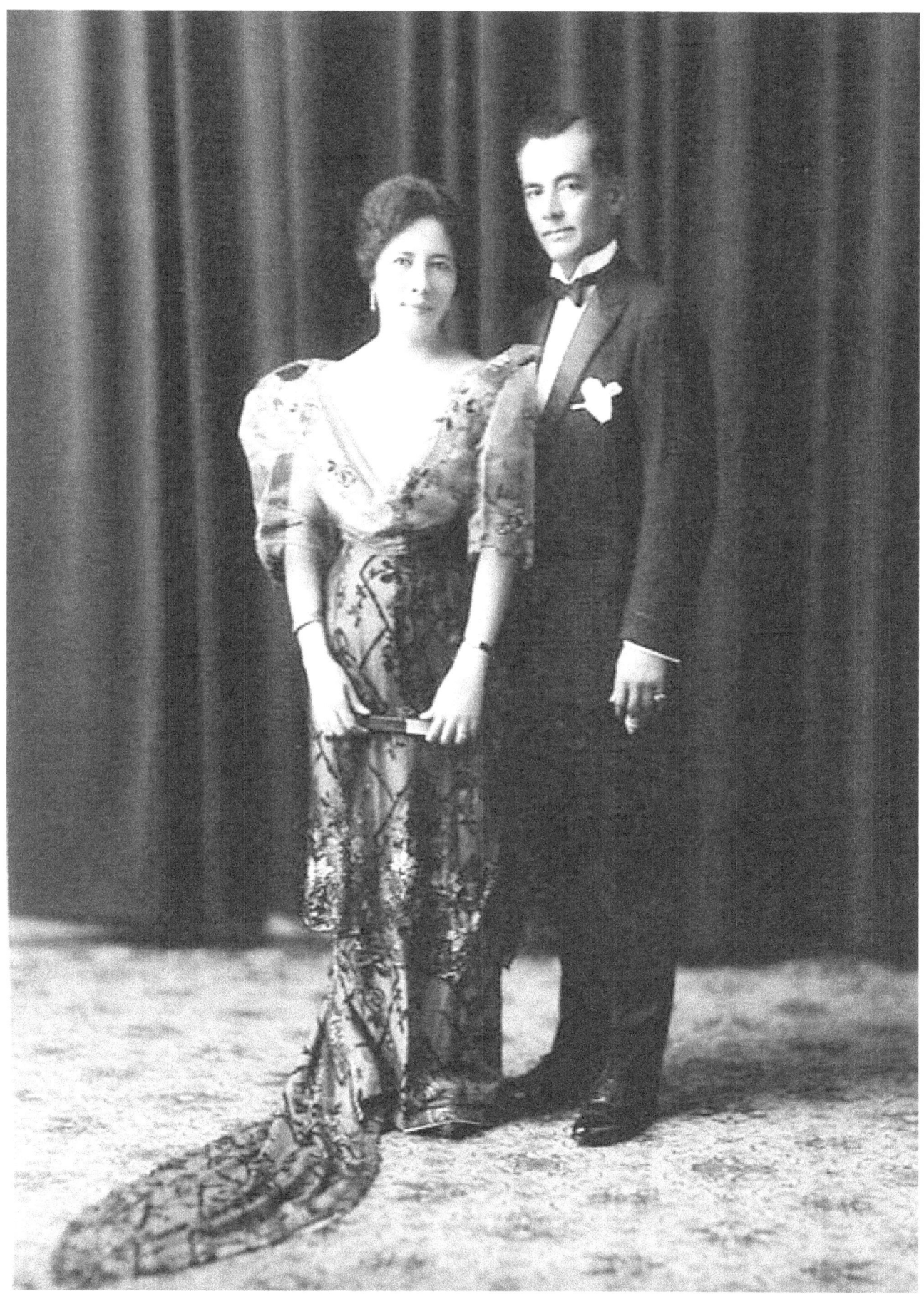

Younger Dona Aurora and Prominent Leader Manuel Quezon, 1920s-30s

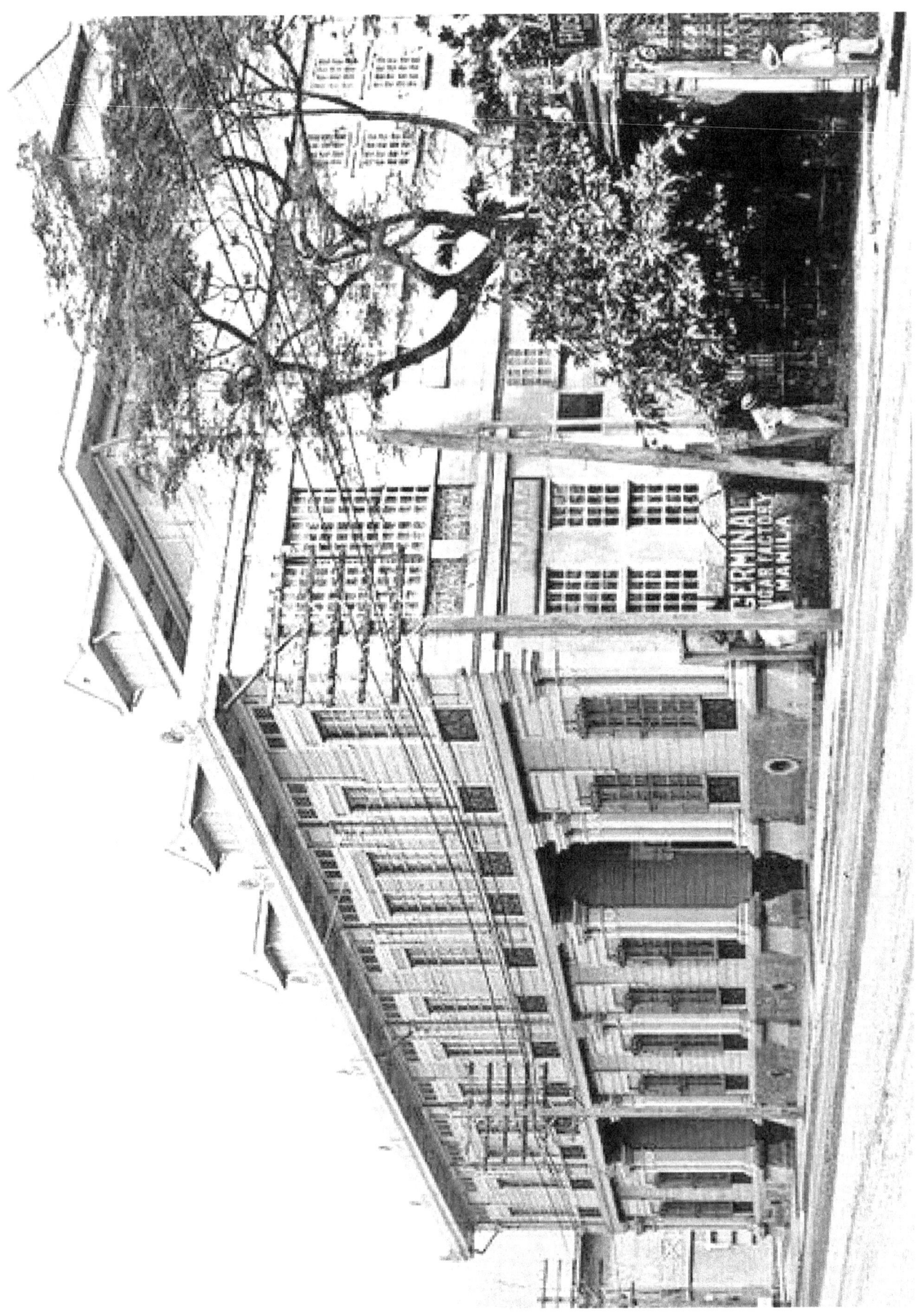

Germinal Cigarette Factory, 1900s (location?)

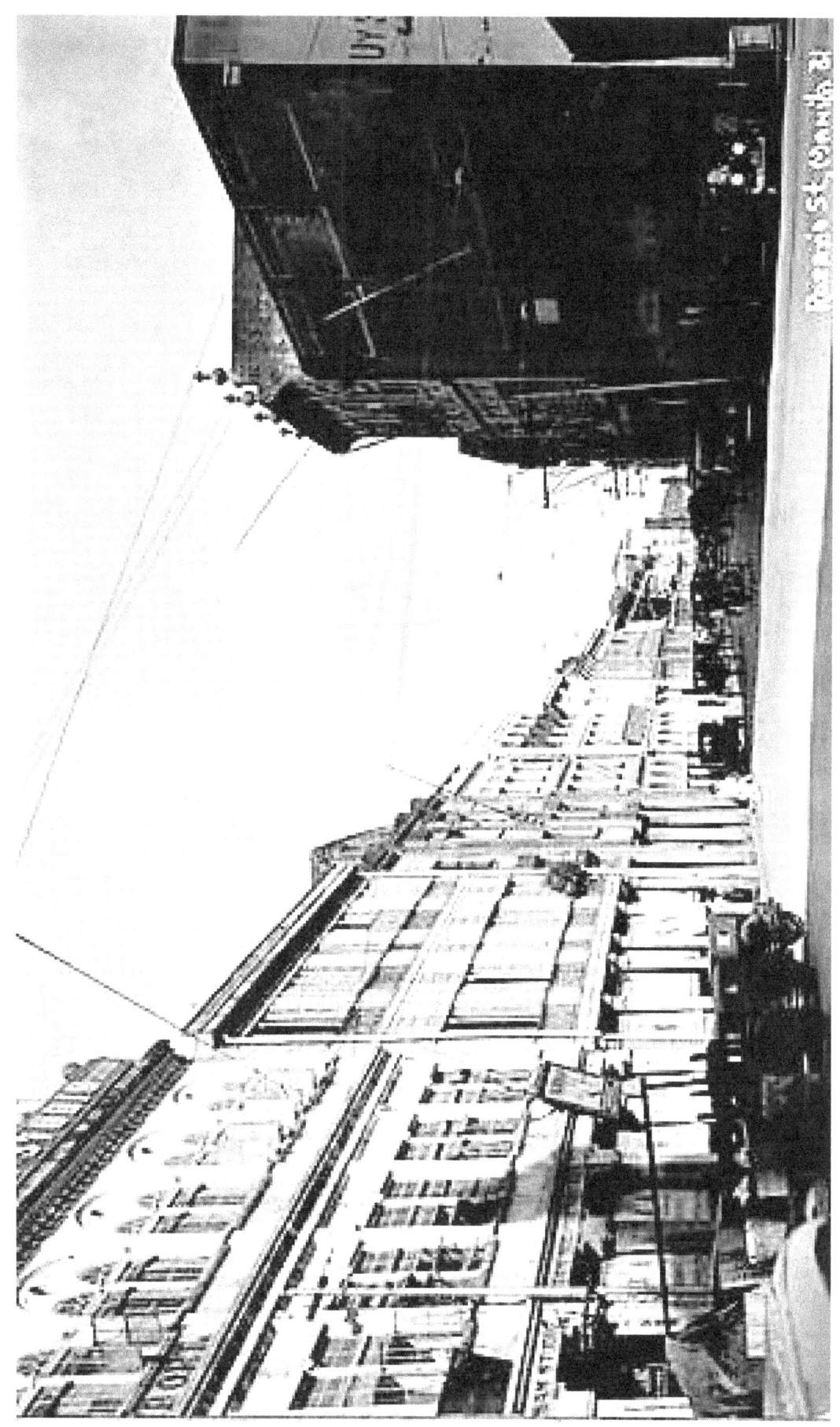

Rosario Street, near Escolta, Business District, 1940s

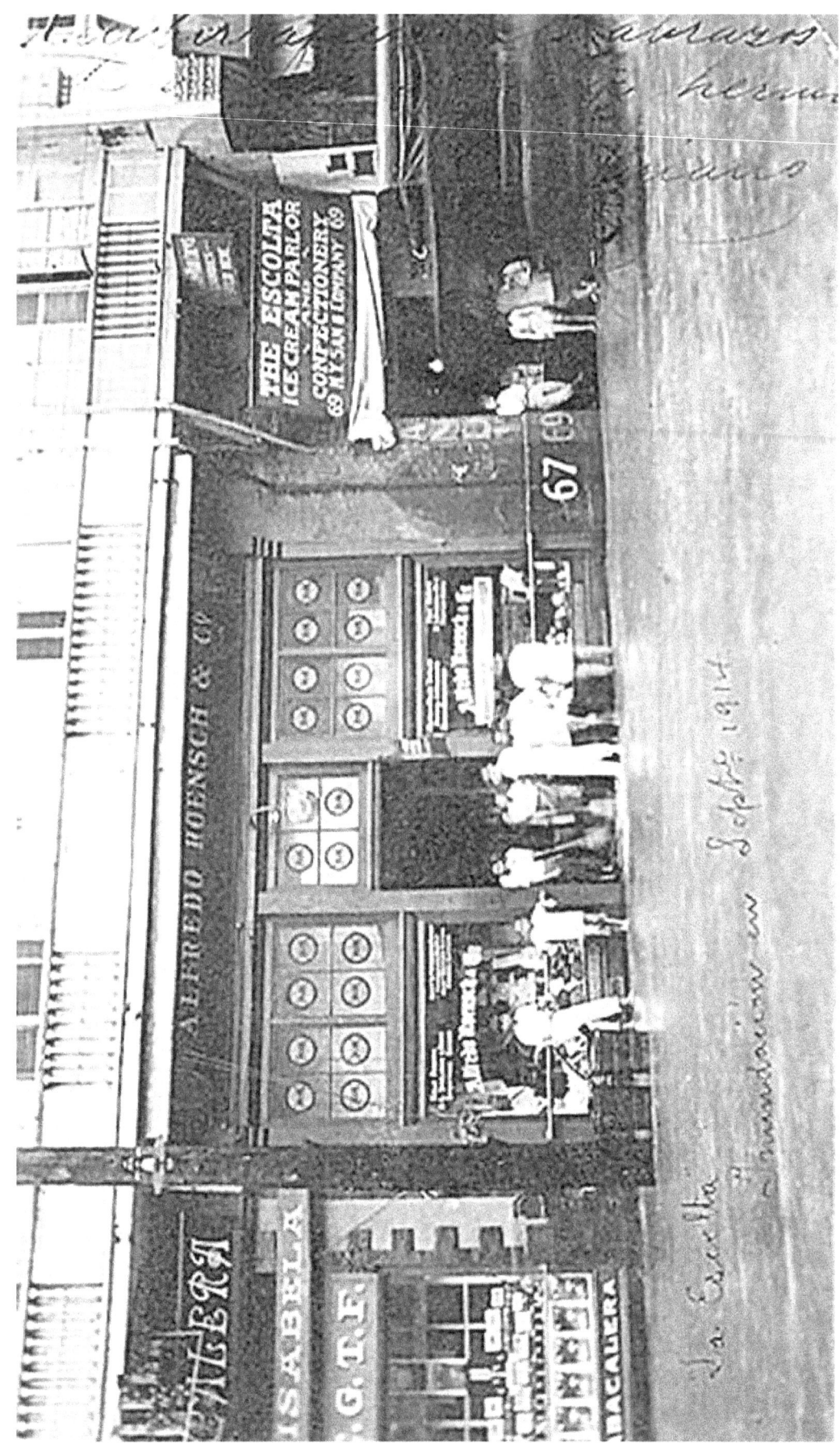

Famous Escolta, 1914 photo

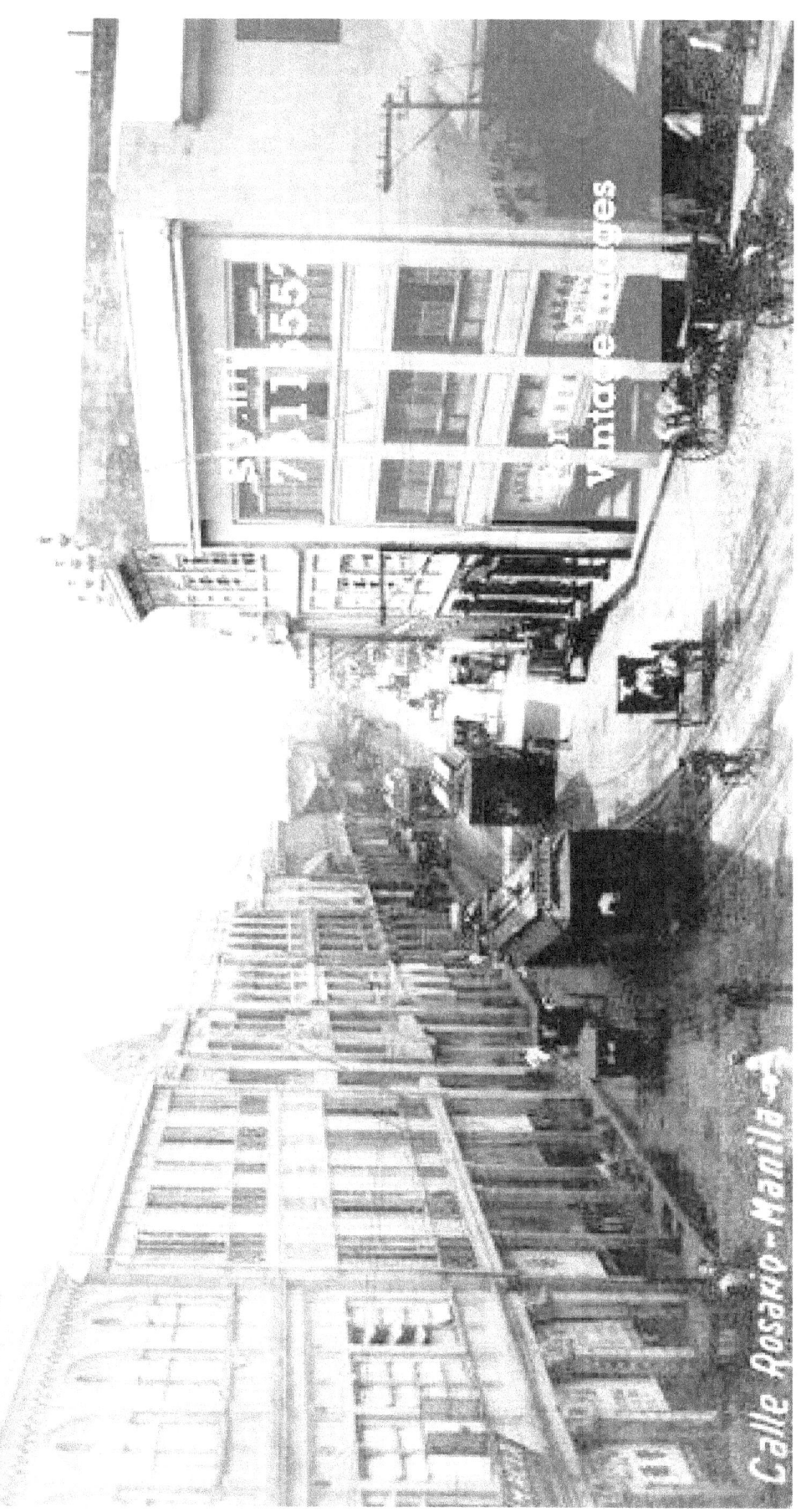

Famous Rosario St. near Escolta, 1900s, tranvia and calesas shown

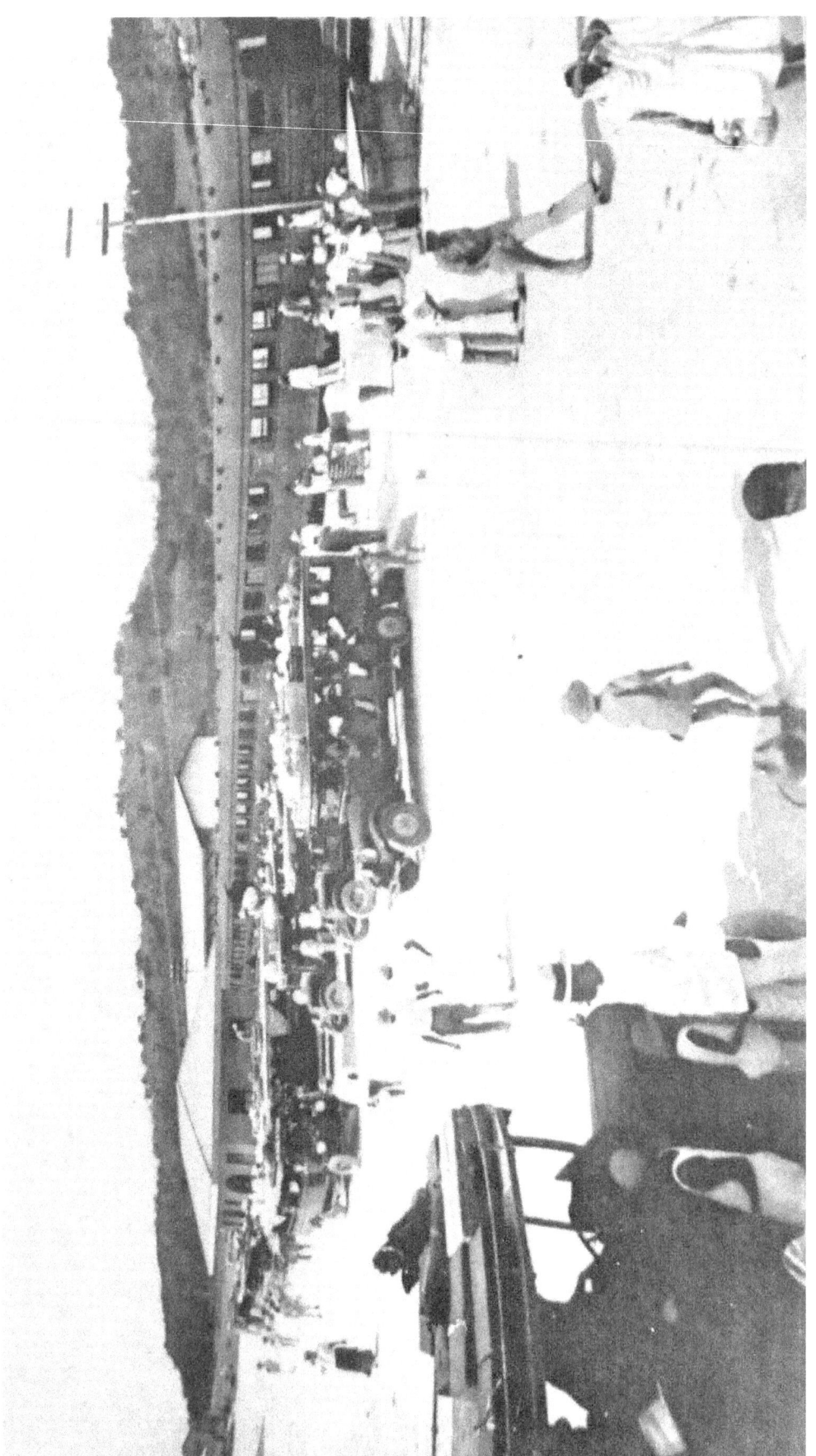

Manila Railroad Station in Bauang, La Union, North Luzon, 1928, typical in Other stations, including South Luzon in Bicol

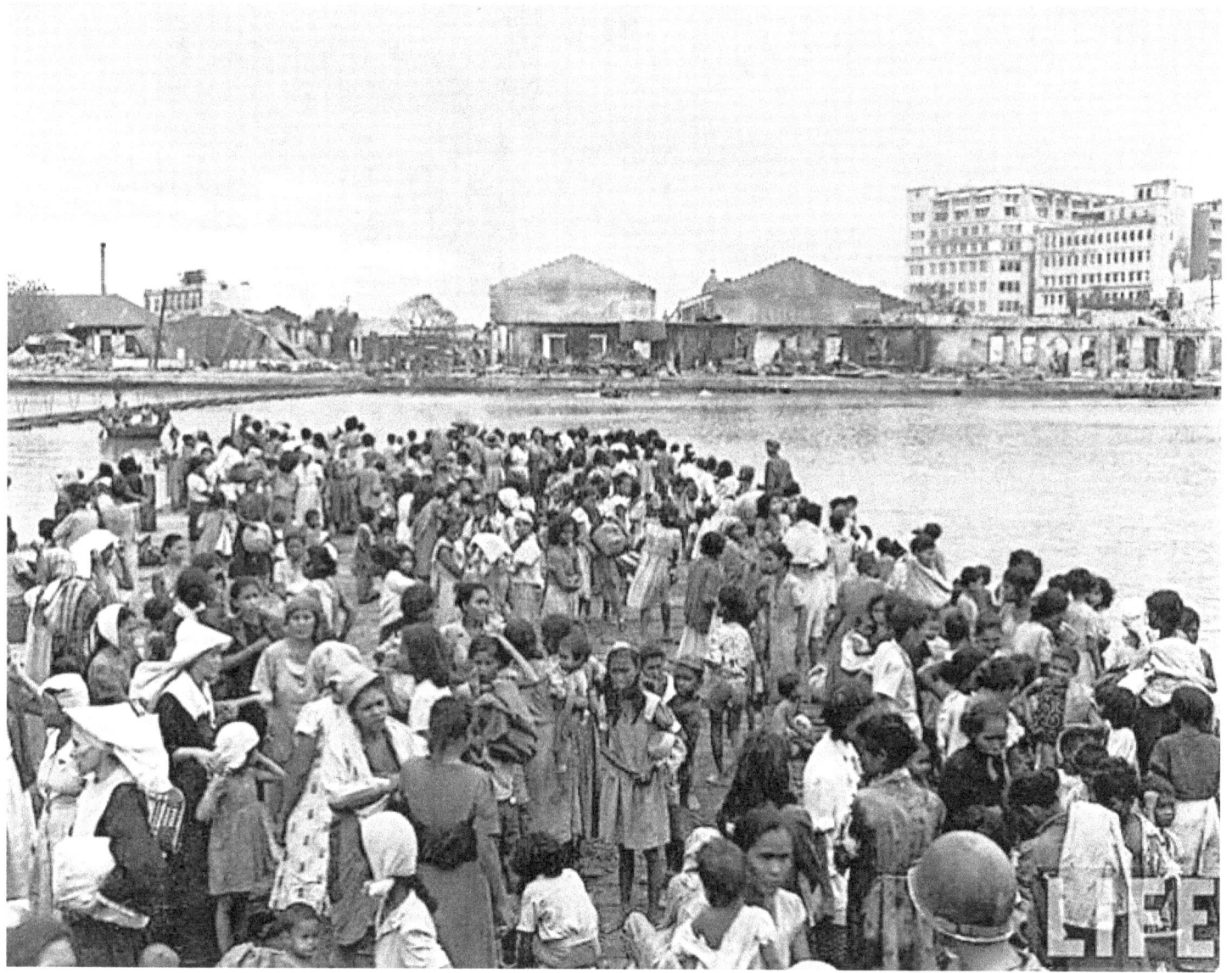
WWII Battle of Manila survivors and local refugees, 1045

(Break)

WELCOME! Thank you for viewing these heritage or nostalgic pictures of individuals, places and events in the history of our beloved country, The Philippines. They say, a picture is worth a thousand words. More info about the person/event can easily be searched in the internet. These old pictures are available in prints, galleries, museums, magazines, and other forms of media. We record them as archives in this format for posterity.

This book can be displayed as coffee table book for family and guests. Each picture can be cut and framed, by buying extra copies. This book is suitable for libraries and schools in Philippines and USA. It is ideal reference material for study of history and celebrities. It is suitable as gift for any occasion. It's a collector's item. Heirs of those shown in pictures may want to own this book for their own families. Pictures are arranged in no particular order. Browse at random.

Most pictures are courtesy of Philippines My Philippines facebook website, but some were derived from various sources, like Museums, Wikipedia and historical websites.

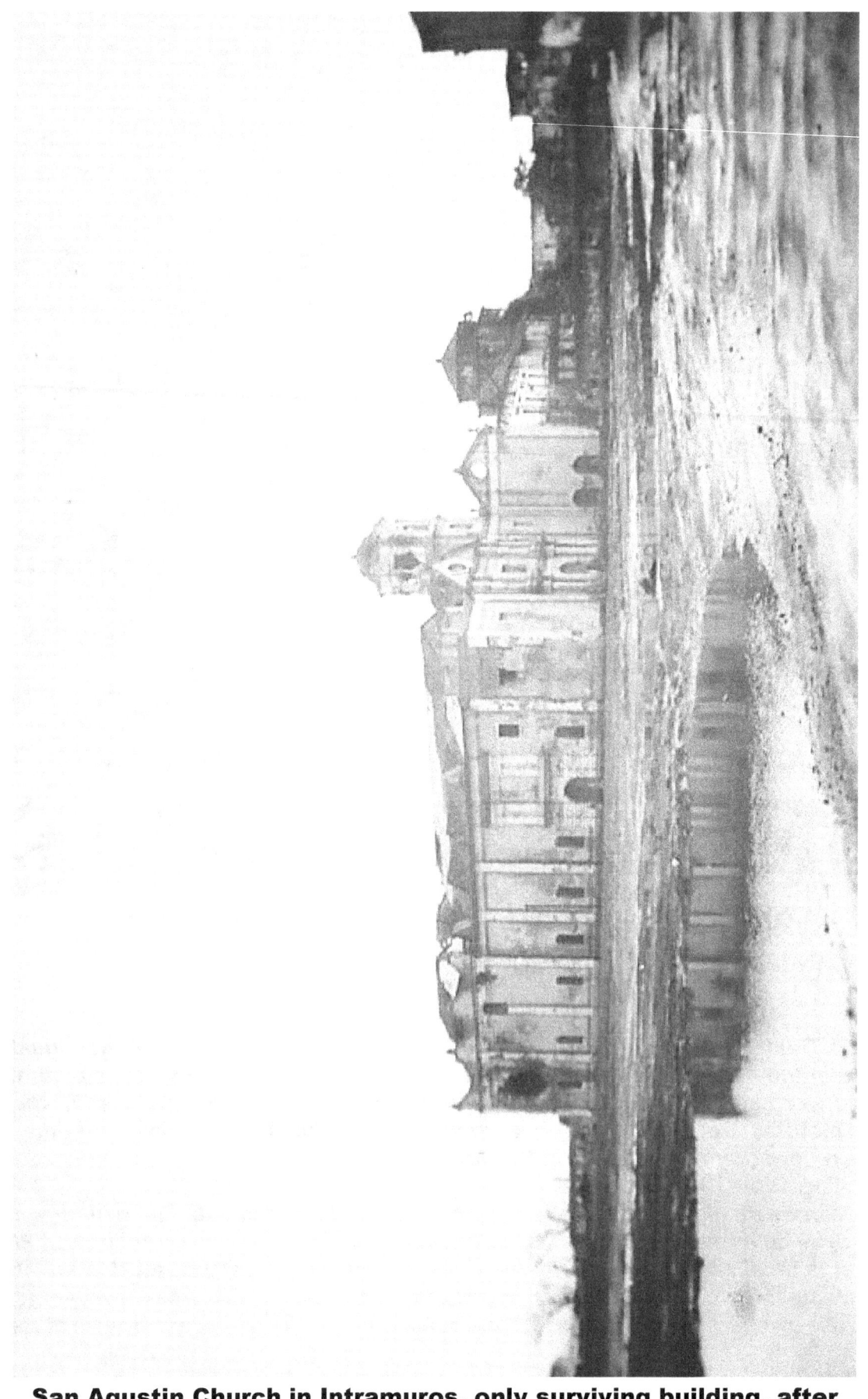

San Agustin Church in Intramuros, only surviving building, after Battle of Manila and Liberation, WWII, 1945

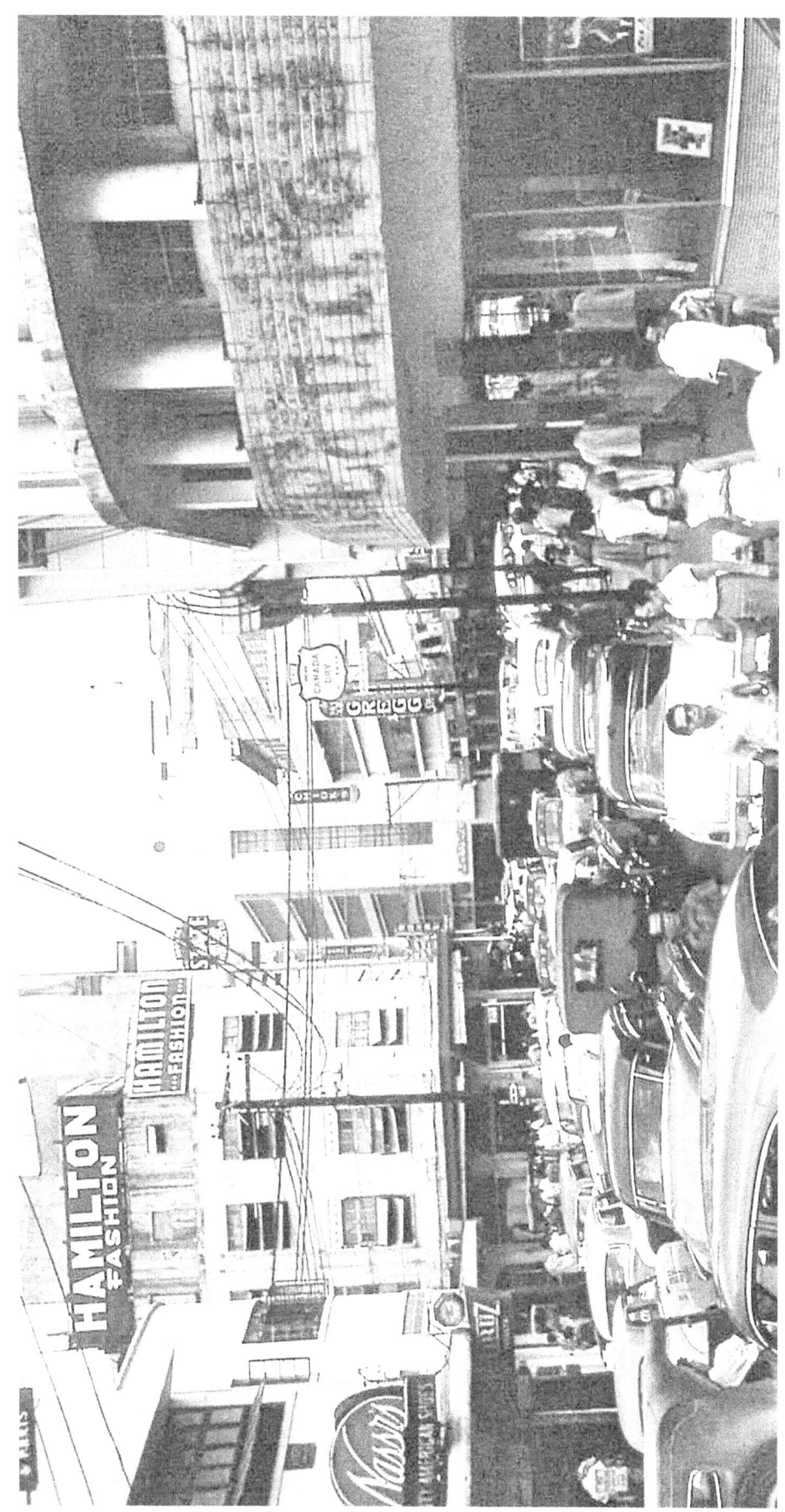

Escolta, Progressive & vibrant, 1957

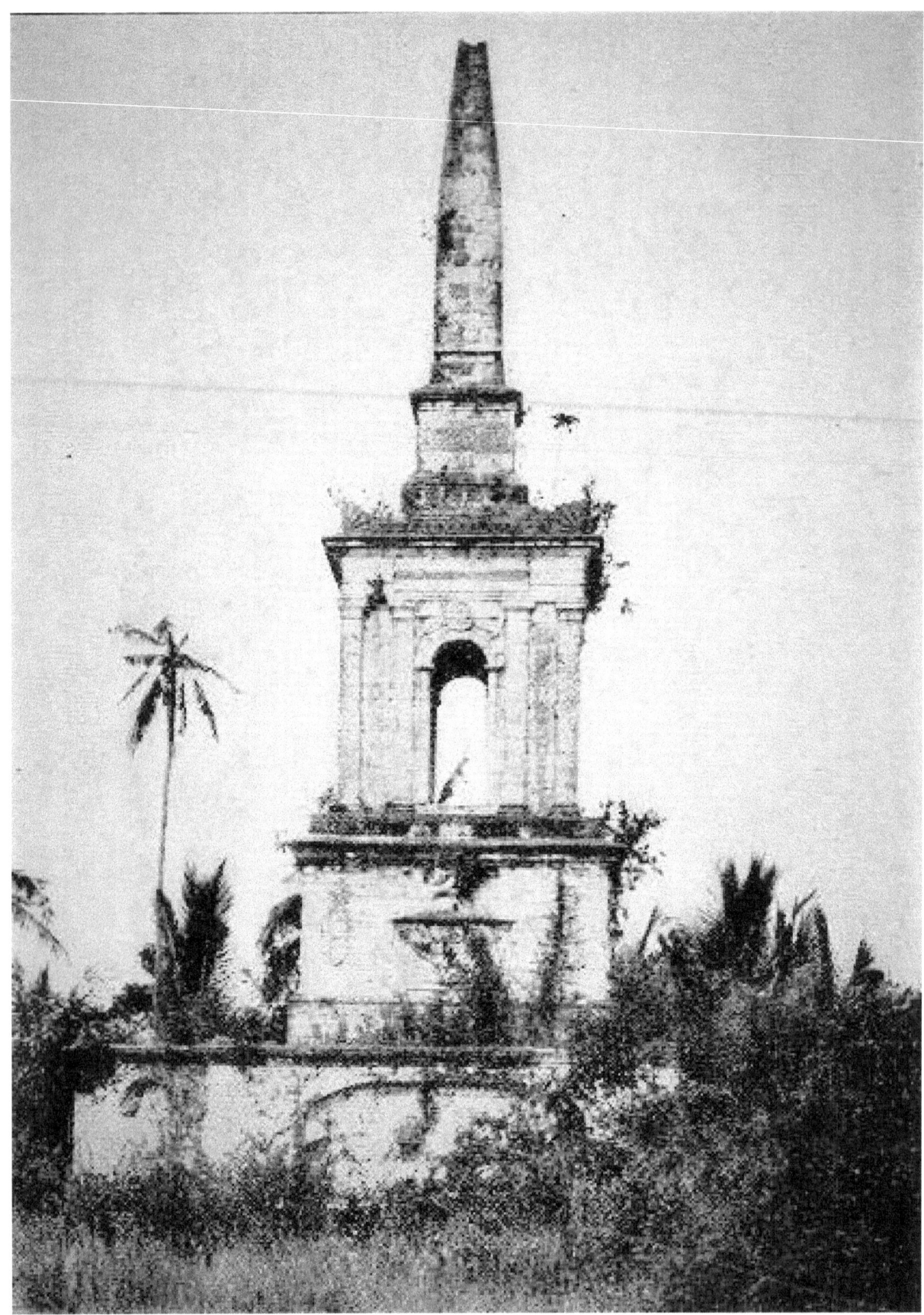

Ferdinand Magellan Monument in Mactan Island, built by Spaniards During Spanish period (Magellan reached Philippines but never returned To Spain in 1521)

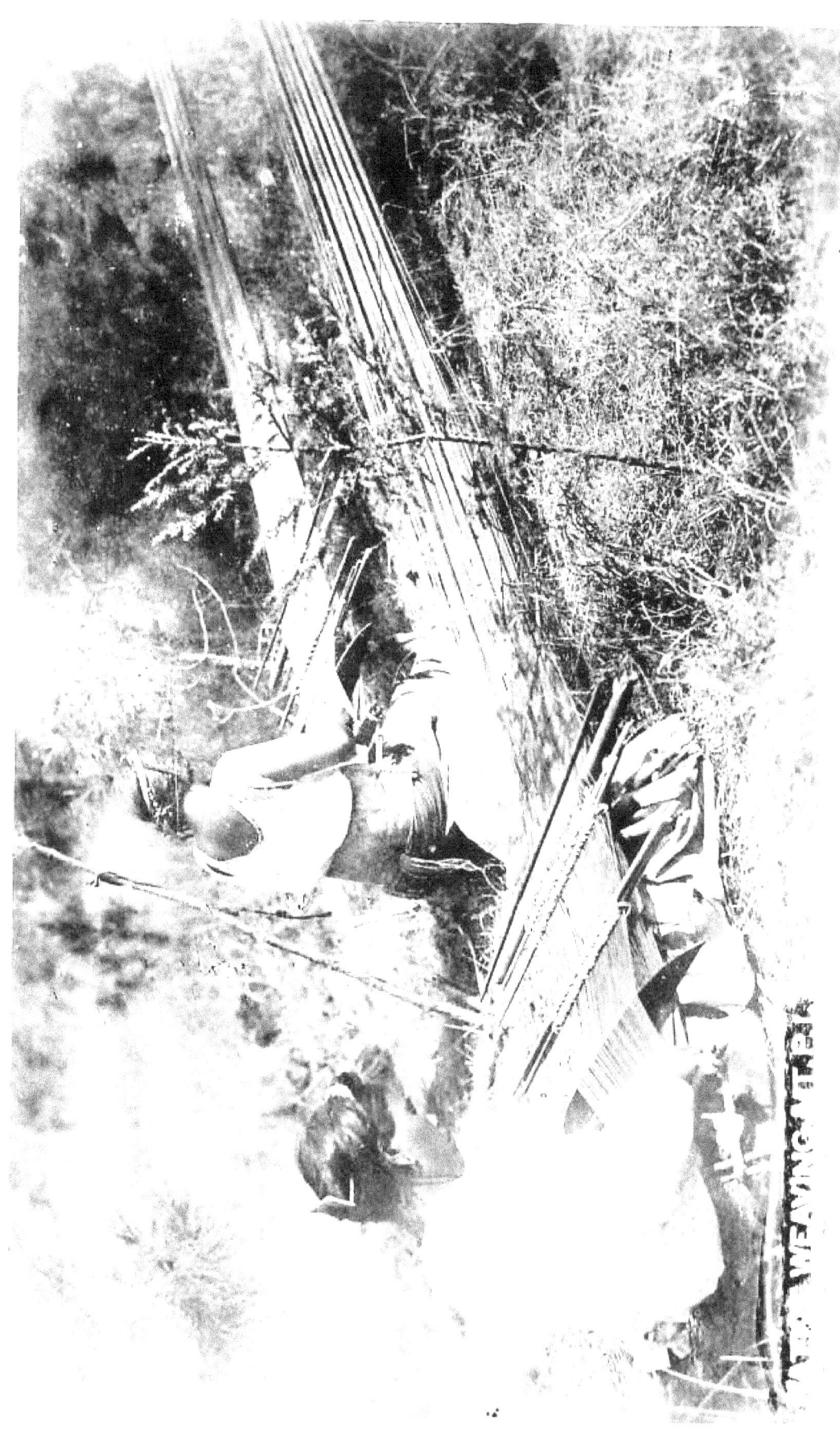

Native women weaving, Mountain Province, 1900s

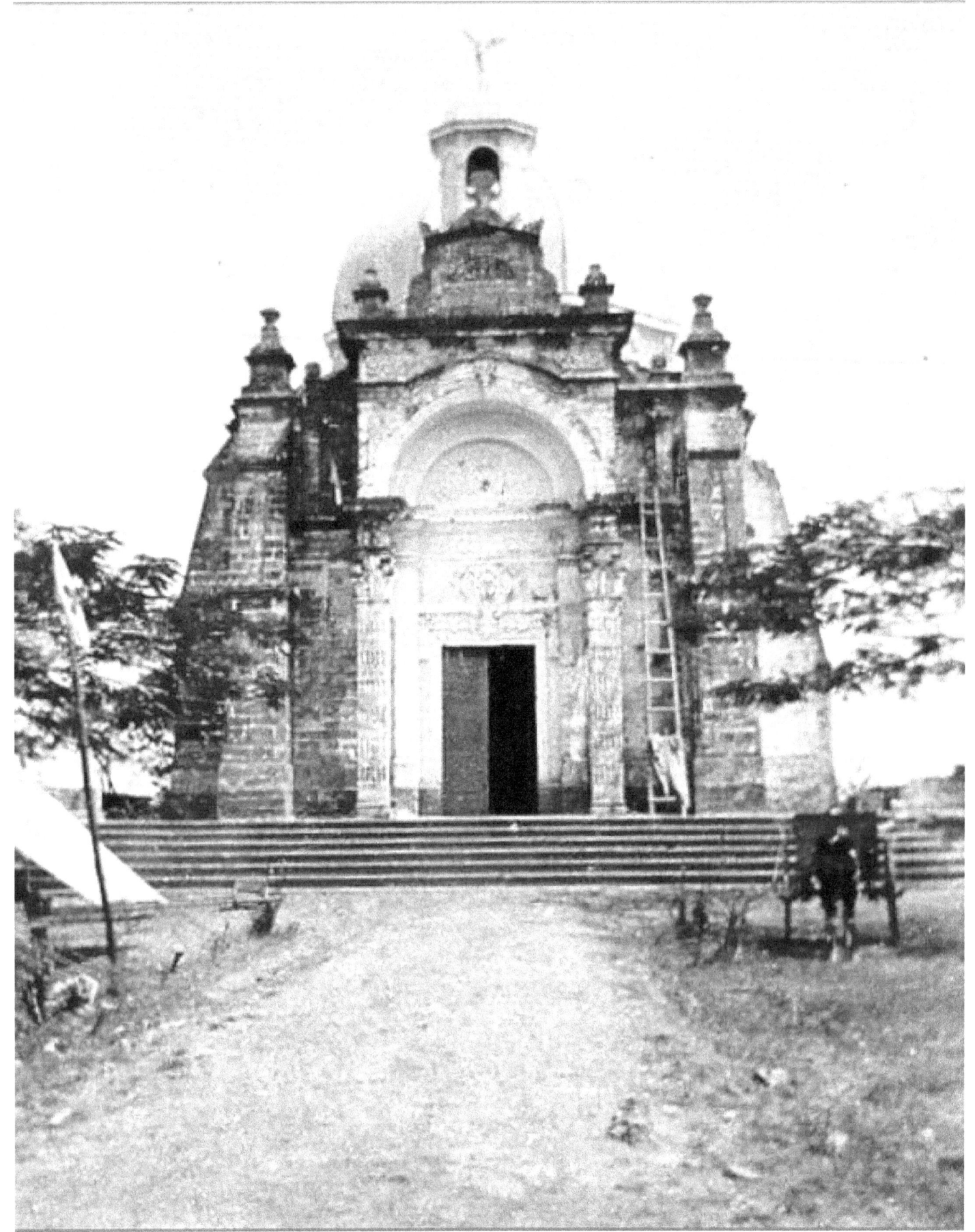
La Loma Chapel & Cemetery, Manila, 1898

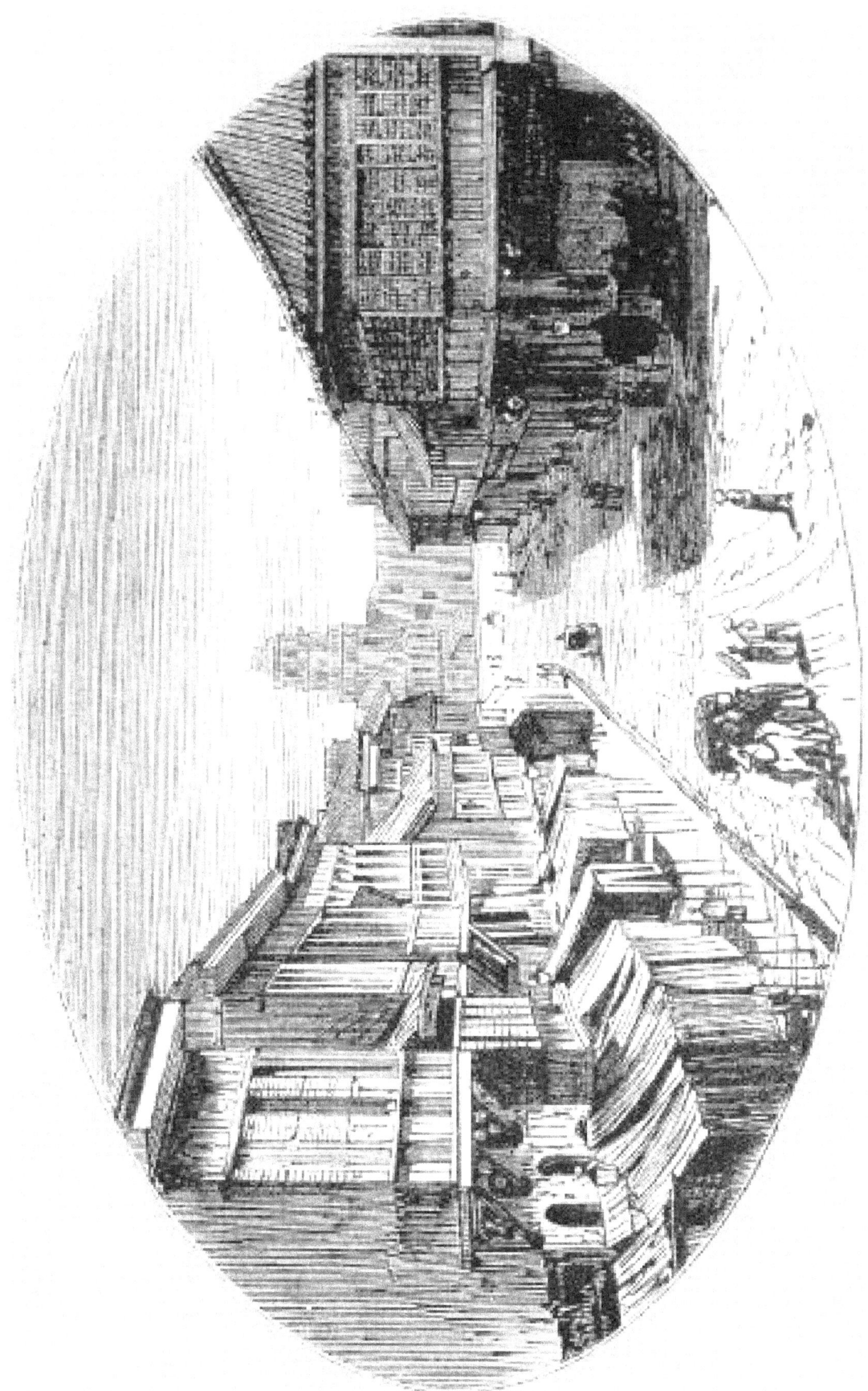

Sketch, Early Escolta, designed by Spaniards Barcelona-style, 18th-19th centuries

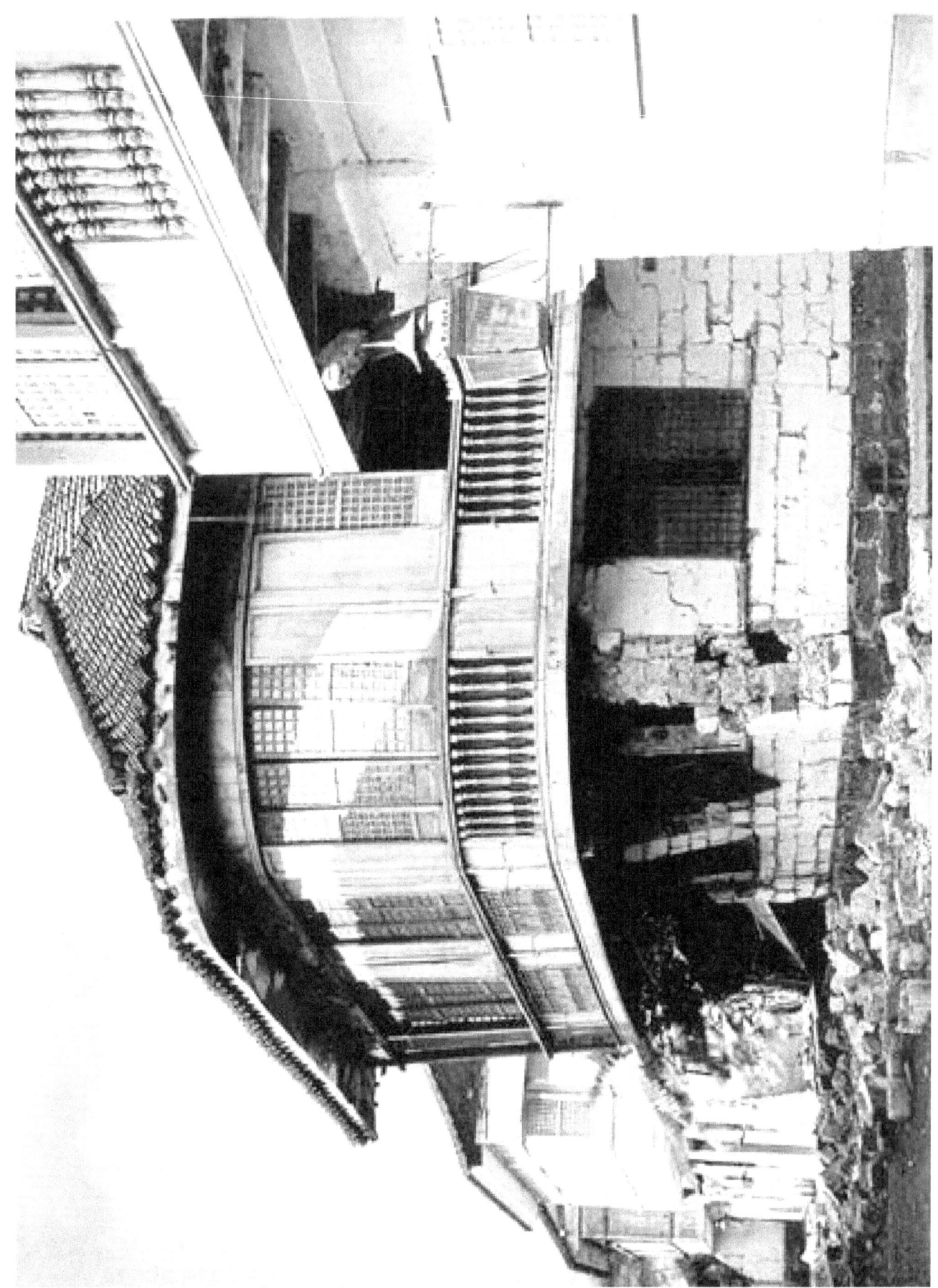

Ageing Spanish-style Homes, Intramuros, Manila, 1900s

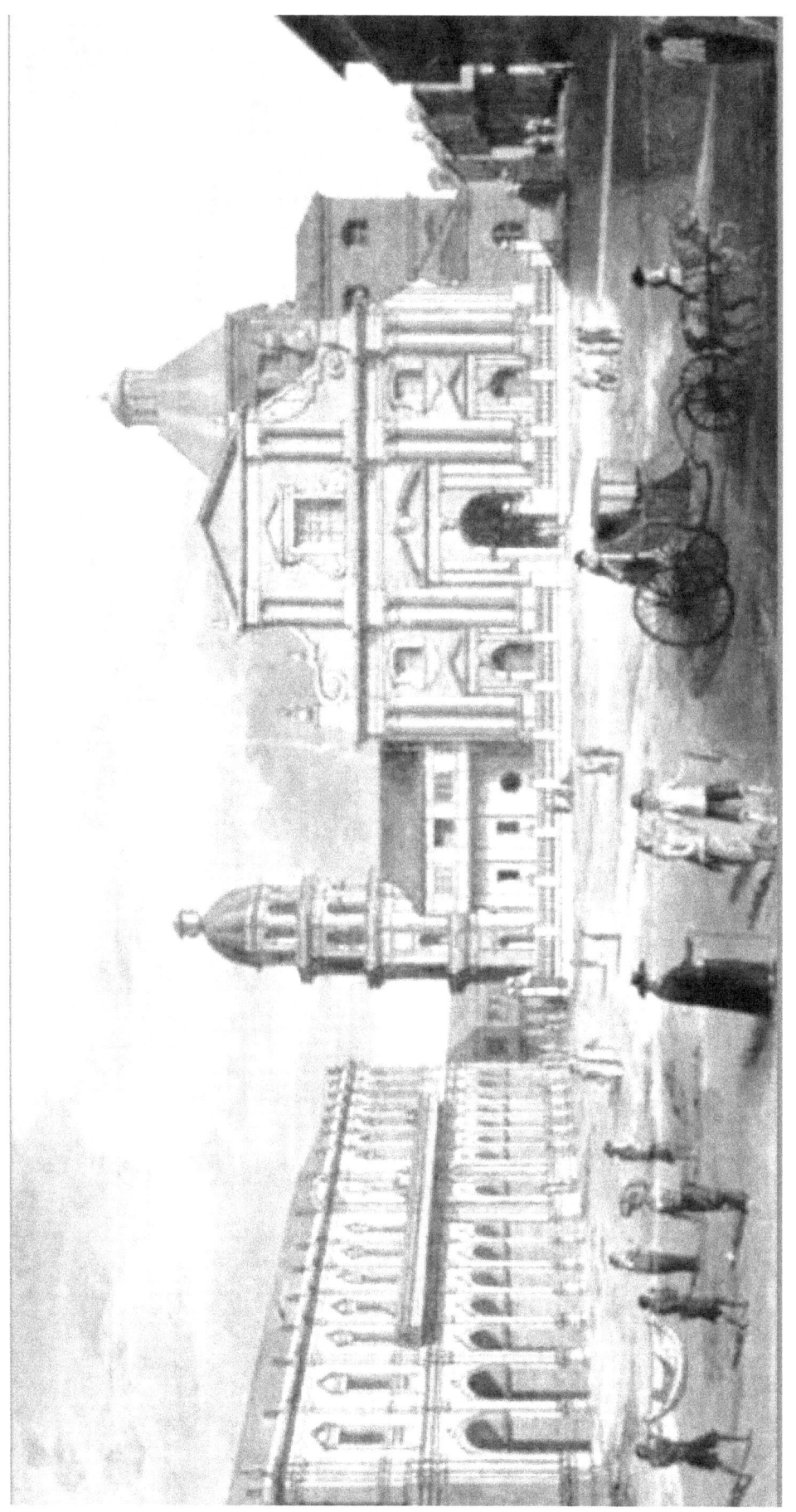

Imposing Building and Church during Spanish times, 17-18-19th centuries

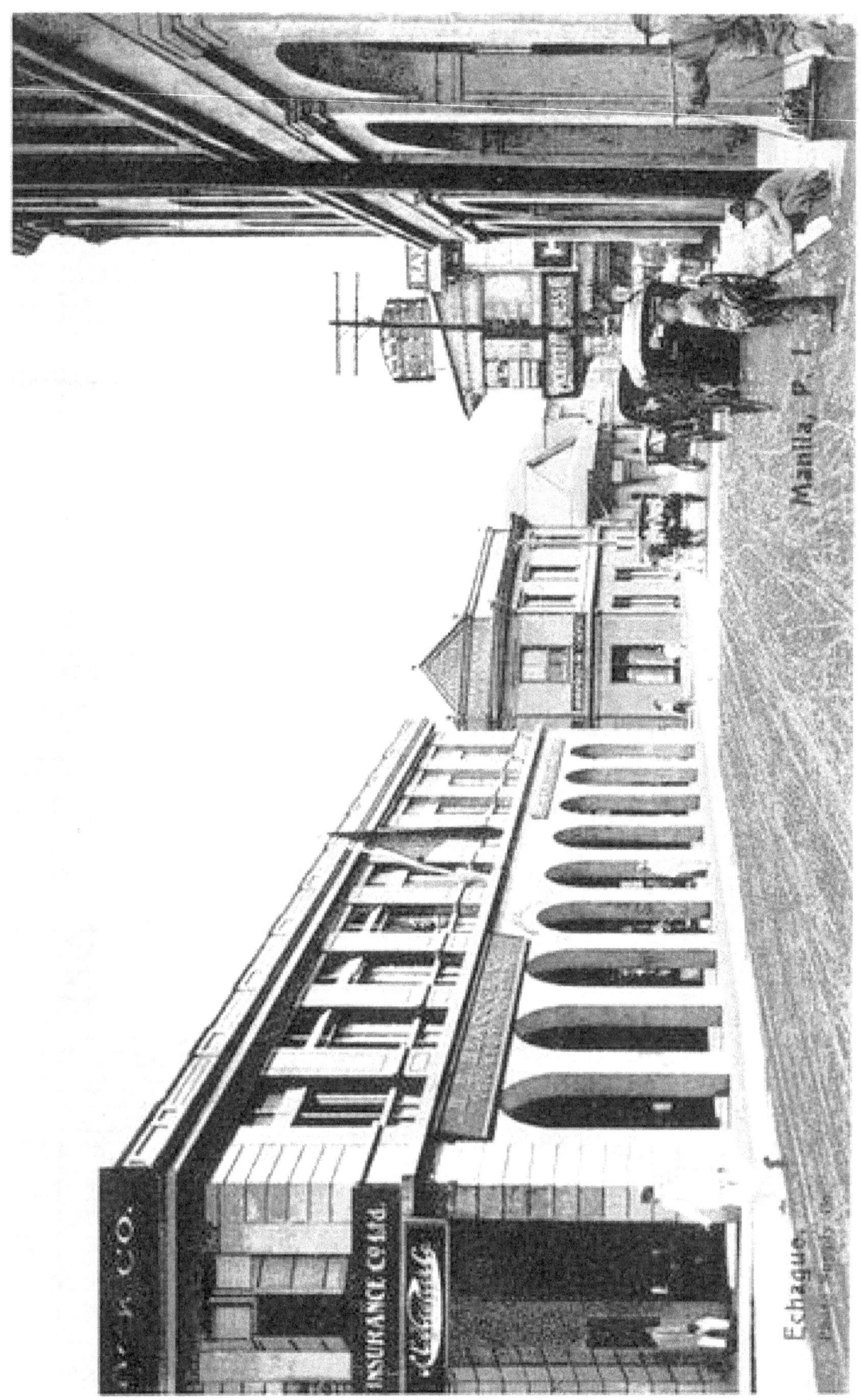

Echague St., near Quiapo, 1920 sketch

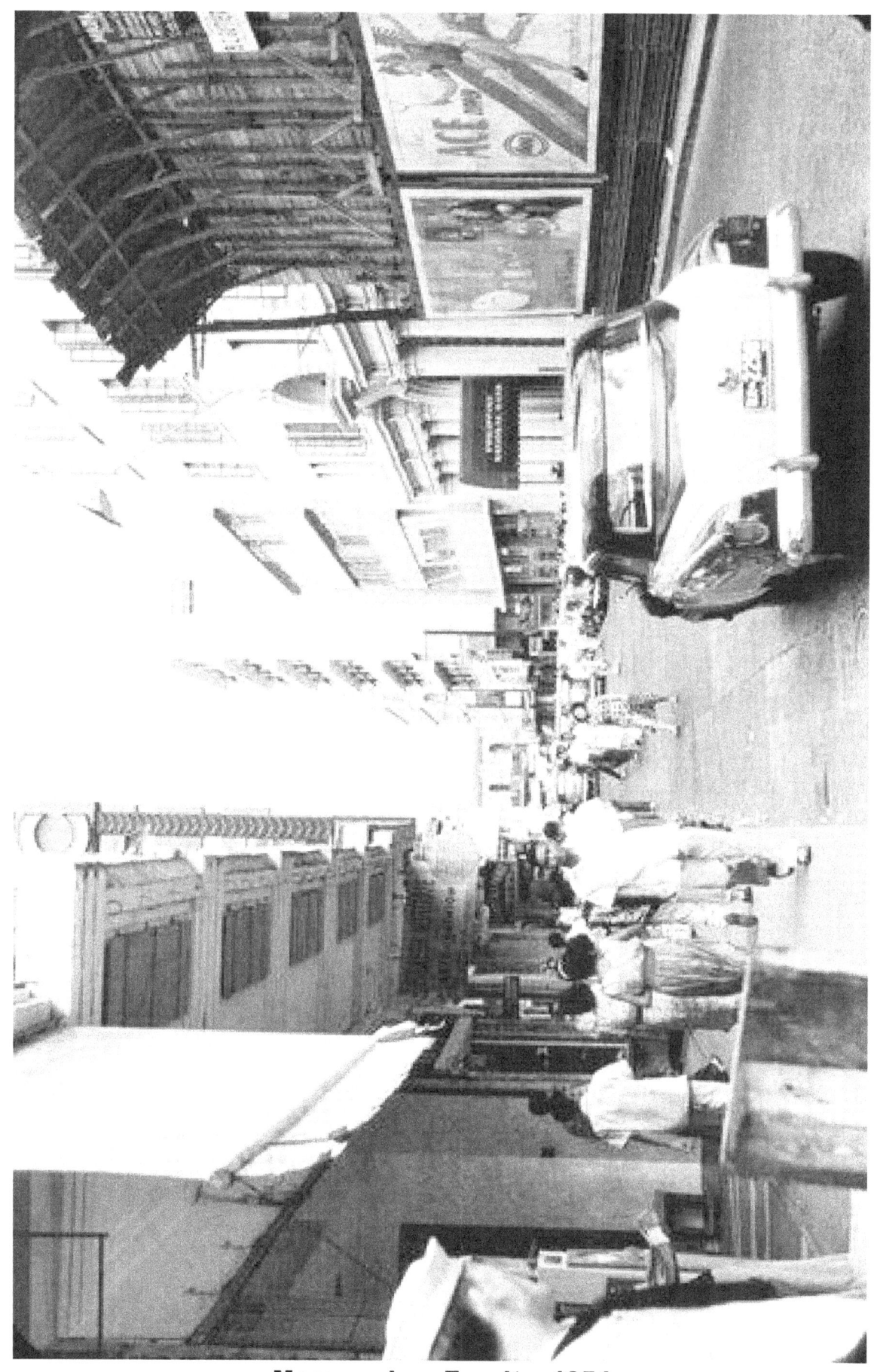
More modern Escolta, 1954

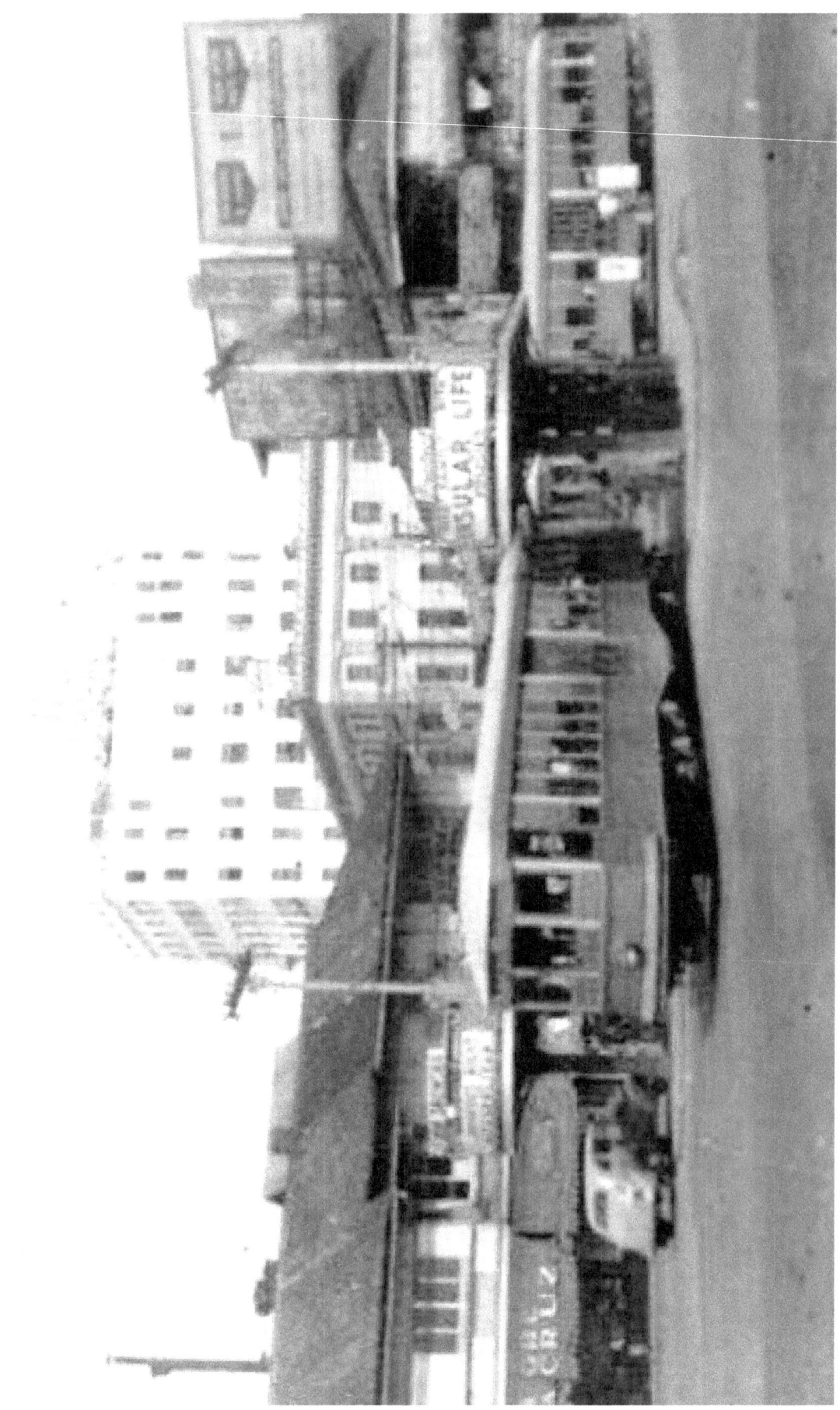

Sta Cruz Plaza, Manila, (tranvia stop), 1930s-40s

www.ingramcontent.com/pod-product-compliance
Lightning Source LLC
Chambersburg PA
CBHW082339220526
45470CB00008B/2569